STANDARD & POOR'S

DICTIONARY OF FINANCIAL TERMS

VIRGINIA B. MORRIS
KENNETH M. MORRIS

LIGHTBULB
PRESS ®

LIGHTBULB PRESS
Project Team

Design Director Dave Wilder
Design Mercedes Feliciano
Editors Michael D. Bromberg, Jackie Day, Sophie Forrester, Mavis Morris
Production and Illustration Krista K. Glasser, Thomas F. Trojan

PICTURE CREDITS

Chicago Board of Trade (page 144); FPG, New York (page 112); NASDAQ (page 135); New York Stock Exchange (pages 50, 206); Alan Rosenburg, New York (pages 22, 83)

ACKNOWLEDGMENTS

Cirrus logo courtesy of MasterCard International (page 51); Dow Jones logo courtesy of Dow Jones & Company (page 62); NASDAQ logo courtesy of NASDAQ (page 100); NYCE logo courtesy of NYCE Corporation (page 51); STAR logo courtesy of STAR Systems (page 51)

*R*ead a financial article on the Web, skim the investment section of a newspaper or magazine, or check the day's events on Wall Street, and chances are you'll come across a term or two that you've heard before but don't quite understand—as well as others that are completely new to you. Words and phrases like *ETFs, market caps, hybrid mortgages, bond swaps, coinsurance, yield curves*, and *total return* are just some of the terms that can leave you perplexed and perhaps a little intimidated.

Being comfortable with these and other financial terms is not only important for understanding the state of the economy and the events that are continually unfolding in the capital markets. The terms are even more important for making sound investment decisions, managing your personal finances intelligently, and planning for a range of financial goals, from paying for a child's college education to living a comfortable retirement.

Ironically, the definitions of investment and personal finance terms that you'll find in many dictionaries are often so cryptic and impersonal that they beg for clearer explanations. That's why, in creating our *Dictionary of Financial Terms*, we've used the straightforward language and practical examples that have made other Lightbulb guides so popular. Beyond defining what a word means, we try to explain what it means *to you*—as an investor, as a credit user, as someone saving for retirement.

This new edition of the *Dictionary of Financial Terms* contains nearly 1,300 words, including many updated definitions and a host of new terms that track the ever-changing landscape of personal finance and the investment markets. We hope that you find the dictionary helpful and that it will provide the key to unlocking the mysteries of the world of money and investing.

Virginia B. Morris
Kenneth M. Morris

Accelerated death benefit

If your life insurance policy has an accelerated death benefit (ADB), you may qualify to use a portion of the death benefit to pay for certain healthcare expenses, such as the costs of a terminal illness or long-term care, while you're still alive.

Using the ADB, you take cash advances from the policy, reducing the death benefit by up to a fixed percentage. The balance is paid to your beneficiaries on your death.

While an accelerated death benefit can help ease current financial burdens, including this option in your policy increases the cost of coverage. And, if you do take money out, it reduces what your beneficiaries receive.

Account balance

Your account balance is the amount of money you have in one of your financial accounts. For example, your bank account balance refers to the amount of money in your bank accounts.

Your account balance can also be the amount of money outstanding on one of your financial accounts. Your credit card balance, for example, refers to the amount of money you owe a credit card company.

With your 401(k), your account balance, also called your accrued benefit, is the amount your 401(k) account is worth on a date that it's valued. For example, if the value of your account on December 31 is $250,000, that's your account balance.

You use your 401(k) account balance to figure how much you must withdraw from your plan each year, once you start taking required distributions after you turn 70½. Specifically, you divide the account balance at the end of your plan's fiscal year by a divisor based on your life expectancy to determine the amount you must take during the next fiscal year.

Accredited investor

An accredited investor is a person or institution that the Securities and Exchange Commission (SEC) defines as being qualified to invest in unregistered securities, such as privately held corporations, private equity investments, and hedge funds.

The qualification is based on the value of the investor's assets, or in the case of an individual, annual income.

Specifically, to be an accredited investor you must have a net worth of at least $1 million or a current annual income of at least $200,000 with the anticipation you'll earn at least that much next year. If you're married, that amount is increased to $300,000.

Institutions are required to have assets worth $5 million to qualify as accredited investors. The underlying principle is that investors with these assets have the sophistication to understand the risks involved in the investment and can afford to lose the money should the investment fail.

Accrued interest

Accrued interest is the interest that accumulates on a fixed-income security between one interest payment and the next.

The amount is calculated by multiplying the coupon rate, also called the nominal interest rate, times the number of days since the previous interest payment.

Interest on most bonds and fixed-income securities is paid twice a year. On corporate and municipal bonds, interest is calculated on 30-day months and a 360-day year. For government bonds, interest is calculated on actual days and a 365-day year.

When you buy a bond or other fixed-income security, you pay the bond's price plus the accrued interest and receive the full amount of the next interest payment, which reimburses you for the accrued interest payment you made when you purchased the bond. Similarly, when you sell a bond, you receive the price of the bond, plus the amount of interest that has accrued since you received the last interest payment.

On a zero-coupon bond, interest accrues over the term of the bond but is paid in a lump sum when you redeem the bond for face value. However, unless you hold the bond in a tax-deferred or tax-exempt account, you owe income tax each year on the amount of interest that the government calculates you would have received, had it been paid.

Accumulation period

The accumulation period refers to the time during which your retirement savings accumulate in a deferred annuity.

Because annuities are federal income tax deferred, all earnings are reinvested to increase the base on which future earnings accumulate, so you have the benefit of compounding.

When you buy a deferred fixed annuity contract, the company issuing the contract promises a fixed rate of return during the accumulation period regardless of whether market interest rates move up or down.

With a deferred variable annuity, the amount you accumulate depends on the performance of the investment alternatives, known as subaccounts or separate account funds, which you select from among those offered in the contract.

At the end of the accumulation period, you can choose to annuitize, agree to some other method of receiving income, or roll over your account value into an immediate annuity. The years in which you receive annuity income are sometimes called the distribution period.

Accumulation unit

Accumulation units are the shares you own in the separate account funds of a variable annuity during the period you're putting money into your annuity.

If you own the annuity in a 401(k) plan, each time you make a contribution that amount is added to one or more of the separate account funds to buy additional accumulation units.

The value of your annuity is figured by multiplying the number of units you own by the dollar value of each unit. During the accumulation phase, that value changes to reflect the changing performance of the underlying investments in the separate account funds.

Acquisition

If a company buys another company outright, or accumulates enough shares to take a controlling interest, the deal is described as an acquisition.

The acquiring company's motive may be to expand the scope of its products and services, to make itself a major player in its sector, or to fend off being taken over itself.

To complete the deal, the acquirer may be willing to pay a higher price per share than the price at which the stock is currently trading. That means shareholders of the target company may realize a substantial gain, so some investors are always on the lookout for companies that seem ripe for acquisition.

Sometimes acquisitions are described, more bluntly, as takeovers and other times, more diplomatically, as mergers. Collectively, these activities are referred to as mergers and acquisitions, or M&A, to those in the business.

Actively managed fund

Managers of actively managed mutual funds buy and sell investments to achieve a particular goal, such as providing a certain level of return or beating a relevant benchmark.

As a result, they generally trade much more frequently than managers of passively managed funds whose goal is to mirror the performance of the index a fund tracks.

While actively managed funds may provide stronger returns than index funds in some years, they typically have higher management and investment fees.

Activities of daily living

To live independently, you must be able to handle certain essential functions, called activities of daily living (ADLs). These standard activities include eating, dressing, bathing, moving from a sitting to a standing position, taking medication, and using the bathroom.

If you are unable to perform two or more these ADLs, you generally qualify to begin receiving benefits from your long-term care insurance policy. Each insurer's list of ADLs may vary slightly, but should always include bathing, as that is often the first activity that a person struggles with.

Cognitive impairments, such as those that result from Alzheimer's disease, are not considered ADLs. A comprehensive long-term care policy will use a different test to determine when policyholders suffering from these impairments qualify to collect benefits.

Adjustable rate mortgage (ARM)

An adjustable rate mortgage is a long-term loan you use to finance a real estate purchase, typically a home.

Unlike a fixed-rate mortgage, where the interest rate remains the same for the term of the loan, the interest rate on an ARM is adjusted, or changed, during its term.

The initial rate on an ARM is usually lower than the rate on a fixed-rate mortgage for the same term, which means it may be easier to qualify for an ARM. You take the risk, however, that interest rates may rise, increasing the cost of your mortgage. Of course, it's also possible that the rates may drop, decreasing your payments.

The rate adjustments, which are based on changes in one of the publicly reported indexes that reflect market rates, occur at preset times, usually once a year but sometimes less often. Typically, rate changes on ARMs are capped both annually and over the term of the loan, which helps protect you in the case of a rapid or sustained increase in market rates.

However, certain ARMs allow negative amortization, which means additional interest could accumulate on the outstanding balance if market rates rise higher than the cap. That interest would be due when the loan matured or if you want to prepay.

Adjusted gross income (AGI)

Your AGI is your gross, or total, income from taxable sources minus certain deductions.

ADJUSTED GROSS INCOME
Gross income
− Special deductions
ADJUSTED GROSS INCOME

Income includes salary and other employment income, interest and dividends, and long- and short-term capital gains and losses. Deductions include unreimbursed business and medical expenses, contributions to a deductible individual retirement account (IRA), and alimony you pay.

You figure your AGI on page one of your federal tax return, and it serves as the basis for calculating the income tax you owe. Your modified AGI is used to establish your eligibility for certain tax or financial benefits, such as deducting your IRA contribution or qualifying for certain tax credits.

Advance-decline (A-D) line

The advance-decline line graphs the ratio of stocks that have risen in value—the advancers—to stocks that have fallen in value—the decliners—over a particular trading period.

The direction and steepness of the A-D line gives you a general idea of the direction of the market. For example, a noticeable upward trend, which is created when there are more advancers than decliners, indicates a growing market.

A downward slope indicates a market in retreat. At times, however, there may be no clear trend in either direction.

Advancer

Stocks that have gained, or increased, in value over a particular period are described as advancers.

If more stocks advance than decline—or lose value—over the course of a trading day, the financial press reports that advancers led decliners. When that occurs over a period of time, it's considered an indication that the stock market is strong.

Affinity fraud

Affinity fraud occurs when a dishonest person plays on your affiliation with a group—such as a house of worship, social club, support group, charity, or veterans' group—as a way to win your confidence in order to sell you something worthless or trick you into handing over cash.

The scammer may actually be a member of the group or may just pretend to be.

Affinity fraud is one the most difficult scams to protect yourself against because being suspicious of colleagues can undermine the reason you belong to a group.

After-hours market

Securities, such as stocks and bonds, may change hands on organized markets and exchanges after regular business hours, in what is known as the after-hours market.

These electronic transactions explain why a security may open for trading at a different price from the one it closed at the day before.

There's also trading in benchmark indexes such as Standard & Poor's 500 Index (S&P 500) and the Dow Jones Industrial Average (DJIA) before US stock markets open. The level of activity and the direction the trading—up or down—is widely interpreted as an early indicator of what's likely to happen in the market during the day.

After-tax contribution

An after-tax contribution is money you put into your 401(k) or other employer sponsored retirement savings plan either instead of or in addition to your pretax contribution.

You make an after-tax contribution if you've chosen to participate in a Roth 401(k) or similar tax-free plan rather than a traditional tax-deferred 401(k).

However, if you make excess deferrals, any earnings on the after-tax amount accumulate tax deferred. The disadvantage is that figuring the tax that's due on your required distributions may be more complicated than if you had made only pretax contributions.

After-tax income

After-tax income, sometimes called post-tax dollars, is the amount of income you have left after federal income taxes (plus state and local income taxes, if they apply) have been withheld.

If you contribute to a nondeductible individual retirement account (IRA), a Roth IRA, or a 529 college savings plan,

purchase an annuity, or invest in a taxable account, you are using after-tax income.

In contrast, if you contribute money to an employer sponsored retirement plan or flexible spending account, you are investing pretax income.

Agency bond

Some federal agencies, including Ginnie Mae (GNMA) and the Tennessee Valley Authority (TVA), raise money by issuing bonds and short-term discount notes for sale to investors.

MONEY FROM AGENCY BONDS CAN REDUCE THE COST OF:

Education

Home buying

Farming

The money raised by selling these debt securities is typically used to make reduced-cost loans available to specific groups, including home buyers, students, or farmers.

Interest paid on the securities is generally higher than you'd earn on Treasury issues, and the bonds are considered nearly as safe from default. In addition, the interest on some—but not all—of these securities is exempt from certain income taxes.

Securities issued by former federal agencies that are now public corporations, including mortgage-buyers Fannie Mae and Freddie Mac, are also sometimes described as agency bonds.

Agent

An agent is a person who acts on behalf of another person or institution in a transaction. For example, when you direct your stockbroker to buy or sell shares in your account, he or she is acting as your agent in the trade.

Agents work for either a set fee or a commission based on the size of the transaction and the type of product, or sometimes a combination of fee and commission.

Depending on the work a particular agent does, he or she may need to be certified, licensed, or registered by industry bodies or government regulators. For instance, insurance agents must be licensed in the state where they do business, and stockbrokers must pass licensing exams and be registered with NASD.

In a real estate transaction, a real estate agent represents the seller. That person may also be called a real estate broker or a Realtor if he or she is a member of the National Association of Realtors. A buyer may be represented by a buyer's agent.

Aggressive-growth fund

Aggressive-growth mutual funds buy stock in companies that show rapid growth potential, including start-up companies and those in hot sectors.

While these funds and the companies they invest in can increase significantly in value, they are also among the most volatile. Their values may rise much higher—and fall much lower—than the overall stock market or the mutual funds that invest in the broader market.

All or none order (AON)

When a trading order is marked AON, the broker who is handling the order must either fill the whole order or not fill it at all.

For example, if you want to buy 1,500 shares at $20 a share and only 1,000 are available at that price, your order won't be filled. However, the order will remain active until you cancel it, and so may be filled at some point in the future.

Alpha

A stock's alpha is an analyst's estimate of its potential price increase based on the rate at which the company's earnings are growing and other aspects of the company's current performance.

For example, if a stock has an alpha of 1.15, that means the analyst expects a 15% price increase in a year when stock prices in general are flat

One investment strategy is to look for stocks whose alphas are high, which means the stocks are undervalued and have the potential to provide a strong return. A stock's alpha is different from its beta, which estimates its price volatility in relation to the market as a whole.

Alternative minimum tax (AMT)

The alternative minimum tax (AMT) was designed to ensure that all taxpayers pay at least the minimum federal income tax for their income level, no matter how many deductions or credits they claim.

The AMT is actually an extra tax, calculated separately and added to the amount the taxpayer owes in regular income tax. Some items that are usually tax exempt become taxable and special tax rates apply. For example, income on certain tax-free bonds is taxable.

Increasing numbers of taxpayers trigger the AMT if they deduct high state and local taxes or mortgage interest expenses, exercise a large number of stock options, or have significant tax-exempt interest.

American Association of Individual Investors (AAII)

The goal of this independent, nonprofit organization is teaching individual investors how to manage their assets effectively.

Headquartered in Chicago, the AAII offers publications, seminars, educational programs, software and videos, and other services and products to its members. The AAII website (www.aaii.org) also provides a wide range of information about investing and personal finance.

American depositary receipt (ADR)

Shares of hundreds of major overseas-based companies, including names such as British Petroleum, Sony, and Toyota, are traded as ADRs on US stock markets in US dollars.

ADRs are actually receipts issued by US banks that hold actual shares of the companies' stocks. They let you diversify into international markets without having to purchase shares on overseas exchanges or through mutual funds.

American depositary share (ADS)

When a company based overseas wants to sell its shares in the US markets, it can offer them through a US bank, which is known as the depositary.

The depositary bank holds the issuing company's shares, known as American depositary shares (ADSs), and offers them to investors as certificates known as American depositary receipts (ADRs). Each ADR represents a specific number of ADSs.

ADRs are quoted in US dollars and trade on US markets just like ordinary shares. While hundreds are listed on the major exchanges, the majority are traded over the counter, usually because they're too small to meet exchange listing requirements.

American Stock Exchange (AMEX)

The AMEX is the second-largest floor-based stock exchange in the United States after the New York Stock Exchange (NYSE).

It operates an auction market in stocks (including overseas stocks), exchange traded funds, and derivatives, including options on many NYSE-traded and over-the-counter (OTC) stocks.

American-style option

A listed option that you can exercise at any point between the day you purchase it and its expiration date is called an American-style option. All equity options are American style, no matter where the exchange on which they trade is located.

In contrast, you can exercise European-style options only on the last trading day before the expiration date, not before. Index options listed on various US exchanges may be either American- or European-style options.

Amortization

Amortization is the gradual repayment of a debt over a period of time, such as monthly payments on a mortgage loan or credit card balance.

To amortize a loan, your payments must be large enough to pay not only the interest that has accrued but also to reduce the principal you owe. The word amortize itself tells the story, since it means "to bring to death."

Analyst

A financial analyst tracks the performance of companies and industries, evaluates their potential value as investments, and makes recommendations on specific securities.

When the most highly respected analysts express a strong opinion about a stock, there is often an immediate impact on that stock's price as investors rush to follow the advice.

Some analysts work for financial institutions, such as mutual fund companies, brokerage firms, and banks. Others work for analytical services, such as Value Line, Inc., Morningstar, Inc., Standard & Poor's, or Moody's Investors Service, or as independent evaluators.

Analysts' commentaries also appear regularly in the financial press, and on radio, television, and the Internet.

Annual percentage rate (APR)

A loan's annual percentage rate, or APR, is what credit costs you each year, expressed as a percentage of the loan amount.

The APR, which is usually higher than the nominal, or named, rate you're quoted for a loan, includes most of a loan's up-front fees as well as the annual interest rate.

You should use APR, which is a more accurate picture of the cost of borrowing than the interest rate alone, to compare various loans you're considering.

Annual percentage yield (APY)

Annual percentage yield is the amount you earn on an interest-bearing investment in a year, expressed as a percentage. For example, if you earn $60 on a $1,000 certificate of deposit (CD) between January 1 and December 31, your APY is 6%.

When the APY is the same as the interest rate that is being paid on an investment, you are earning simple interest. But when the APY is higher than the interest rate, the interest is being compounded, which means you are earning interest on your accumulating interest.

Annual renewable term insurance

If your term life insurance is an annual renewable policy, you can renew your coverage each year without filling out a new application or passing a physical exam.

However, the premium, or the amount you pay for the policy, isn't fixed, and goes up each time you renew. Policies with five- or ten-year terms may also be renewable, with comparable increases in their premiums.

Annual report

By law, each publicly held corporation must provide its shareholders with an annual report showing its income and balance sheet.

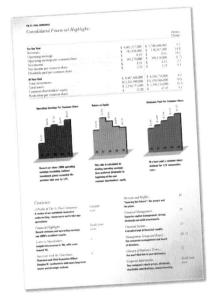

In most cases, it contains not only financial details but also a message from the chairman, a description of the company's operations, and an overview of its achievements.

Most annual reports are glossy affairs that also serve as marketing pieces. Copies are generally available from the company's investor relations office, and annual reports may even appear on the company's website. The company's 10-K report is a more comprehensive look at its finances.

Annuitant

An annuitant is a person who receives income from an annuity. If you receive a distribution from an annuity that you or your employer buys with your 401(k) assets, you're the annuitant.

Similarly, you're the annuitant if you take distributions from a tax-deferred individual retirement annuity or from an individual annuity you buy with after-tax income.

If your beneficiary receives annuity income after your death, he or she becomes the annuitant. It's also possible to buy an annuity naming someone other than the buyer—a disabled child, for example—as annuitant.

Annuitization

Annuitization means that you convert part or all of the money in a qualified retirement plan or nonqualified annuity contract into a stream of regular income payments, either for your lifetime or the lifetimes of you and your joint annuitant.

Once you choose to annuitize, the payment schedule and the amount is generally fixed and can't be altered.

If you have a qualified retirement plan, such as a 401(k), you generally have three major options when you retire. You can annuitize, roll over the account balance to an IRA, or take the money all at once as a lump sum distribution.

If you have a nonqualified deferred annuity, you have a choice of annuitizing, taking a lump sum, setting up a systematic withdrawal plan, or arranging some other payout method that the contract allows.

Annuitize

When you annuitize, you choose to convert the assets in your deferred annuity or other retirement savings account into a stream of regular income payments that are guaranteed to last for your lifetime or the combined lifetimes of yourself and another person, called your joint annuitant.

You typically annuitize when you retire. But, if you own a nonqualified annuity, you may begin receiving income at 59½ without risking an early withdrawal penalty, or you can postpone the decision to annuitize well beyond normal retirement age.

One reason people may give for choosing not to annuitize is that they're afraid if they die shortly after they begin receiving payments, they will forfeit a large portion of the annuity's value. To avoid that situation, some people choose to annuitize with what's called a period certain payout, guaranteeing that they or their beneficiaries will receive income for at least a minimum period, typically 5, 10, or 20 years.

You should be aware that the promise to pay lifetime income is contingent on the claims-paying ability of the company providing the annuity contract. That's why you'll want to check the ratings that independent analysts give your annuity company before you annuitize your contract.

Annuity

Originally, an annuity simply meant an annual payment. That's why the retirement income you receive from a defined benefit plan each year, usually in monthly installments, is called a pension annuity.

But an annuity is also an insurance company product that's designed to allow you to accumulate tax-deferred assets that can be converted to a source of lifetime annual income.

When a deferred annuity is offered as part of a qualified plan, such as a traditional 401(k), 403(b), or tax-deferred annuity (TDA), you can contribute up to the annual limit and typically begin to take income from the annuity when you retire.

You can also buy a nonqualified deferred annuity contract on your own. With nonqualified annuities, there are no federal limits on annual contributions and no required withdrawals, though you may begin receiving income without penalty when you turn 59½.

An immediate annuity, in contrast, is one you purchase with a lump sum when you are ready to begin receiving income, usually when you retire. The payouts begin right away and the annuity company promises the income will last your lifetime.

With all types of annuities, the guarantee of lifetime annuity income depends on the claims-paying ability of the company that sells the annuity contract.

Annuity principal

The annuity principal is the sum of money you use to buy an annuity and the base on which annuity earnings accumulate.

If you're buying a deferred annuity, you may make a one-time—or single premium—purchase, or you may build your annuity principal with a series of regular or intermittent payments.

For example, if you own an annuity in an employer-sponsored retirement plan, you add to your principal each time you defer some of your income into your account—typically every time you're paid.

When you buy an immediate annuity, you commit your annuity principal as a lump sum, and that amount is one of the key factors that determines the amount of your annuity income.

Annuity unit

Annuity units are the shares you own in variable annuity subaccounts, also called annuity funds or separate account funds, during the period you're receiving income from the annuity.

The number of your annuity units is fixed at the time that you buy the income annuity contract, or when you annuitize your deferred variable annuity.

While the number of units does not change, the value of each unit fluctuates to reflect the performance of the underlying investments in the subaccount. That's why the income you receive from a variable annuity may differ from month to month.

Appreciation

When an asset such as stock, real estate, or personal property increases in value without any improvements or modification having been made to it, that's called appreciation.

Some personal assets, such as fine art or antiques, may appreciate over time, while others—such as electronic equipment—usually lose value, or depreciate.

Certain investments also have the potential to appreciate. A number of factors can cause an asset to appreciate, among them inflation, uniqueness, or increased demand.

Approved charge

With traditional fee-for-service health insurance, the insurance company sets an approved or allowable amount for each medical procedure or office visit.

If your bill exceeds the approved charge, the difference between the approved charge and the claim that's submitted to the insurance company for reimbursement is considered an excess charge. You are responsible for that amount in addition to a percentage of the approved charge.

Medicare establishes approved charges for medical procedures and office visits. If you participate in Original Medicare, there's a legal limit on what a doctor, laboratory, or other medical provider can charge in excess of the approved amount.

Arbitrage

Arbitrage is the technique of simultaneously buying at a lower price in one market and selling at a higher price in another market to make a profit on the spread between the prices.

Although the price difference may be very small, arbitrageurs, or arbs, typically trade regularly and in huge volume, so they can make sizable profits.

But the strategy, which depends on split-second timing, can also backfire if interest rates, prices, currency exchange rates, or other factors move in ways the arbitrageurs don't anticipate.

Arbitration

Arbitration is a way to resolve conflicts between parties or individuals, and may be considered a middle ground between the more cooperative, informal nature of mediation and the more expensive, involved, and lengthy process of litigation.

Usually, when you open a brokerage account, you sign an agreement to use arbitration to resolve possible conflicts with the firm and waive the right to sue for damages in court.

Arbitration is binding, which means you can't appeal the decision or try for a different result by going to court. Most investment-related arbitration claims are handled by either NASD, the main self-regulatory body that supervises brokers, or the New York Stock Exchange (NYSE).

In arbitration, a trained impartial arbitrator or panel of arbitrators reviews the evidence, decides on the outcome, and sets any award. While arbitration is usually less expensive than litigation, arbitration and attorney fees make it a more expensive option than mediation.

Arithmetic index

An arithmetic index gives equal weight to the percentage price change of each stock that's included in the index.

In computing the index, the percentage changes of all the stocks are added, and the total is divided by the number of stocks. The percentage price changes of large companies aren't counted more heavily, as they are in a market-capitalization weighted index.

An arithmetic index is a more accurate measure of total stock market performance than an index that stresses relatively few high-priced or large-company stocks. However, some analysts point out that it may also produce higher total return figures than other indexing methods.

The best known arithmetic index in the United States is the one computed by Value Line, Inc., which tracks the approximately 1,700 stocks. Standard & Poor's also calculates an arithmetic version of the S&P 500 index.

Ask

The ask price (a shortening of asked price) is the price at which a market maker or broker offers to sell a security or commodity.

The price another market maker or broker is willing to pay for that security is called the bid price, and the difference between the two prices is called the spread.

Bid and ask prices are typically reported to the media for commodities and over-the-counter (OTC) transactions.

In contrast, last, or closing, prices are reported for exchange-traded and national market securities.

With open-end mutual funds, the ask price is the net asset value (NAV), or the price you get if you sell, plus the sales charge, if one applies.

Asset

Assets are everything you own that has any monetary value, plus any money you are owed.

They include money in bank accounts, stocks, bonds, mutual funds, equity in real estate, the value of your life insurance policy, and any personal property that people would pay to own.

When you figure your net worth, you subtract the amount you owe, or your liabilities, from your assets. Similarly, a company's assets include the value of its physical plant, its inventory, and less tangible elements, such as its reputation.

Asset allocation

Asset allocation is a strategy, advocated by modern portfolio theory, for reducing risk in your investment portfolio in order to maximize return.

Specifically, asset allocation means dividing your assets among different broad categories of investments, called

asset classes. Stock, bonds, and cash are examples of asset classes, as are real estate and derivatives such as options and futures contracts.

AGGRESSIVE
85% Stocks
10% Bonds
5% Cash

MODERATE
65% Stocks
25% Bonds
10% Cash

CONSERVATIVE
40% Stocks
40% Bonds
20% Cash

Most financial services firms suggest particular asset allocations for specific groups of clients and fine-tune those allocations for individual investors.

The asset allocation model—specifically the percentages of your investment principal allocated to each investment category you're using—that's appropriate for you at any given time depends on many factors, such as the goals you're investing to achieve, how much time you have to invest, your tolerance for risk, the direction of interest rates, and the market outlook.

Ideally, you adjust or rebalance your portfolio from time to time to bring the allocation back in line with the model you've selected. Or, you might realign your model as your financial goals, your time frame, or the market situation changes.

Asset class

Different categories of investments are described as asset classes. Stock, bonds, and cash—including cash equivalents—are major asset classes. So are real estate, derivative investments, such as options and futures contracts, and precious metals.

When you allocate the assets in your investment portfolio, you decide what proportion of its total value will be invested in each of the different asset classes you're including.

Asset management account (AMA)
All-in-one asset management accounts provide the financial advantages of an investment account combined with the convenience of an interest-bearing checking account.

AMAs generally offer check-writing and ATM privileges, credit cards, direct deposit, and automatic transfer between accounts, as well as access to reduced-rate loans and other perks. There are usually annual fees and minimum account requirements.

AMAs are offered by many brokerage firms and mutual fund companies, and are also known as central asset accounts (CAAs) or cash management accounts (CMAs).

Asset-backed bond
Asset-backed bonds, also known as asset-backed securities, are secured by loans or by money owed to a company for merchandise or services purchased on credit.

For example, an asset-backed bond is created when a securities firm bundles debt, such as credit card or car loans, and sells investors the right to receive the payments made on those loans.

Assignment
Assignment occurs when someone who has written, or sold, a listed option receives a notice that the option has been exercised and he or she must fulfill the terms of the contract by buying the underlying instrument if the option was a put or selling the underlying instrument if the option was a call.

Making the assignment is a two-step process. When an option listed on a US exchange is exercised, the Options Clearing Corporation (OCC) notifies a member broker-dealer firm with clients who have sold options in that series that one of those clients must meet the obligation to buy or sell. The firm, in turn, selects an individual client following its particular methodology, such as chronological order of sale or random choice.

As the writer of an in-the-money option, you should expect assignment, unless you close out your position with an offsetting contract. However, there is no guarantee that you will realize a profit or avoid a loss.

Assignment also means transferring property you own, such as stock and real estate, to someone else by using the document that's appropriate to the type of property. Similarly, property of a financially troubled entity can be assigned, or transferred, to a creditor and sold to offset losses.

At-the-money
At-the-money is another way of saying at the current price. Options whose exercise price is the same or almost the same as the current market price of the underlying stock or futures contract are considered at-the-money.

Auction market
Auction market trading, sometimes known as open outcry, is the way the major exchanges, such as the New York Stock Exchange (NYSE) and the Chicago Mercantile Exchange (CME), have traditionally handled buying and selling.

Brokers acting for buyers compete against each other on the exchange floor, as brokers acting for sellers do, to get the best price. While the trading can be quite intense, it is orderly because the participants adhere to exchange rules.

Audit
An audit is a professional, independent examination of a company's financial statements and accounting documents following generally accepted accounting principles (GAAP).

An IRS audit, in contrast, is an examination of a taxpayer's return, usually to question the accuracy or acceptability of the information the return reports.

Audit committee
The corporate audit committee is the liaison between the company's management, the board of directors, internal and external auditors, and any other accounting experts advising the company on audit issues.

In particular, the audit committee is responsible for hiring and managing external auditors. Since 2002, when Congress passed the Sarbanes-Oxley Act, implementing stringent financial oversight regulations, the role of the audit committee has become increasingly important.

An audit committee is composed of a subgroups from the corporation's board of directors. Members of the audit committee must be independent, which means they have no ties to the company's management team.

In general, they cannot receive any compensation, such as consulting or advisory fees, except for a board of director's fee. They may not be able to own shares in the company or be affiliated in any other way with the company. Nor can they be affiliated with or have an interest in the external auditing company.

Automatic enrollment

Your employer has the right to sign you up for your company's 401(k) plan, in what's known as an automatic enrollment. If you don't want to participate, you must refuse, in writing, to be part of the plan.

In an automatic enrollment, the company determines the percentage of earnings you contribute and how your contribution is invested, choosing among a number of potential alternatives. You have the right to change either or both of those choices if you stay in the plan.

Automatic exercise

If you hold a call option, automatic exercise may occur if the contract is in-the-money by a certain amount.

In this case, an in-the-money contract is one where the strike price—the price at which you would purchase the underlying instrument if the contract were exercised—is lower than the market price of that instrument. Generally speaking, exercising your option in this situation would produce a profit on the transaction.

Certain options may be subject to automatic exercise authorized by the Options Clearing Corporation (OCC) unless you instruct them otherwise. Your brokerage firm may also have an automatic exercise policy.

Average

A stock market average is a mathematical way of reporting the composite change in prices of the stocks that the average includes.

Each average is designed to reflect the general movement of the broad market or a certain segment of the market and often serves as a benchmark for the performance of individual stocks in its sphere.

A true average adds the prices of the stocks it covers and divides that amount by the number of stocks.

However, many averages are weighted, which usually means they count stocks with the largest market capitalizations more heavily than they do others. Weighting reflects the impact that the stocks of the biggest companies have on the markets and on the economy in general.

The Dow Jones Industrial Average (DJIA), which tracks the performance of 30 large-company stocks, is the most widely followed market average in the United States.

Average annual yield

Average annual yield is the average yearly income on an investment, expressed as a percentage.

You can calculate the average annual yield by adding all the income you received on an investment and dividing that amount by the number of years the money was invested. So if you receive $60 interest on a $1,000 bond each year for ten years, the average annual yield is 6% ($60 ÷ $1,000 = 0.06 or 6%).

Average daily balance

The average daily balance method is one of the ways that the finance charge on your credit card may be calculated.

The credit card company issuer divides the balance you owe each day by the number of days in your billing cycle and multiplies the result by the interest rate to find the finance charge for each day in the period.

If this is the method your creditor uses, the larger the payment you make and the earlier in the cycle you make it, the smaller your finance charge will be.

Baby bond

Bonds whose par values are less than $1,000 are often described as baby bonds, or, in the case of municipal bonds, as mini-munis.

Small companies that may not be able to attract institutional investors, such as banks and mutual fund companies, may offer baby bonds to raise cash from individual investors.

Some municipalities also use baby bonds to foster involvement in government activities by making it possible for more people to invest.

Baccalaureate bond

Baccalaureate bonds are tax-free zero coupon bonds issued by certain states specifically to help families accumulate assets to meet college tuition costs.

The bonds are usually sold in small denominations, so that you can buy several, with maturity dates that correspond with the dates that tuition payments are due.

In some states, baccalaureate bond-holders receive a small tuition discount if they use the bonds to pay for attending an in-state school.

Back-end load

Some mutual funds impose a back-end load, or a contingent deferred sales charge, if you sell shares in the fund during the first six or seven years after you purchase them.

The charge is a percentage of the value of the assets you're selling. The percentage typically declines each year the charge applies and then is dropped.

However, the annual asset-based management fee is higher on back-end load funds, also known as Class B shares, than on front-end load funds, where you pay the sales charge at the time you purchase.

Back test

A back test simulates the investment return that an investment strategy would have produced over a specific period.

For example, someone who wanted to evaluate a strategy of buying after stock splits might test the effect of having purchased 500 additional shares in the large-cap stocks in a hypothetical portfolio each time one of the stocks split during the period from 1957 to the present.

Back testing is sometimes used to support a current investment strategy by demonstrating that it would have enjoyed strong past performance. Critics point out that the testing period that's chosen has a significant impact on the results and that past performance doesn't guarantee future returns.

Back-up withholding

Back-up withholding is triggered when a bank, brokerage firm, or other institution pays interest, dividends, or other income that must be reported on IRS Form 1099 to a payee who does not provide a tax identification number (TIN), typically a Social Security number, or provides an incorrect number.

While income that's reported on Form 1099 is not normally subject to withholding, in this instance, the payer must withhold 28% of the gross amount as income tax.

You can avoid back-up withholding in most cases by providing a correct TIN using IRS form W-9. But if the IRS determines you have underreported your investment income, it may require back-up withholding even if the payer has your TIN.

Backwardation

If the price of a futures contract that expires in the near term is higher than the price of a contract with the same terms that expires at a later date, the relationship between the two is called backwardation.

More typically, the contract with the longer-term expiration commands a higher price. That relationship is called contango.

Balance of trade

The difference between the value of a country's imports and exports during a specific period of time is called the balance of trade.

If a country exports more than it imports, it has a surplus, or favorable balance of trade. A trade deficit, or unfavorable balance, occurs when a country imports more than it exports.

Balance sheet

A balance sheet is a statement of a company's financial position at a particular moment in time. This financial report shows the two sides of a company's financial situation—what it owns and what it owes.

What the company owns, called its assets, is always equal to the combined value of what the company owes, called its liabilities, and the value of its shareholders' equity. Expressed as an equation,

a company's balance sheets shows assets = liabilities + shareholder value.

If the company were to dissolve, then its debts would be paid, and any assets that remained would be distributed to the shareholders as their equity. Bankruptcy occurs in situations where there is nothing left to distribute to the shareholders, and the company balance sheet is in fact unbalanced because the company owes more than it owns.

Balanced fund

Balanced funds are mutual funds that invest in a portfolio of common stocks, preferred stocks, and bonds to meet their investment goal of seeking a strong return while moderating risk.

Balanced funds generally produce more income than stock funds, though their total return may be less than stock fund returns in a strong stock market.

In a flat or falling stock market, however, disappointing returns on equity investments may be offset by a stronger performance from a balanced fund's fixed-income investments.

Balanced funds are sometimes described as a type of asset allocation fund, which provides the opportunity to spread your money among asset classes with one investment.

Balloon mortgage

With a balloon mortgage, you make monthly payments over the mortgage term, which is typically five, seven, or ten years, and a final installment, or balloon payment, that is significantly larger than the usual monthly payments.

In some cases, you pay only interest on the loan during the mortgage term, and the entire principal is due in the balloon payment.

Many balloon mortgages offer a conversion feature that lets you extend the loan at a new interest rate. For instance, some balloon mortgages convert to a 30-year fixed-rate mortgage at the end of their original term.

You might choose a balloon mortgage if you anticipate being able to refinance at a favorable rate at the end of the term or if you're confident you'll have enough money to pay off the loan in a lump sum. But you may risk losing your home when the balloon payment is due if you can afford to buy the home only because of the comparatively smaller monthly payments that may be available with a balloon mortgage.

Bankruptcy

Bankruptcy means being insolvent, or unable to pay your debts. In that case, you can file a bankruptcy petition to seek a legal resolution.

Chapter 7 bankruptcy, which allows you to discharge your unsecured debts but may result in your losing your home, car, or other secured debt, is available only to those whose earn less than the median for their state or qualify because of special circumstances.

With Chapter 11 bankruptcy, also called reorganization bankruptcy, you work with the court and your creditors to repay debt over three to five years.

However, some debts are not reduced by a declaration of bankruptcy, including past due federal income taxes, alimony, and higher education loans. Similarly, when you hear that a company is re-organizing or is "in Chapter 11," it means it has filed for bankruptcy.

Barbell strategy

When you use a barbell strategy, you invest equivalent amounts in short-term and long-term bonds, creating the shape that gives the strategy its name. The goal is to earn more interest than intermediate-term bonds would provide without taking more risk.

For example, you might buy a port-folio of bonds, with some that mature within a year or two and an equal number that mature in 30 years. When the shorter-term bonds come due, you replace them with other short-term bonds.

It's a different approach from laddering your bond investment, often with a portfolio of intermediate-term bonds, so that your bonds mature in a rolling pattern every few years.

Basis

Basis is the total cost of buying an investment or other asset, including the price, commissions, and other charges.

If you sell the asset, you subtract your basis, also known as your cost basis, from the selling price to determine your capital gain or capital loss. If you give the asset away, the recipient's basis is the same amount as yours.

But if you leave an asset to a beneficiary in your will, the person receives the asset at a step-up in basis, which means the basis of the asset is reset to its market value as of the time of your death.

Basis point

Yields on bonds, notes, and other fixed-income investments fluctuate regularly, typically changing only a few hundredths of a percentage point.

These small variations are measured in basis points, or gradations of 0.01%, or one-hundredth of a percent, with 100 basis points equaling 1%. For example, when the yield on a bond changes from 6.72% to 6.65%, it has dropped 7 basis points.

Similarly, small changes in the interest rates charged for mortgages or other loans are reported in basis points, as are the fees you pay on various investment products, such as annuities and mutual funds. For example, if the average management fee is 1.4%, you might hear it expressed as 140 basis points.

Your percentage of ownership in certain kinds of investments may also be stated in basis points, and in this case each basis point equals 0.01% of the whole investment.

Basis price

When you sell a security, such as a stock or bond, or real estate, the price you use to calculate your capital gains is known as your basis price.

In the case of a security, it includes the purchase price plus any commissions you paid to buy or sell. For real estate, it includes purchase price, certain closing costs at purchase and sale, and the costs of qualifying improvements to the property.

Bear market

A bear market is sometimes described as a period of falling securities prices and sometimes, more specifically, as a market where prices have fallen 20% or more from the most recent high.

A bear market in stocks is triggered when investors sell off shares, generally because they anticipate worsening economic conditions and falling corporate profits.

A bear market in bonds is usually the result of rising interest rates, which prompts investors to sell off older bonds paying lower rates.

Bear spread

A bear spread is an options strategy that you use when you anticipate a decline in the price of the underlying instrument, such as a stock or an index.

As in any spread, you purchase one option and write another on the same underlying item. Both options are identical except for one element, such as the strike price or the expiration date.

For example, with a vertical bear call spread, you buy a call with a higher strike price and sell a call with a lower strike price. With a vertical bear put, you buy a put at a higher price and sell a put at a lower price.

In either case, if you're right about the behavior of the underlying instrument—for example, if a stock whose price you expect to fall does lose value—you could have a net profit. If you're wrong, you could have a net loss cushioned by the income from the sale of one of the legs of the spread.

Bearer bond

A bearer bond is a certificate that states the security's par value, the rate at which interest will be paid, and the name of the bond's owner.

In the past, bearer bonds came with detachable coupons that had to be presented to the issuer to receive the interest payments. That practice explains why a bond's interest rate is often referred to as its coupon rate.

Unlike most bonds issued in the United States since 1983, which are registered electronically, a bearer bond isn't registered, and there's no record of

ownership. This means it can be sold or redeemed by the person or organization that holds it.

Bearer form

When securities are issued as paper certificates and the issuing corporation has no record of the owner, the securities are in bearer form.

The bearer, or holder, of the certificate is considered the owner, and when ownership changes hands a physical transfer of the certificate is required.

The securities may have attached coupons, which the holder must present or send in to the issuer or issuer's agent—typically a bank or brokerage firm—to receive interest or dividend payments.

Bearer securities are rare in the United States today because of the convenience, simplicity, and added security of electronic registration, known as book entry form. When book entry securities are traded, records of ownership are electronically updated, and the buyer's and seller's brokerage accounts are automatically debited and credited, similar to when you pay bills online.

Behavioral finance

Behavioral finance combines psychology and economics to explain why and how investors act and to analyze how that behavior affects the market.

Behavioral finance theorists point to the market phenomenon of hot stocks and bubbles, from the Dutch tulip bulb mania that caused a market crash in the 17th century to the more recent examples of junk bonds in the 1980s and Internet stocks in the 1990s, to validate their position that market prices can be affected by the irrational behavior of investors.

Behavioral finance is in conflict with the perspective of efficient market theory, which maintains that market prices are based on rational foundations, like the fundamental financial health and performance of a company.

Beige book

Beige book is the colloquial name for the Federal report that is formally titled Summary of Commentary on Current Economic Conditions by Federal Reserve District.

The beige book is prepared eight times per year by the Federal Reserve Board, in preparation for the Federal Open Market Committee (FOMC) meetings, at which its members discuss the state of the economy and determine whether any changes ought to be made to the discount rate and whether the money supply should be tightened or loosened.

The report is based on information provided by each Federal Reserve Bank on its particular district and includes opinion and analysis from economists, bank directors, business people, and other market experts in each district. Economic forecasters use the beige book to predict whether and how the Fed will act after the FOMC meeting.

Bellwether

A market bellwether is a security whose changing price is considered a signal that the market is changing direction.

It gets its name from the wether, or castrated ram, that walks at the head of a shepherd's flock. The distinctive tone of the bell around the wether's neck signals the flock's position.

There's not an official list of these trend setters, or market barometers, and they do change as the overall markets and the fortunes of individual companies change.

Benchmark

An investment benchmark is a standard against which the performance of an individual security or group of securities is measured.

For example, the average annual performance of a class of securities over time is a benchmark against which current performance of members of that class and the class itself is measured.

When the benchmark is an index tracking a specific segment of the market, the changing value of the index not only measures the strength or weakness of its segment but is the standard against which the performance of individual investments within the segment are measured.

For example, the Standard & Poor's 500 Index (S&P 500) and the Dow Jones Industrial Average (DJIA) are the most widely followed benchmarks, or indicators, of the US market for large-company stocks and the funds that invest in those stocks.

There are other indexes that serve as benchmarks for both broader and narrower segments of the US equities markets, of international markets, and of other types of investments such as bonds, mutual funds, and commodities.

Individual investors and financial professionals often gauge their market expectations and judge the performance of individual investments or market sectors against the appropriate benchmarks. In a somewhat different way, the changing yield on the 10-year US Treasury bond is considered a benchmark of investor attitudes.

For example, a lower yield is an indication that investors are putting money into bonds, driving up the price, possibly because they expect stock prices to drop. Conversely, a higher yield indicates investors are putting their money elsewhere.

Originally the term benchmark was a surveyor's mark indicating a specific height above sea level.

Beneficial owner

When your stocks are registered in street name, the brokerage firm has title to the stocks but you are the beneficial owner, or the person who actually benefits from owning the stock.

Beneficiary

A beneficiary is the person or organization who receives assets that are held in your name in a retirement plan, or are paid on your behalf by an insurance company, after your death.

If you have established a trust, the beneficiary you name receives the assets of the trust.

A life insurance policy pays your beneficiary the face value of your policy minus any loans you haven't repaid when you die. An annuity contract pays the beneficiary the accumulated assets as dictated by the terms of the contract.

A retirement plan, such as an IRA or 401(k), pays your beneficiary the value of the accumulated assets or requires the beneficiary to withdraw assets either as a lump sum or over a period of time, depending on the plan. Some retirement plans require that you name your spouse as beneficiary or obtain written permission to name someone else.

You may name any person or institution—or several people and institutions—as beneficiary or contingent beneficiary of a trust, a retirement plan, annuity contract, or life insurance policy. A contingent beneficiary is one who inherits the assets if the primary beneficiary has died or chooses not to accept them.

Beta

Beta is a measure of an investment's relative volatility. The higher the beta, the more sharply the value of the investment can be expected to fluctuate in relation to a market index.

For example, Standard & Poor's 500 Index (S&P 500) has a beta coefficient (or base) of 1. That means if the S&P 500 moves 2% in either direction, a stock with a beta of 1 would also move 2%.

Under the same market conditions, however, a stock with a beta of 1.5 would move 3% (2% increase x 1.5 beta = 0.03, or 3%). But a stock with a beta lower than 1 would be expected to be more stable in price and move less. Betas as low as 0.5 and as high as 4 are fairly common, depending on the sector and size of the company.

However, in recent years, there has been a lively debate about the validity of assigning and using a beta value as an accurate predictor of stock performance.

Bid

The bid is the price a market maker or broker is willing to pay for a security, such as a stock or bond, at a particular time. In the real estate market, a bid is the amount a buyer offers to pay for a property.

Bid and ask

Bid and ask is better known as a quotation or quote.

Bid is the price a market maker or broker offers to pay for a security, and ask is the price at which a market maker or dealer offers to sell. The difference between the two prices is called the spread.

Big Board

The Big Board is the nickname of the New York Stock Exchange (NYSE), the oldest stock exchange in the United States and the one with the largest trading floor.

Common and preferred stock, bonds, exchange traded funds, warrants, rights. and other investment products are all traded on the Big Board, which dates back to 1792.

Blind pool

If the general partner of a limited partnership does not say which investments the partnership will make, the investment is known as a blind pool.

In a blind pool equipment leasing partnership, for example, you don't know what type of equipment the partnership is planning to acquire for leasing, and in a blind pool real estate investment trust (REIT), you don't know which properties the partnership will purchase.

When you invest in a blind pool limited partnership, your evaluation of the partnership's prospects is based on the investment track record of the general partner. In contrast, in a specified pool limited partnership, you can assess the partnership's prospects on a more concrete analysis of the costs and projected revenues.

However, there is no evidence that the average performance of blind pools differs significantly from the performance of comparable specified pool partnerships.

Blind trust

A blind trust is created when a third party, such as an investment adviser or other trustee, assumes complete control of the assets held in a trust.

Elected officials often set up blind trusts to reassure the public that political decisions are not being made for personal financial benefit.

Block trade

When at least 10,000 shares of stock or bonds valued at $200,000 or more are bought or sold in a single transaction, it is called a block trade.

Institutional investors, including mutual funds and pension funds, typically trade in this volume, and most individual investors do not.

Blue chip stock

Blue chip stock is the common stock of a large, well-regarded US company. The companies in that informal category are collectively known as blue chip companies. Blue chips have a long-established record of earning profits and paying dividends regardless of the economic climate.

They take their name from the most valuable poker chips. In the United Kingdom, in contrast, comparable firms are called alpha companies.

Blue sky laws

Blue sky laws require companies that sell stock, mutual funds, and other financial products to register new issues with the appropriate public agency.

The companies must also provide financial details of each offering in writing so that investors have the information they need to make informed buy and sell decisions.

These laws are state rather than federal laws, and owe their origin—at least in legend—to a frustrated judge who equated the value of a worthless stock offering to a patch of blue sky.

Boiler room

A boiler room is a location used by con artists to contact potential victims out-of-the-blue—an approach known as cold calling—in an attempt to sell high-risk investments that may or may not be legitimate.

Boiler room scammers typically use high-pressure tactics to close an immediate sale and are unwilling to provide written information about either the investment they are pushing or themselves.

Bond

Bonds are debt securities issued by corporations and governments.

Bonds are, in fact, loans that you and other investors make to the issuers in return for the promise of being paid interest, usually but not always at a fixed rate, over the loan term. The issuer also promises to repay the loan principal at maturity, on time and in full.

Because most bonds pay interest on a regular basis, they are also described as fixed-income investments. While the term bond is used generically to describe all debt securities, bonds are specifically long-term investments, with maturities longer than ten years.

Bond fund

A bond mutual fund sells shares in the fund to investors and uses the money it raises to invest in a portfolio of bonds to meet its investment objective—typically to provide regular income.

The appeal of bond funds is that you can usually invest a much smaller amount of money than you would need to buy a portfolio of bonds, making it easier to diversify your fixed-income investments.

Unlike individual bonds, however, bond funds have no maturity date and no guaranteed interest rate because their portfolios aren't fixed. Also unlike individual bonds, they don't promise to return your principal.

You can choose among a variety of bond funds with different investment strategies and levels of risk. Some funds invest in long-term, and others in short-term, bonds. Some buy government bonds, while others buy corporate bonds or municipal bonds. Finally, some buy investment-grade bonds, while others focus on high-yield bonds.

Bond rating

Independent agencies, such as Standard & Poor's (S&P) and Moody's Investors Service, assess the likelihood that bond issuers are likely to default on their loans or interest payments.

Ratings systems differ from one agency to another but usually have at least 10 categories, ranging from a high of AAA (or Aaa) to a low of D. Bonds ranked BBB (or Baa) or higher are considered investment-grade bonds.

Bond swap

In a bond swap, you buy one bond and sell another at the same time.

For example, you might sell one bond at a loss at year's end to get a tax write-off while buying another to keep the same portion of your portfolio allocated to bonds.

You may also sell a bond with a lower rating to buy one with a higher rating, or sell a bond that's close to maturity so you can buy a bond that won't mature for several years.

Book value

Book value is the net asset value (NAV) of a company's stocks and bonds.

Finding the NAV involves subtracting the company's short- and long-term liabilities from its assets to find net assets. Then you'd divide the net assets by the number of shares of common stock, preferred stock, or bonds to get the NAV per share or per bond.

Book value is sometimes cited as a way of determining whether a company's assets cover its outstanding obligations and equity issues.

Further, some investors and analysts look at the price of a stock in relation to its book value, which is provided in the company's annual report, to help identify undervalued stocks. Other investors discount the relevance of this information.

Book-entry security

Book-entry securities are stocks, bonds, and similar investments whose ownership is recorded electronically rather than in certificate form.

When you sell the security, the records are updated, deleting you as an owner and adding the purchaser. This means you don't have to keep track of paper documents, and they can't be lost or stolen.

The Depository Trust & Clearing Corporation (DTCC) acts as a clearing-house for book-entry securities.

Bottom fishing

Investors using a bottom-fishing strategy look for stocks that they consider undervalued because the prices are low.

The logic of bottom fishing is that stock prices sometimes fall further than a company's actual financial situation warrants, especially in the aftermath of bad news. Bottom-fishing investors hope the stock will rebound dramatically and provide a healthy profit.

Bottom-up investing

When you use a bottom-up investing strategy, you focus on the potential of individual stocks, bonds, and other investments.

Using this approach, for example, means you pay less attention to the economy as a whole, or to the prospects of the industry a company is in, than you do to the company itself.

If your investing method is bottom up, you read research reports, examine the company's financial stability, and evaluate what you know about its products and services in great detail.

Bourse

Bourse is the French term for a stock exchange, meaning, literally, purse. The national stock market of France, a totally electronic market, is known as the Paris Bourse.

The term is used throughout Europe and worldwide as a synonym for stock exchange, though it generally isn't used in the United States.

Brady bond

These bonds of Latin American countries, named for former US Secretary of the Treasury Nicholas Brady, are issued in US dollars and backed by US Treasury zero coupon bonds.

The bonds were originally issued in exchange for commercial bank loans that were in default. Their changing prices in the secondary market reflect the level of confidence investors have in the economies of the issuing nations.

Breakout

Stock prices fluctuate constantly, but each stock typically moves within a fairly narrow range. That means the stock's average price changes gradually, if at all. But sometimes a stock's price breaks out of its limits, and jumps or tumbles suddenly.

Usually the breakout is fueled by a particular event. The company may realize a commercial success, such as a drug company discovering a new cure for a major disease. Or a breakout may reflect a financial development, such as a new alliance with a successful partner.

Breakpoint

A breakpoint is the level at which your account balance in a mutual fund company or the size of a new investment in the company's funds qualifies you to pay a reduced sales charge.

Fund companies that charge a percentage of the amount you invest as a front-end load, or sales charge, may offer this cost saving. They are not required to do so, but if they do use breakpoints, they must ensure that all clients who qualify get the discount.

In most cases, the first breakpoint is $25,000, with further reductions for each additional $25,000 or $50,000 purchase. For example, if the standard load were 5.5%, it might drop to 5.25% at $25,000, to 5% at $50,000, and perhaps to as low as 2.5% with an investment of $250,000.

In calculating breakpoints, some fund companies will combine the value of all of your investments in the mutual funds

they offer. Other companies count the investments of all the members of your household or give you credit for purchases you intend to make in the future.

Broker

A broker acts as an agent or intermediary for a buyer and a seller. The buyer, seller, and broker may all be individuals, or one or more may be a business or other institution.

For example, a stockbroker works for a brokerage firm, and handles client orders to buy or sell stocks, bonds, commodities, and options in return for a commission or asset-based fee.

Stockbrokers must pass a uniform examination administered by the NASD and must register with the Securities and Exchange Commission (SEC).

A floor broker handles buy and sell orders on the floor of a securities or commodities exchange. A real estate broker represents the seller in a real estate transaction and receives a commission on the sale.

If as a real estate buyer you hire someone to represent your interests, that person is known as a buyer's agent. A mortgage or insurance broker acts as an intermediary in finding a mortgage or insurance policy for his or her client and also receives a commission.

Broker-dealer

A broker-dealer (B/D) is a license granted by the Securities and Exchange Commission (SEC) that entitles the licensee to buy and sell securities for its clients' accounts. The firm may also act as principal, or dealer, trading securities for its own inventory.

Some broker-dealers act in both capacities, depending on the circum-stances of the trade or the type of security being traded. For example, your order to purchase a particular security might be filled from the firm's inventory.

That's perfectly legal, though you must be notified that it has occurred. B/Ds range in size from independent one-person offices to large brokerage firms.

Brokerage account

To buy and sell securities through a broker-dealer or other financial services firm, you establish an account, generally known as a brokerage account, with that firm.

In a full-service brokerage firm, a registered representative or account executive handles your buy and sell instructions and often provides investment advice.

If your account is with a discount firm, you are more likely to give your orders to the person who answers the telephone when you call.

And if your account is with an online firm, you give orders and get confirmations electronically.

In all three cases, the firm provides updated information on your investment activity and portfolio value, and handles the required paperwork. And in some cases, your brokerage account may be part of a larger package of financial services known as an asset management account.

Brokerage firm

Brokerage firms, also known as broker-dealers, are licensed by the Securities and Exchange Commission (SEC) to buy and sell securities for clients and for their own accounts.

When a brokerage firm sells securities it owns, it is said to be acting as a principal in that transaction.

Firms frequently maintain research departments for their own and their clients' benefit. They may also provide a range of financial products and services, including financial planning, asset management, and educational programs.

Brokerage firms come in all sizes, from one- or two-person offices to huge firms with offices around the world. They are sometimes differentiated as full-service or discount firms, based on pricing structure and client relationships.

Some brokerage firms exist entirely online, and nearly all firms offer you the option of placing orders electronically rather than over the telephone. In most cases, trading electronically is substantially less expensive than giving buy and sell orders by phone.

Brokerage window

A 401(k) account that permits its plan participants to buy and sell investments through a designated brokerage account is said to offer a brokerage window.

Any securities trades you authorize for your account are made through this brokerage account. Transaction fees are subtracted as those orders are executed.

Bucket shop

A bucket shop is an illegal brokerage firm whose salespeople pose as legitimate brokers and attempt to sell you securities.

Typically, a bucket shop broker doesn't actually purchase the securities you agree to buy and that you pay for. Rather, the con artists pocket your money and move on, disappearing before you realize you have been scammed.

Budget

A budget is a written record of income and expenses during a specific time frame, typically a year.

You use a budget as a spending plan to allocate your income to cover your expenses and to track how closely your actual expenditures line up with what you had planned to spend.

An essential part of personal budgeting is creating an emergency fund, which you can use to cover unexpected expenses. You also want to budget a percentage of your income for saving and investing, just as you budget for food, housing, and clothing.

Businesses and governments also create budgets to govern their expenditures for a fiscal year—though like individuals they make regular adjustments to reflect financial reality. And, like individuals, businesses and governments can find themselves in trouble if their spending outpaces their income.

Bull market

A prolonged period when stock prices as a whole are moving upward is called a bull market, although the rate at which those gains occur can vary widely from bull market to bull market.

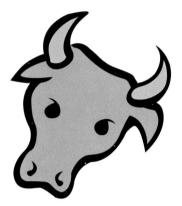

The duration of a bull market, the severity of the falling market that follows, and the time that elapses until the next upturn are also different each time. Well-known bull markets began in 1923, 1949, 1982, and 1990.

Bull spread

A bull spread is an options strategy that you use when you anticipate an increase in the price of the underlying instrument, such as a stock or an index.

As in any spread, you purchase one option and write another on the same underlying item. Both options are identical except for one element, such as the strike price or the expiration date.

For example, with a vertical bull call spread, you buy a call with a lower strike price and sell a call with a higher strike price. With a vertical bull put, you buy a put at a lower price and sell a put at a higher price.

In either case, if you're right about the behavior of the underlying instrument, you could have a net profit. For example, you would make money if a stock whose price you expect to increase does gain value. If you're wrong, you could have a net loss cushioned by the income from the sale of one of the legs of the spread.

Buydown

When you make an up-front cash payment to reduce your monthly payments on a mortgage loan, it's called a buydown.

In a temporary buydown, your payments during the buydown period are calculated at a lower interest rate than the actual rate on your loan, which makes the payments smaller.

For example, if you prepay $6,000, your rate might be reduced by a total of six percentage points, or one percent for each thousand dollars, spread over three years.

Instead of an 8% rate in the first year, it would be 5%. In the second year, it would be 6%, and in the third year 7%. On a $100,000 loan with a 30-year term, a reduction from 8% to 5% would reduce your monthly payments in the first year from about $734 to about $535.

The extra cash you prepaid would be used to make up the difference between the amounts due calculated at the lower rates and the actual cost of borrowing—in this case about $200 a month in the first year. Then, in the fourth year, you would begin to pay at the actual loan rate and your payments would increase.

In a permanent buydown, which is less common, your rate might be reduced by about 0.25% for each thousand dollars, or point, you prepaid, but the reduction would last for the life of the loan.

You might choose to do a buydown if you had extra cash at the time you were ready to buy, but a smaller income than would normally allow you to qualify to buy the home you want.

In most cases, lenders require that your housing costs be no more than 28% of your income. You might be able to reach that level if your initial payments were less at the time of purchase. In other cases, a home builder who is having trouble selling new properties might offer buydowns through a local lender to encourage reluctant buyers to take advantage of lower payments in the first years they own their homes.

Buy side

Institutional money managers, such as mutual funds, pension funds, and endowments, are the buy side of Wall Street.

Buy-side institutions use proprietary research to make investments for the portfolios they manage and don't interact with or make recommendations to individual investors.

In contrast, sell-side institutions such as brokerage firms act as agents for individual investors when they buy and sell securities, and make their research available to their clients.

Buy-and-hold

Buy-and-hold investors take a long-term view of investing, generally keeping a bond from date of issue to date of maturity and holding onto shares of a stock through bull and bear markets.

Among the advantages of following a buy-and-hold strategy are increased opportunity for your assets to compound and reduced trading costs. Among the risks are continuing to hold investments that are no longer living up to reasonable expectations.

Buyback

When a company purchases shares of its own publicly traded stock or its own bonds in the open market, it's called a buyback.

The most common reason a company buys back its stock is to make the stock more attractive to investors by increasing its earnings per share. While the actual earnings stay the same, the earnings per share increase because the number of shares has been reduced.

Companies may also buy back shares to pay for acquisitions that are financed with stock swaps or to make stocks available for employee stock option plans.

They may also want to decrease the risk of a hostile takeover by reducing the number of shares for sale, or to discourage short-term trading by driving up the share price.

Companies may buy back bonds when they are selling at discount, which is typically the result of rising interest rates. By paying less than par in the open market, the company is able to reduce the cost of redeeming the bonds when they come due.

Buyer's agent

A buyer's agent represents a buyer in a real estate transaction, negotiating with the seller's agent for a lower price or a contract with more favorable terms.

A real estate agent or broker, on the other hand, represents the seller. Although that agent customarily shows the property to prospective buyers, his or her primary obligation is to the seller.

Bylaws

Bylaws are the self-imposed rules governing an incorporated company. The bylaws cover details such as the structure of the company, what the company's goals are, and how often shareholders meet.

They also explain the voting process and how officers, committees, and board members are chosen. A company can put almost any provisions in its bylaws, as long as the rules don't break federal or local law.

Cafeteria plan

Some employers offer cafeteria plans, more formally known as flexible spending plans, which give you the option of participating in a range of tax-saving benefit programs.

If you enroll in the plan, you choose the percentage of your pretax income to be withheld from your paycheck, up to the limit the plan allows. You allocate your money to the parts of the plan you want to participate in.

For example, you can set aside money to pay for medical expenses that aren't covered by insurance, for child care, or for additional life insurance coverage. As you incur these kinds of expenses, you are reimbursed from the amount you have put into the plan.

Since you owe no income tax on the money you contribute, you actually have more cash available for these expenses than if you were spending after-tax dollars.

However, you must estimate the amount you're going to contribute before the tax year begins, and you forfeit any money you've set aside but don't spend. For example, if you've set aside $1,500 for medical expenses but spend only $1,400, you lose the $100.

In some plans the deadline for spending the money in your flexible spending account is December 31. Other plans provide up to a three-month extension.

Call

In the bond markets, a call is an issuer's right to redeem bonds it has sold before the date they mature. With preferred stocks, the issuer may call the stock to retire it, or remove it from the marketplace.

In either case, it may be a full call, redeeming the entire issue, or a partial call, redeeming only a portion of the issue.

When a bank makes a secured loan, it reserves the right to demand full repayment of the loan—referred to as calling the loan—should the borrower default on interest payments.

Finally, when the term refers to options contracts, holding a call gives you the right to buy the underlying instrument at a specific price by a specific date. Selling a call obligates you to deliver the underlying instrument if the call is exercised and you're assigned to meet the call.

Call option

Buying a call option gives you, as owner, the right to buy a fixed quantity of the underlying product at a specified price, called the strike price, within a specified time period.

For example, you might purchase a call option on 100 shares of a stock if you expect the stock price to increase but prefer not to tie up your investment principal by investing in the stock. If the price of the stock does go up, the call option will increase in value.

You might choose to sell your option at a profit or exercise the option and buy the shares at the strike price. But if the stock price at expiration is less than the strike price, the option will be worthless. The amount you lose, in that case, is the premium you paid to buy the option plus any brokerage fees.

In contrast, you can sell a call option, which is known as writing a call. That gives the buyer the right to buy the underlying investment from you at the strike price before the option expires. If you write a call, you are obliged to sell if the option is exercised and you are assigned to meet the call.

Callable bond

A callable bond can be redeemed by the issuer before it matures if that provision is included in the terms of the bond agreement, or deed of trust.

Bonds are typically called when interest rates fall, since issuers can save money by paying off existing debt and offering new bonds at lower rates. If a bond is called, the issuer may pay the bondholder a premium, or an amount above the par value of the bond.

Cap
A cap is a ceiling, or the highest level to which something can go.

For example, an interest rate cap limits the amount by which an interest rate can be increased over a specific period of time. A typical cap on an adjustable rate mortgage (ARM) limits interest rate increases to two percentage points annually and six percentage points over the term of the loan.

In a different example, the cap on your annual contribution to an individual retirement account (IRA) is $4,000 for 2006 and 2007 and $5,000 in 2008, provided you have earned at least that much. If you're 50 or older, you can make an additional catch-up contribution of $1,000 each year.

Capital
Capital is money that is used to generate income or make an investment. For example, the money you use to buy shares of a mutual fund is capital that you're investing in the fund.

Companies raise capital from investors by selling stocks and bonds and use the money to expand, make acquisitions, or otherwise build the business.

The term capital markets refers to the physical and electronic environments where this capital is raised, either through public offerings or private placements.

Capital appreciation
Any increase in a capital asset's fair market value is called capital appreciation. For example, if a stock increases in value from $30 a share to $60 a share, it shows capital appreciation.

Some stock mutual funds that invest for aggressive growth are called capital appreciation funds.

Capital gain
When you sell an asset at a higher price than you paid for it, the difference is your capital gain. For example, if you buy 100 shares of stock for $20 a share and sell

them for $30 a share, you realize a capital gain of $10 a share, or $1,000 in total.

If you own the stock for more than a year before selling it, you have a long-term capital gain. If you hold the stock for less than a year, you have a short-term capital gain.

Most long-term capital gains are taxed at a lower rate than your other income while short-term gains are taxed at your regular rate. There are some exceptions, such as gains on collectibles, which are taxed at 28%. The long-term capital gains tax rates are 15% for anyone whose marginal federal tax rate is 25% or higher, and 5% for anyone whose marginal rate is 10% or 15%.

CAPITAL GAIN	
What you sold for	$3,000
− What you paid	− $2,000
CAPITAL GAIN	$1,000

You are exempt from paying capital gains tax on profits of up to $250,000 on the sale of your primary home if you're single and up to $500,000 if you're married and file a joint return, provided you meet the requirements for this exemption.

Capital gains distribution
When mutual fund companies sell investments that have increased in value, the profits, or capital gains, are passed on to their shareholders as capital gains distributions.

These distributions are made on a regular schedule, often at the end of the year and are taxable at your regular rate unless the funds are held in a tax-deferred or tax-free account.

Most funds offer the option of automatically reinvesting all or part of your capital gains distributions to buy more shares.

Capital gains tax (CGT)
A capital gains tax is due on profits you realize on the sale of a capital asset, such as stock, bonds, or real estate.

Long-term gains, on assets you own more than a year, are taxed at a lower rate than ordinary income while short-term gains are taxed at your regular rate.

The long-term capital gains tax rates on most investments is 15% for anyone whose marginal federal tax rate is 25% or higher, and 5% for anyone whose marginal rate is 10% or 15%. There are some exceptions. For example, long-term gains on collectibles are taxed at 28%.

You are exempt from capital gains tax on profits of up to $250,000 on the sale of your primary home if you're single and up to $500,000 if you're married and file a joint return, provided you meet the requirements for this exemption.

Capital loss

When you sell an asset for less than you paid for it, the difference between the two prices is your capital loss.

For example, if you buy 100 shares of stock at $30 a share and sell when the price has dropped to $20 a share, you will realize a capital loss of $10 a share, or $1,000.

Although nobody wants to lose money on an investment, there is a silver lining. You can use capital losses to offset capital gains in computing your income tax. However, you must use short-term losses to offset short-term gains and long-term losses to offset long-term gains.

CAPITAL LOSS	
What you paid	$3,000
− What you sold for	− $2,000
CAPITAL LOSS	$1,000

If you have a net capital loss in any year—that is, your losses exceed your gains—you can usually deduct up to $3,000 of this amount from regular income on your tax return. You may also be able to carry forward net capital losses and deduct on future tax returns.

Capital markets

Capital markets are the physical and electronic markets where equity and debt securities, commodities, and other investments are sold to investors.

When you place an order through a brokerage firm, trade online, or use a dividend reinvestment plan (DRIP), you're participating in a capital market.

Corporations use capital markets to raise money through public offerings of stocks and bonds or private placements of securities to institutional investors, such as mutual fund companies.

Capital preservation

Capital preservation is a strategy for protecting the money you have available to invest by choosing insured accounts or fixed-income investments that promise return of principal.

The downside of capital preservation over the long term is that by avoiding the potential risks of equity investing, you exposure yourself to inflation risk.

That's the case because your investments are unlikely to increase enough in value to offset the gradual loss of purchasing power that's a result of even moderate inflation.

Car insurance

Car insurance covers theft of and damage to your car or damage that your car causes, plus liability protection in case you are sued as a result of an accident. Your state may require proof of insurance before you can register your car.

As a car owner, you pay premiums set by the insurance company based on the value of your car and the risk the company believes you pose. The insurance company agrees to cover your losses, subject to a deductible and the limits specified in the contract.

Some states have insurance pools that allow car owners who have been turned down elsewhere to obtain coverage.

Cash balance plan

A cash balance retirement plan is a defined benefit plan that has many of the characteristics of a defined contribution plan.

The benefit that you'll be entitled to builds up as credits to a hypothetical account. The hypothetical account is credited with hypothetical earnings, based on a percentage of your current pay.

These plans are portable, which means you can roll them over from one employer to another when you change jobs. That makes them popular with younger and mobile workers.

But they are often unpopular with older workers whose employers switch from a defined benefit to cash balance plan because their pensions may be less than with traditional defined benefit plans.

Cash basis accounting

Cash basis accounting is one of two ways of recording revenues and expenses. Using this method, a company records income on its books when it receives a payment and expenses when it makes a payment.

In accrual accounting, by comparison, a company counts revenue as it's earned and expenses as they're incurred.

For example, when a magazine company sells annual subscriptions, it receives the cash for the subscriptions at the beginning of the year, but it doesn't earn the whole amount of the subscription cost until it has sent the subscriber a full year's issues of the magazine.

In cash basis accounting, paid subscriptions are recorded as revenue when the company receives the payments. In accrual accounting, the company records revenue only as the subscription is fulfilled.

A $24 subscription for 12 monthly issues of a magazine would result in immediate revenue of $24 in cash basis accounting, versus an accrual of $2 of revenue each month under accrual accounting.

Cash equivalent

Short-term, low-risk investments, such as US Treasury bills or short-term certificates of deposit (CDs), are considered cash equivalents.

The Financial Accounting Standards Board (FASB) defines cash equivalents as highly liquid securities with maturities of less than three months. Liquid securities typically are those that can be sold easily with little or no loss of value.

Cash flow

Cash flow is a measure of changes in a company's cash account during an accounting period, specifically its cash income minus the cash payments it makes.

For example, if a car dealership sells $100,000 worth of cars in a month and spends $35,000 on expenses, it has a positive cash flow of $65,000. But if it takes in only $35,000 and has $100,000 in expenses, it has a negative cash flow of $65,000.

Investors often consider cash flow when they evaluate a company, since without adequate money to pay its bills, it will have a hard time staying in business.

You can calculate whether your personal cash flow is positive or negative the same way you would a company's. You'd subtract the money you receive (from wages, investments, and other income) from the money you spend on expenses (such as housing, transportation, and other costs).

If there's money left over, your cash flow is positive. If you spend more than you have coming in, it's negative.

Cash market

In a cash market, buyers pay the market price for securities, currency, or commodities "on the spot," just as you would pay cash for groceries or other consumer products.

Cash markets are also called spot markets. A cash market is the opposite of a futures market, where commodities or financial products are scheduled for delivery and payment at a set price at a specified time in the future.

In a cash market, ownership is transferred promptly, and payment is made upon delivery.

Cash settlement

To settle a futures contract where the underlying asset is a financial instrument, such as a stock index or interest rate rather than a physical commodity, you deliver cash.

In contrast, when you settle a futures contract on other commodities, you deliver the physical product. But because index values or interest rates are intangible, physical delivery is not possible.

The way you calculate the amount due is defined in the contract. When the underlying instrument is an index, this usually involves multiplying the value of the index times a fixed amount. For example, the cash settlement of a contract on the Standard & Poor's MidCap 400 Index is determined by multiplying the value of the index times $500.

However, in the vast majority of cases, futures contracts are offset before the settlement date, and no delivery is required.

Cash surrender value

The cash surrender value of a permanent life insurance policy is the amount you receive if you cancel or surrender your policy before you die.

It's a portion of the money that accumulates tax-deferred in your cash value account during the period you pay premiums on the policy, minus fees and expenses.

Generally the only portion of the cash surrender value that's subject to income tax is the amount that exceeds what you paid in premiums during the time the policy was in force, though you should check with your tax adviser.

Cash value

Cash value is the amount that an account is worth at any given time.

For example, the cash value of your 401(k) or IRA is what the account is worth at the end of a period, such as the end of a business day, or at the end of the plan year, often December 31.

The cash value of an insurance policy is the amount the insurer will pay you, based on your policy's cash reserve, if you cancel your policy. The cash value is the difference between the amount you paid in premiums and the actual cost of insurance plus other expenses.

Cash value account

If you have a permanent life insurance policy, part of each premium you pay goes into a tax-deferred account called the cash value account.

You can borrow against the money that accumulates in this account, though any outstanding balance at the time of your death reduces the death benefit your beneficiary receives.

If you cancel or surrender your policy, or if you stop paying the premiums, you are entitled to receive a portion of your cash value account. That amount is your cash surrender value.

Catastrophic illness insurance

Many health insurance policies cap, or limit, the amount they will pay to cover medical expenses. But you can buy catastrophic illness insurance to cover medical expenses above the maximum your regular health insurance will pay.

Catch-up contribution

You are entitled to make an annual catch-up contribution to your employer sponsored retirement savings plan and individual retirement account (IRA) if you're 50 or older.

The catch-up amounts, which are larger for employer plans than for IRAs, increase from time to time based on the rate of inflation.

You are eligible to make catch-up contributions whether or not you have contributed the maximum amount you were eligible for in the past. And if you participate in an employer plan and also put money in an IRA, you are entitled to use both catch-up options.

Earnings on catch-up contributions accumulate tax deferred, just as other earnings in your account do. And when your primary contributions are tax deferred, so are your catch-up contributions.

Health savings accounts (HSAs), which you're eligible to open if you have a high deductible health plan (HDHP), allow catch-up contributions if you're at least 55. Your eligibility to make any contributions to an HSA ends when you turn 65.

Ceiling

If there is an upper limit, or cap, on the interest rate you can be charged on an adjustable-rate loan, it's known as a ceiling.

Even if interest rates in general rise higher than the interest-rate ceiling on your loan, the rate you're paying can't be increased above the ceiling.

However, according to the terms of some loans, lenders can add some of the interest they weren't allowed to charge you because of the ceiling to the total amount you owe. This is known as negative amortization.

That means, despite a ceiling, you don't escape the consequences of rising rates, though repayment is postponed, often until the end of the loan's original term.

Ceiling can also refer to a cap on the amount of interest a bond issuer is willing to pay to float a bond. Or, it's the highest price a futures contract can reach on any single trading day before the market locks up, or stops trading, that contract.

Central bank

Most countries have a central bank, which issues the country's currency and holds the reserve deposits of other banks in that country. It also either initiates or carries out the country's monetary policy, including keeping tabs on the money supply.

In the United States, the 12 regional banks that make up the Federal Reserve System act as the central bank. This multibank structure was deliberately developed to ensure that no single region of the country could control economic decision-making.

Central Registration Depository (CRD)

The Central Registration Depository (CRD) is an automated database maintained by NASD.

The database contains records and information about registered securities employees, including employment history, licensing status, the firms that employ them, and any disciplinary actions taken against them.

You can access some of the information about a broker's regulatory background and registration in the database free of charge through NASD's BrokerCheck service at www.nasd.com. You can generally obtain even more extensive information from the CRD through your state's securities regulator.

Certificate of Accrual on Treasury Securities (CATS)

CATS are US Treasury zero-coupon bonds that are sold at deep discount to par, or face value. Like other zeros, the interest isn't actually paid during the bond's term but accumulates so that you receive face value at maturity.

You can use CATS in your long-term portfolio to provide money for college tuition or retirement. For example, you may purchase them in a tax-deferred IRA or a tax-free Roth IRA or Coverdell education savings account (ESA).

As with other zeros, CATS prices can be volatile, so you risk losing some of your principal if you sell before maturity. And like other federal government issues, the interest is free of state and local income tax but subject to federal income tax.

Certificate of deposit (CD)

CDs are time deposits. When you purchase a CD from a bank, up to $100,000 is insured by the Federal Deposit Insurance Corporation (FDIC).

You generally earn compound interest at a fixed rate, which is

determined by the current interest rate and the CD's term, which can range from a week to five years.

However, rates can vary significantly from bank to bank. You usually face a penalty if you withdraw funds before your CD matures, often equal to the interest that has accrued up to the time you make the withdrawal.

Check hold

When you deposit a check, your bank or other financial institution may delay crediting the money to your account during what's called the check hold period.

The number of days that your bank can legally hold your funds depends on the type of check you deposit and, at some banks, on the type of deposit slip you use.

Under federal law, certain deposits must be available by the next business day, including checks payable by the US Treasury or a Federal Reserve Bank, US Postal Service money orders, cashier's checks, and electronic payments.

Other deposits can be subject to a check hold of one to five business days, depending on whether the check is drawn on a local or non-local bank, and the size of the deposit. The law does require banks to make the first $100 of your deposit available on the next business day.

Your bank must inform you of its check hold policy, although you should keep in mind that banks can impose longer holds if your account has been open less than 30 days.

Check truncation

To process payments faster and more efficiently, many banks no longer transport paper checks, but replace them with digital images—called substitute checks—that can be transferred electronically, in a system called check truncation.

When you receive your account statements, the bank may send you substitute checks in place of cancelled checks, each formatted on a separate piece of paper, with the words "This is a legal copy of your check" appearing next to the image.

Most banks destroy original checks once they've archived the substitutes. However, many banks send out either a line item statement or an image statement with photocopies of multiple cancelled checks on each page.

If you need to verify a payment, you can request a substitute check from your bank. There may be a fee for this service.

Checking account

Checking accounts are transaction accounts that allow you to authorize the transfer money to another person or organization either by writing a check that includes the words "Pay to the order of" or by making an electronic transfer.

Banks and credit unions provide transaction accounts, as do brokerage firms and other financial services companies that offer banking services.

Money in transaction accounts is insured by the Federal Deposit Insurance Corporation (FDIC) up to $100,000 per depositor in each banking institution. However, the FDIC doesn't insure money market mutual funds that offer check-writing privileges.

Churning

If a broker intentionally mishandles buying and selling securities in your investment account, it's known as churning.

The broker might buy and sell securities at an excessive rate, or at a rate that's inconsistent with your investment goals or the amount of money you have invested.

One indication of potential churning is that you're paying more in commissions than you are earning on your investments. Churning is illegal but is often hard to prove.

Circuit breaker

After the stock market crash of 1987, stock and commodities exchanges established a system of trigger-point rules known as circuit breakers. They temporarily restrict trading in stocks, stock options, and stock index futures when prices fall too far, too fast.

Currently, trading on the New York Stock Exchange (NYSE) is halted when the Dow Jones Industrial Average (DJIA) drops 10% any time before 2:30 p.m., sooner if the drop is 20%.

But trading could resume, depending on the time of day the loss occurs. However, if the DJIA drops 30% at any point in the day, trading ends for the day.

The actual number of points the DJIA would need to drop to hit the trigger is set four times a year, at the end of each quarter, based on the average value of the DJIA in the previous month.

The only time the circuit breakers have been triggered was on October 27, 1997, when the DJIA fell 554 points, or 7.2%, and the shut-down level was lower. In fact, the DJIA has dropped as much as 10% in a single day only three times in its history.

Claim

You file an insurance claim when you send your insurance company paperwork asking the company to pay for any of the expenses your policy covers.

Clearance

Clearance is the first half of the process that completes your order to buy or sell a security. During clearance, the details on both sides of the transaction are compared electronically to ensure that the order to buy and the order to sell correspond.

For example, in a stock transaction, the Committee on Uniform Securities

Identification Procedures (CUSIP) number, the number of shares, and the price per share must match.

Next, transactions within each broker-dealer are netted down, or offset, by matching its clients' buy orders against sell orders from others of its clients or among a group of affiliated firms. Their records are then updated to reflect the new ownership and account balances.

Any unmatched orders are forwarded to the National Securities Clearing Corporation (NSCC), which instructs selling broker-dealers to provide the relevant securities and the buying broker-dealer to send the cash.

Clearing firm

Clearing firms handle the back-office details of securities transactions between broker-dealers, making the settlement process streamlined and efficient.

In brief, when a broker's order to buy or sell a security has been filled, the clearing firm electronically compares and verifies the details of that trade. Then it nets down the trades to minimize the number of securities that must be received or delivered at settlement.

Cleared trades are settled within a specific time after the trade date, based on the type of security being traded.

Clearinghouse

Clearing corporations, or clearinghouses, provide operational support for securities and commodities exchanges. They also help ensure the integrity of listed securities and derivatives transactions in the United States and other open markets.

For example, when an order to buy or sell a futures or options contract is executed, the clearinghouse compares the details of the trade. Then it delivers the product to the buyer and ensures that payment is made to settle the transaction.

Closed-end fund

Closed-end mutual funds are actively managed funds that raise capital only once, by issuing a fixed number of shares. Like other mutual funds, however, fund managers buy and sell individual investments in keeping with their investment objectives.

The shares are traded on an exchange and their prices fluctuate throughout the trading day, based on supply, demand, and the changing values of their underlying holdings. Most single country funds are closed-end funds.

Closely held

A closely held corporation is one in which a handful of investors, often the people who founded the company, members of the founders' families, or sometimes the current management team, own a majority of the outstanding stock.

Closing costs

When you purchase real estate, there are expenses—known as closing costs—you pay to finalize the transaction, over and above the cost of the property.

In some cases, the seller may offer to pay certain closing costs to attract buyers or close the sale more quickly. Closing costs vary depending on the area where the property is located and are either prepaid or non-recurring.

Prepaid costs are expenses that recur periodically, including home insurance premiums and real estate taxes.

Non-recurring costs pay for securing a mortgage and transferring the property, and may include a filing fee to record the transfer of ownership, mortgage tax, attorneys' fees, credit check fees, title search and title insurance expenses, home inspection fees, an appraisal fee, and any points, or up-front interest charges, you have agreed to pay the lender.

The lender will give you a good faith estimate (GFE) of your closing costs before the closing date, so you'll know approximately how much money you need to have available at closing—usually 5% to 10% of your mortgage.

Many closing costs are tax deductible, so it's a good idea to consult with your tax adviser.

Closing price

The closing price of a stock, bond, option, or futures contract is the last trading price before the exchange or market on which it is traded closes for the day.

With after-hours trading, however, the opening price at the start of the next trading day may be different from the closing price the day before.

When a security is valued as part of an estate or charitable gift, its value is set at the closing price on the day of the valuation of the estate.

Closing statement

A closing statement, also called a HUD1 or settlement sheet, is a legal form your closing or settlement agent uses to itemize all of the costs you and the seller will have to pay at closing to complete a real estate transaction.

Your total cost should be similar to the amount in the good faith estimate (GFE) provided by your lender.

It's important to review the closing statement with your real estate agent and settlement agent. Mistakes do occasionally happen, so be sure to ask questions if there are any charges you don't understand.

Coinsurance

When your healthcare insurance has a coinsurance provision, you and your insurer divide the responsibility for paying doctor and hospital bills by splitting the costs on a percentage basis.

With an 80/20 coinsurance split, for example, your insurer would pay 80%, or $80 of a covered $100 medical bill, and you would pay 20%, or $20.

Some policies set a cap on your out-of-pocket expenses, so that the insurance company covers 95% to 100% of the cost once you have paid the specified amount.

Coinsurance may also apply when you buy insurance on your home or other real estate. In that case, insurers may require you to insure at least a minimum percentage of your property's value— usually about 80%—and may reduce what they will cover if you file a claim but have failed to meet the coinsurance requirement.

Coinsurance also describes a situation in which two insurers split the risk of providing coverage, often in cases when the dollar amount of the potential claims is larger than a single insurer is willing to handle. This type of coinsurance is also called reinsurance.

Collateral

Assets with monetary value, such as stock, bonds, or real estate, which are used to guarantee a loan, are considered collateral.

If the borrower defaults and fails to fulfill the terms of the loan agreement, the collateral, or some portion of it, may become the property of the lender.

For example, if you borrow money to buy a car, the car is the collateral. If you default, the lender can repossess the car and sell it to recover the amount you borrowed.

Loans guaranteed by collateral are also known as secured loans.

Collateralized mortgage obligation (CMO)

CMOs are fixed-income investments backed by mortgages or pools of mortgages.

A conventional mortgage-backed security has a single interest rate and maturity date. In contrast, the pool of mortgages in a CMO is divided into four tranches, each with a different interest rate and term.

Owners of the first three tranches receive regular interest payments and principal is repaid to reflect the order in which the tranches mature. The fourth tranche is usually a deep-discount zero coupon bond on which interest accrues until maturity, when the full face value is repaid.

CMOs usually involve high-quality mortgages or those guaranteed by the government. Their yield may be lower than those of other mortgage-backed investments.

However, the way in which they are repaid makes them especially attractive to institutional investors including insurance companies and pension funds.

The risk, as with all mortgage-backed securities, is that a change in interest rates can affect the rate of repayment and the market value of the CMO.

Collectible

When you invest in objects rather than in capital assets such as stocks or bonds, you are putting your money into collectibles. Collectibles can run the gamut from fine art, antique furniture, stamps, and coins to baseball cards and Barbie dolls.

Their common drawback, as an investment, is their lack of liquidity. If you need to sell your collectibles, you may not be able to find a buyer who is willing to pay what you believe your investment is worth. In fact, you may not be able to find a buyer at all.

On the other hand, collectibles can provide a sizable return on your investment if you have the right thing for sale at the right time.

CollegeSure CD

CollegeSure CDs are certificates of deposit designed to let you prepay future college costs at today's rates, plus a premium based on the child's age and the amount you invest.

The CDs, which are issued by the College Savings Bank of Princeton (NJ), pay annual interest rates linked to increases in an index of average college costs and are available with terms from one to twenty-two years.

While these CDs are insured by the Federal Deposit Insurance Corporation (FDIC), the interest they pay is taxable, unless you own them within a Coverdell education savings account (ESA), participating state 529 plan, or Roth IRA.

With the Roth IRA option, the account must be open for at least five years and you must be at least 59½ to qualify for tax-free withdrawals.

CollegeSure CDs are sold in whole or partial units. At maturity, each whole unit is guaranteed to pay the average cost of one year of tuition, fees, and room and board at a four-year private college. If you decide to purchase only a partial unit, it will be worth only that portion of the average yearly college cost at maturity.

If the intended beneficiary decides not to go to college, you can get the entire principal and interest calculated at the guaranteed rate back when the CD matures and use it for any purpose.

However, if you choose to cash in the CD before its maturity date, you'll owe a penalty of 10% of the principal during the first three years of its term. The penalty drops to 5% for the remaining years of the CD's term, except for the last year, which carries a 1% penalty.

Commercial bank

Commercial banks offer a full range of retail banking products and services, such as checking and savings accounts, loans, credit cards, and lines of credit to individuals and businesses.

Most commercial banks also sell certain investments and many offer full brokerage and financial planning services.

Commercial paper

To help meet their immediate needs for cash, banks and corporations sometimes issue unsecured, short-term debt instruments known as commercial paper.

Commercial paper usually matures within a year and is an important part of what's known as the money market.

It can be a good place for investors—institutional investors in particular—to put their cash temporarily. That's because these investments are liquid and essentially risk-free, since they are typically issued by profitable, long-established, and highly regarded corporations.

Commission

Securities brokers and other sales agents typically charge a commission, or sales charge, on each transaction.

With traditional, full-service brokers, the charge is usually a percentage of the total cost of the trade, though some brokers may offer favorable rates to frequent traders.

Online brokerage firms, on the other hand, usually charge a flat fee for each transaction, regardless of the value of the trade. The flat fee may have certain limits, however, such as the number of shares being traded at one time.

The commissions on some transactions, such as stock trades, are reported on your confirmation slip. But commissions on other transactions are not reported separately.

In the case of cash value life insurance, for example, the commission may be as large as a year's premium.

Committee on Uniform Securities Identifying Procedures (CUSIP)

The Committee on Uniform Securities Identifying Procedures (CUSIP) assigns codes and numbers to all securities traded in the United States.

The CUSIP identification number is used to track the securities when they are bought and sold. You'll find the CUSIP number on a confirmation statement from your broker, for example, and on the face of a stock certificate.

Commodity

Commodities are bulk goods and raw materials, such as grains, metals, livestock, oil, cotton, coffee, sugar, and cocoa, that are used to produce consumer products.

The term also describes financial products, such as currency or stock and bond indexes.

Commodities are bought and sold on the cash market, and they are traded on the futures exchanges in the form of futures contracts.

Commodity prices are driven by supply and demand. When a commodity is plentiful—tomatoes in August, for example—prices are comparatively low. When a commodity is scarce because of a bad crop or because it is out of season, the price will generally be higher.

You can buy options on many commodity futures contracts to participate in the market for less than it might cost you to buy the underlying futures contracts. You can also invest through commodity funds.

Commodity Futures Trading Commission (CFTC)

The CFTC is the federal agency that regulates the US futures markets, as the Securities and Exchange Commission (SEC) regulates the securities markets.

The agency's five commissioners are appointed by the US president for staggered five-year terms.

The agency is responsible for maintaining fair and orderly markets, enforcing

market regulations, and ensuring that customers have the information they need to make informed decisions.

Commodity exchanges also regulate themselves, but any changes they want to make must be approved by the CFTC before they go into effect.

Common stock

When you own common stock, your shares represent ownership in the corporation and give you the right to vote for the company's board of directors and benefit from its financial success.

You may receive a portion of the company's profits as dividend payments if the board of directors declares a dividend. You also have the right to sell your stock and realize a capital gain if the share value increases.

But if the company falters and the price falls, your investment could lose some of or all its value.

Community property

In nine US states, any assets, investments, and income that are acquired during a marriage are considered community property. That is, they are owned jointly by the married couple.

For example, if you're married, live in one of these states, and buy stock, half the value of that stock belongs to your spouse even if you paid the entire cost of buying it. In a divorce, the value of the community property is divided equally.

However, property you owned before you married or that you received as a gift is generally not considered community property.

The community property states are Arizona, California, Idaho, Louisiana, Nevada, New Mexico, Texas, Washington, and Wisconsin.

Competitive trader

Competitive traders, also known as registered competitive traders or floor traders, buy and sell stocks for their own accounts on the floor of an exchange.

Traders must follow very specific rules governing when they can buy and sell. But since they trade in large volumes and do not pay commissions on their transactions, they can profit from small differences between the prices at which they buy and sell.

Composite trading

Composite trading figures report end-of-day price changes, closing prices, and the daily trading volume for stocks, warrants, and options listed on a stock exchange.

The New York Stock Exchange (NYSE) total also includes transactions on regional exchanges and listed securities traded over-the-counter.

Since trading continues on some of those exchanges after the close of business in New York, the composite figures give a comprehensive picture of the day's activities but do not include after-hours transactions.

Compound interest

When the interest you earn on an investment is added to form the new base on which future interest accumulates, it is compound interest.

For example, say you earn 5% compound interest on $100 every year for five years. You'll have $105 after one year, $110.25 after two years, $115.76 after three years, and $127.63 after five years.

Without compounding, you earn simple interest, and your investment doesn't grow as quickly. For example, if you earned 5% simple interest on $100 for five years, you would have $125. A larger base or a higher rate provide even more pronounced differences.

Compound interest earnings are reported as annual percentage yield (APY), though the compounding can occur annually, monthly, or daily.

Compounding

Compounding occurs when your investment earnings or savings account interest is added to your principal, forming a larger base on which future earnings may accumulate.

As your investment base gets larger, it has the potential to grow faster. And the longer your money is invested, the more you stand to gain from compounding.

For example, if you invested $10,000 earning 8% annually and reinvested all your earnings, you'd have $21,589 in your account after 10 years.

If instead of reinvesting you withdrew the earnings each year, you would have collected $800 a year, or $8,000 over the 10 years. The $3,589 difference is the benefit of 10 years of compound growth.

Comptroller of the Currency

The Office of the Comptroller of the Currency, housed in the US Department of the Treasury, charters, regulates, and oversees national banks.

The comptroller ensures bank integrity, fosters economic growth, promotes competition among banks, and guarantees that people have access to adequate financial services.

The comptroller does this by enforcing the Community Reinvestment Act and federal fair lending laws, which mandate that access. The comptroller is appointed by the US president and confirmed by the Senate.

Conduit IRA

A conduit IRA is another name for a rollover IRA, which you establish with money you roll over from a 401(k), 403(b), or other retirement savings plan.

Assets in a conduit IRA continue to be tax deferred until they are withdrawn and may be transferred into a new employer's plan if the plan allows transfers.

Confirmation

When you buy or sell a stock or bond, your brokerage firm will send you a confirmation, or printed document, with the details of the transaction.

Confirmations include the price, any fees, and the trade and settlement dates. Stock confirmations also include the commission if it applies. These documents are your backup for calculating capital gains and losses.

You'll also receive a confirmation to reaffirm orders you place, such as a good 'til canceled order to buy or sell a certain stock at a stop or limit price.

In addition, activity in your trading account, such as stock splits, spinoffs, or mergers will trigger a confirmation notice.

Conglomerate

A conglomerate is a corporation whose multiple business units operate in different, often unrelated, areas.

A conglomerate is generally formed when one company expands by acquiring other firms, which it brings together under a single management umbrella.

In some, but not all, cases, the formerly independent elements of the conglomerate retain their brand identities, though they are responsible to the conglomerate's management.

Some conglomerates are successful, with different parts of the whole contributing the lion's share of the profits in different phases of the economic cycle, offsetting weaker performance by other units.

Other conglomerates are never able to meld the parts into a functioning whole. In those cases, the parent company may sell or spin off various divisions into new independent companies.

Conscience fund

Conscience funds, also known as socially responsible funds, allow you to invest in companies whose business practices are in keeping with your personal values.

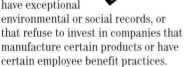

For example, you can choose mutual funds that invest in companies that have exceptional environmental or social records, or that refuse to invest in companies that manufacture certain products or have certain employee benefit practices.

Each fund explains the principles it follows in its prospectus and describes the screens, or set of criteria, it uses to identify its investments.

Consensus recommendation

A consensus recommendation for an individual stock compiles ratings from a number of analysts who track that stock. The recommendation is expressed as either the mean or median of the separate recommendations.

Calculating the consensus is a multi-step process that involves grouping the terms that analysts use to recommend buying, selling, or holding, generally into three or five categories, assigning a scale, and computing the result either by averaging the numbers for the mean or identifying the median, which is the point at which half the views are higher and half are lower.

A consensus recommendation provides a snapshot of current thinking about a stock, so it can serve as a benchmark against which you can compare a single analyst's opinion to gauge how mainstream it is.

But like any statistical mean or median, a consensus recommendation can distort strong differences at either end of the scale. Further, if the report accompanying the consensus view doesn't point out significant differences in the viewpoints of the various analysts it includes, you won't be able to tell where the most respected analysts stand on the stock.

In addition, you should be aware that the consensus recommendation for any given stock might differ from one research company to the next. This is because the mathematical formula that assigns weights to the individual recommendations will vary, based in part on how many levels of differentiation the research company uses and how it interprets the words that analysts use to express their opinions.

Consumer confidence index

The consumer confidence index is released each month by the Conference Board, an independent business research organization.

It measures how a representative sample of 5,000 US households feel about the current state of the economy, and what they anticipate the future will bring. The survey focuses specifically on the participants' impressions of business conditions and the job market.

Economic observers follow the index because when consumer attitudes are positive they are more likely to spend money, contributing to the very economic growth they anticipate. But if consumers are worried about their jobs, they may spend less, contributing to an economic slowdown.

Consumer price index (CPI)

The consumer price index (CPI) is compiled monthly by the US Bureau of Labor Statistics and is a gauge of inflation that measures changes in the prices of basic goods and services.

Some of the things it tracks are housing, food, clothing, transportation, medical care, and education.

The CPI is used as a benchmark for making adjustments in Social Security payments, wages, pensions, and tax brackets to keep them in tune with the buying power of the dollar. It's often incorrectly referred to as the cost-of-living index.

Contango

The price of a futures contract tends to reflect the cost of storage, insurance, financing, and other expenses incurred by the producer as the commodity awaits delivery.

So, typically, the further in the future the maturity date, the higher the price of the contract. That relationship is described as contango.

If the opposite is true, and the price of a longer-term contract is lower than the price of one with a closer expiration date, the relationship is described as backwardation.

Contingency order

A contingency order to buy or sell a security or other investment product is one that has strings attached.

Specifically, it is an order, such as a stop order, a stop-limit order, or an all-or-none order, that is to be executed only if the condition or conditions that the order specifies are met.

For example, if you gave a stop-limit order to sell a particular stock if the price fell to $30—the stop price—but not to sell if the transaction price were less than $27—the limit price—execution would be contingent on the stock price being between $27 and $30.

Broker-dealers aren't required to accept contingency orders, but if they do accept them they are required to abide by the terms of the order.

Contingent beneficiary

A contingent beneficiary receives the proceeds of an insurance policy, term-certain annuity, individual retirement account (IRA), employer-sponsored retirement savings plan, will, or trust if the primary beneficiary dies before the benefit is paid or if he or she declines to accept the benefit.

For example, if you name your spouse as the primary beneficiary of your IRA, you might name your children as contingent beneficiaries. Then, if your spouse is not alive at your death, your children inherit your IRA directly.

It's often a good idea to name as contingent beneficiary someone who is younger than you and your primary beneficiary, increasing the chances that the contingent beneficiary will outlive you. Or, if you choose, you might name an institution or a trust as contingent beneficiary.

You have the right to change your designation of contingent beneficiaries, except in the case of an irrevocable trust or a life insurance policy whose terms and conditions were established in a court ruling.

A contingent beneficiary may also be someone who is entitled to inherit assets if he or she meets the terms of the will or trust granting those assets.

Contingent deferred sales load

A contingent deferred sales load, also called a back-end load, is a sales charge some mutual funds impose when you sell shares in the fund within a certain period of time after you buy them.

These shares are typically identified as Class B shares, and the period that the load applies is often as long as seven to ten years, as determined by the fund.

The charge is a percentage of the amount of the investment you're liquidating. It typically begins at a certain level—say 7%—and drops by a percentage point each year until it disappears entirely.

Information about the charge and how long it's levied is provided in the fund's prospectus.

Continuous net settlement

In continuous net settlement, most securities transactions are finalized, or cleared and settled, within a broker-age firm.

The firm's clients' orders to buy and sell are offset, or matched against each other, so that at the end of the trading day only those positions that haven't been offset internally remain to be settled.

In a simplified example, all the shares of Stock A that a firm's clients bought are netted against all the shares that its clients sold by reallocating ownership on the firm's books. Payment is handled in a similar fashion, as money is transferred from the buyers' account to the sellers'.

If the firm has more buys than sells or the other way around, as is likely, it either delivers shares or receives them and makes a payment or receives it.

Clearing and settlement for transactions that aren't offset are handled by an automated system through two branches of the Depository Trust and Clearing Corporation (DTCC), the National Securities Clearing Corporation (NSCC), and the Depository Trust Company (DTC).

Contrarian

An investor who marches to a different drummer is sometimes described as a contrarian. In other words, if most investors are buying large-cap growth stocks, a contrarian is concentrating on building a portfolio of small-cap value stocks.

This approach is based, in part, on the idea that if everybody expects something to happen, it probably won't.

In addition, the contrarian believes that if other investors are fully committed to a certain type of investment, they're not likely to have cash available if a better one comes along. But the contrarian would.

Contrarian mutual funds use this approach as their investment strategy, concentrating on building a portfolio of out-of-favor, and therefore often under-valued, investments.

Conversion price

A conversion price is the predetermined price, set at the time of issue, at which you can exchange a convertible bond or other convertible security for common stock.

The number of shares that you'll receive at conversion is calculated by dividing the face value of the security by the conversion price. However, that number changes if the stock has split or has paid dividends.

Convertible bond

Convertible bonds are corporate bonds that give you the alternative of converting their value into common stock of that company or redeeming them for cash when they mature.

The details governing the conversion, such as the number of shares of stock you would receive, are set when the bonds are issued.

A convertible bond has a double appeal for investors. Its market value goes up if the stock price rises, but falls only to what it would be as a conventional bond if the stock price falls. In other words, the upside potential is considered greater than the downside risk.

While convertible bonds typically provide lower yields than conventional bonds from the same issuer, they may provide higher yields than the underlying stock.

You can buy convertibles through a broker or choose a mutual fund that invests in them.

Convertible hedge

When you use a convertible hedge, you buy a convertible bond, which you can exchange under certain circumstances for shares of the company's common stock. At the same time, you sell short the common stock of the same company.

As in any hedge, your goal is to make more money on one of the transactions than you lose on the other. For example, if the price of the stock falls, you're in a position to make money on the short sale while at the same time knowing that the convertible bond will continue to be at least as valuable as other bonds the company has issued.

On the other hand, if the stock gains value, you hope to be able to realize more profit from either selling the convertible or exchanging it for shares you can sell than it costs you to have borrowed and repaid the shares you sold short.

There are no guarantees this strategy or any other hedging strategy will work, especially for an individual investor who faces the challenge of identifying an appropriate security to hedge and the appropriate time to act.

Convertible term

A convertible term life insurance policy can be converted into a permanent life policy at some point in the future without requiring you to pass a health screening exam.

A convertible term policy is generally more expensive than a regular term policy from the same insurance provider.

Like other term insurance policies, a convertible term policy remains in force for a specific period of time, or term, and can usually be renewed for an additional term, though the premiums typically increase with each renewal.

Cook the books

When a company cooks the books, it is deliberately—and illegally—providing false information about its financial situation to bolster its stock price, often by overstating profits and hiding losses.

A company may also cook the books to reduce its tax liability, but then it stirs in the opposite direction by underreporting profits and overstating losses.

Cooling-off period

In the financial industry, a cooling-off period applies when a new issue is being brought to market. During this time, also known as the quiet period, investment bankers and underwriters aren't permitted to discuss the issue with the public.

In the consumer world, during a cooling-off period, you can cancel your obligation to purchase a product or take a loan without penalty if you change your mind.

Different kinds of transactions are governed by different cooling-off rules. For example, one federal rule allows you to cancel home improvement loans and second mortgages within three days of signing.

Another gives you three days to return purchases you make at places other than a merchant's usual place of business, such as at a trade show.

The law governing your cooling-off rights, sometimes known as buyers' remorse rules, is included in the fine print on any agreement you sign.

Cooperative (co-op)

A co-op is a corporation that owns a particular residential property. The shareholders are the tenants who, instead of owning an individual unit, own shares in the corporation, which gives them the right to live in that unit.

Copayment

If you have a managed-care health insurance plan, your copayment is the fixed amount you pay—often $10 to $25—for each in-network doctor's office visit or approved medical treatment

In some plans, the copayment to see a specialist to whom you're referred is higher than the copayment to visit your primary care physician. Some plans may not require copayments for annual physicals and certain diagnostic tests.

If you see an out-of-network provider, you are likely to be responsible for a percentage of the approved charge, called coinsurance, plus any amount above the approved charge.

Core earnings

Core earnings differ in several ways from more traditional measures of earnings. Most notably, they treat company stock options as an expense and exclude any income that comes from the company's pension fund investments.

Standard & Poor's (S&P) developed the core earnings measure to give investors a more uniform way to compare earnings numbers.

Otherwise, it may be difficult to compare numbers since companies often use different formulas to calculate their earnings.

Cornering the market

If someone tries to buy up as much of a particular investment as possible in order to control its price, that investor is trying to corner the market.

Not only is it difficult to make this strategy work in a complex economic environment, but the practice is illegal in US markets.

Corporate bond

Corporate bonds are debt securities issued by publicly held corporations to raise money for expansion or other business needs.

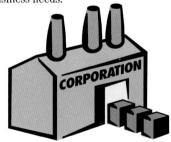

Corporate bonds typically pay a higher rate of interest than federal or municipal government bonds, but the interest you earn is generally fully taxable.

You may be able to buy corporate bonds at issue through your brokerage firm, usually at the offering price of $1,000 per bond, though you may have to buy several bonds of the same issue rather than just one.

You can buy bonds on the secondary market at their current market price, which may be higher or lower than par. However, most individual investors buy corporate bonds though a mutual fund that specializes in those issues.

Correction

A correction is a drop—usually a sudden and substantial one of 10% or more—in the price of an individual stock, bond, commodity, index, or the market as a whole.

Market analysts anticipate market corrections when security prices are high in relation to company earnings and other indicators of economic health.

When a market correction is greater than 10% and the prices do not begin to recover relatively promptly, some analysts point to the correction as the beginning of a bear market.

Correlation

In investment terms, correlation is the extent to which the values of different types of investments move in tandem with one another in response to changing economic and market conditions.

Correlation is measured on a scale of – 1 to +1. Investments with a correlation of + 0.5 or more tend to rise and fall in value at the same time. Investments with a negative correlation of – 0.5 to – 1 are more likely to gain or lose value in opposing cycles.

Correspondent

A correspondent is a financial institution, such as a bank or brokerage firm, that handles transactions on behalf of another financial institution that it can't complete on its own.

For example, if a US bank has a client who needs to make a payment to a supplier located overseas, the US bank would use its relationship with a correspondent bank in the supplier's home country to credit the supplier's bank account with money from its own client's account that had been transferred through an international payment system.

Cost basis

The cost basis is the original price of an asset—usually the purchase price plus commissions. You use the cost basis to calculate capital gains and capital losses, depreciation, and return on investment.

If you inherit assets, such as stocks or real estate, your cost basis is the asset's value on the date the person who left it to you died (or the date on which his or her estate was valued). This new valuation is known as a step-up in basis.

For example, if you buy a stock at $20 a share and sell it for $50 a share, your cost basis is $20. If you sell, you owe capital gains tax on the $30-a-share profit.

If you inherit stock that was bought at $20 a share but valued at $50 a share when that person died, your cost basis would be $50 a share, and you'd owe no tax if you sold it at that price.

Cost-of-living adjustment (COLA)

A COLA results in a wage or benefit increase that is designed to help you keep pace with increased living costs that result from inflation.

COLAs are usually pegged to increases in the consumer price index (CPI). Federal government pensions, some state pensions, and Social Security are usually adjusted annually, but only a few private pensions provide COLAs.

Council of Economic Advisors (CEA)

The Council of Economic Advisors' job is to assist and advise the president of the United States on economic policy. The CEA differs from other government agencies in its academic orientation and emphasis on contemporary developments in economic thought.

The Council consists of a chairman and two staff members, appointed by the president and confirmed by the Senate, plus a staff of about ten economists and ten younger scholars. The Council's chairman frequently speaks on behalf of the administration on economic issues and policies.

Countercyclical stock

Stocks described as countercyclical tend to continue to maintain their value and provide regular income when the economy is slowing down or staying flat.

Companies whose stocks fit into this category are those whose products are always in demand, such as food or utilities. They may also be companies whose services reduce the expenses of other companies, such as providers of temporary office help.

Or they could be financial services companies that specialize in cash equivalent or other stable value investments. By including some countercyclical stocks in your equity portfolio, you can balance the potential volatility of cyclical investments.

Counterparty

In any financial contract, the persons or institutions entering the contract on the opposite sides of the transaction are called the counterparties.

For example, if you sign a contract to sell an item that you produce to a buyer, you and the buyer are counterparties to the contract.

Similarly, the counterparties in financial transactions known as forwards or swaps are the banks or corporations that make deals between themselves to protect future cash flows or currency values.

Counterparty risk

Counterparty risk is the risk that the person or institution with whom you have entered a financial contract—who is a counterparty to the contract—will default on the obligation and fail to fulfill that side of the contractual agreement.

In other words, counterparty risk is a type of credit risk. Counterparty risk is the greatest in contracts drawn up directly between two parties and least in contracts where an intermediary acts as counterparty.

For example, in the listed derivatives market, the industry's or the exchange's clearinghouse is the counterparty to every purchase or sale of an options or futures contract. That eliminates the possibility that the buyer or seller won't make good on the transaction.

The clearinghouse, in turn, protects itself from risk by requiring market participants to meet margin requirements. In contrast, there is no such protection in the unlisted derivatives market where forwards and swaps are arranged.

Coupon

Originally, bonds were issued with coupons, which you clipped and presented to the issuer or the issuer's agent—typically a bank or brokerage firm—to receive interest payments.

Bonds with coupons are also known as bearer bonds because the bearer of the coupon is entitled to the interest.

Although most new bonds are electronically registered rather than issued in certificate form, the term coupon has stuck as a synonym for interest in phrases like the coupon rate.

When interest accumulates rather than being paid during the bond's term, the bond is known as a zero coupon.

Coupon rate

The coupon rate is the interest rate that the issuer of a bond or other debt security promises to pay during the term of a loan. For example, a bond that is paying 6% annual interest has a coupon rate of 6%.

The term is derived from the practice, now discontinued, of issuing bonds with detachable coupons.

To collect a scheduled interest payment, you presented a coupon to the issuer or the issuer's agent. Today, coupon bonds are no longer issued. Most bonds are registered, and interest is paid by check or, increasingly, by electronic transfer.

Covered option

When you sell call options on stock that you own, they are covered options. That means if the option holder exercises the option, you can deliver your stock to meet your obligation if you are assigned to complete the transaction.

Similarly, if you sell put options on stock and have enough cash on hand make the required purchase if the option holder exercises, the options are covered. Covered puts are also known as cash-secured puts.

One appeal of selling a covered call is that you collect the premium but don't risk potentially large losses. Otherwise, you may have to buy the stock at a higher market price in order to meet your obligation to deliver stock at the strike price if the option is exercised.

The downside is that if your stock is called away from you, you'll no longer be in a position to profit from any potential dividends or increases in price.

Crash

A crash is a sudden, steep drop in stock prices. The downward spiral is intensified as more and more investors, seeing the bottom falling out of the market, try to sell their holdings before these investments lose all their value.

The two great US crashes of the 20th century, in 1929 and 1987, had very different consequences. The first was followed by a period of economic stagnation and severe depression. The second had a much briefer impact. While some investors suffered huge losses in 1987, recovery was well under way within three months.

In the aftermath of each of these crashes, the federal government instituted a number of changes designed to reduce the impact of future crashes.

Credit

Credit generally refers to the ability of a person or organization to borrow money, as well as the arrangements that are made for repaying the loan and the terms of the repayment schedule.

If you are well qualified to obtain a loan, you are said to be credit-worthy.

Credit is also used to mean positive cash entries in an account. For example, your bank account may be credited with interest. In this sense, a credit is the opposite of a debit, which means money is taken from your account.

Credit bureau

The three major credit bureaus—Equifax, Experian, and TransUnion—collect information about the way you use credit and make it available to anyone with a legitimate business need to see it, including potential lenders, landlords, and current or prospective employers.

The bureaus keep records of the credit accounts you have, how much you owe, your payment habits, and the lenders and other businesses that have accessed your credit report.

Credit bureaus, also known as credit reporting agencies, store other information about you as well, such as your present and past addresses, Social Security number, employment history, and information in the public record, including bankruptcies, liens, and any judgments against you.

However, there are certain things, by law, your credit report can't include, including your age, race, religion, political affiliation, or health records.

You are entitled to a free copy of your credit report from each of the three major credit bureaus once a year, but you have to request them through the Annual Credit Report Request Service (www.annualcreditreport.com or 877-322-8228).

If you've recently been denied credit, are unemployed, on public assistance, or have a reason to suspect identity theft or credit fraud, you're also entitled to a free report. In those cases, you should contact the credit bureaus directly.

Credit limit

A credit limit, also known as a credit line, is the maximum amount of money you can borrow under a revolving credit agreement.

For instance, if you have a credit card with a credit limit of $3,000, and you charge $1,000, you can spend $2,000 more before you reach your credit  limit. And if you repay the $1,000 before the end of the month without making additional purchases, your credit limit is back up to $3,000 again.

Most credit issuers charge additional fees or penalties if you exceed your credit limit.

Credit line

A credit line, or line of credit, is a revolving credit agreement that allows you to write checks or make cash withdrawals of amounts up to your credit limit.

When you use the credit—sometimes called accessing the line—you owe interest on the amount you borrow. But when that amount has been repaid you can borrow it again.

A home equity line of credit (HELOC) is secured by your home, but other credit lines, such as an overdraft arrangement linked to your checking account, are unsecured. In general, the interest rate on a secured credit line is less than the rate on an unsecured line.

Credit rating

Your credit rating is an independent statistical evaluation of your ability to repay debt based on your borrowing and repayment history.

If you always pay your bills on time, you are more likely to have good credit and therefore may receive favorable terms on a loan or credit card, such as relatively low finance charges.

If your credit rating is poor because you have paid bills late or have defaulted on a loan, you may be offered less favorable terms or may be denied credit altogether.

A corporation's credit rating is an assessment of whether it will be able to meet its obligations to bond holders and other investors. Credit rating systems for corporations generally range from AAA or Aaa at the high end to D (for default) at the low end.

Credit report

A credit report is a summary of your financial history. Potential lenders will use your credit report to help them evaluate whether you are a good credit risk.

The three major credit-reporting agencies are Experian, Equifax, and Transunion. These agencies collect certain types of information about you, primarily your use of credit and information in the public record, and sell that information to qualified recipients.

As a provision of the Fair and Accurate Credit Transaction Act (FACT Act), you are entitled to a free copy of your credit report each year from each of the credit reporting agencies.

You also have a right to see your credit report at any time if you have been turned down for a loan, an apartment, or a job because of poor credit. You may also question any information the credit reporting agency has about you and ask that errors be corrected.

If the information isn't changed following your request, you have the right to attach a comment or explanation, which must be sent out with future reports.

Credit score

Your credit score is a number, calculated based on information in your credit report, that lenders use to assess the credit risk you pose and the interest rate they will offer you if they agree to lend you money.

Most lenders use credit scores rather than credit reports since the scores reduce extensive, detailed information about your financial history to a single number.

There are actually two competing credit scoring systems, FICO, which has been the standard, and VantageScore, which was developed by the three major credit bureaus.

Their formulas give different weights to particular types of credit-related behavior, though both put the most emphasis on paying your bills on time. They also have different scoring systems, ranging from 300 to 850 for FICO to 501 to 999 for AdvantageScore. The best—or lowest—interest rates go to applicants with the highest scores.

Because your credit score and credit report are based on the same information, it's very unlikely that they will tell a different story. It's smart to check your credit report at least once a year, which you can do for free at www.annualcreditreport.com or by calling 877-322-8228.

It may be a good idea to review your score if you anticipate applying for a major loan, such as a mortgage, in the next six months to a year. That allows time to bring your score up if you fear it's too low.

Credit union

Credit unions are financial cooperatives set up by employee and community associations, labor unions, church groups, and other organizations. They provide affordable financial services to members of the sponsoring organization.

In some cases, they're created in rural or economically disadvantaged areas, where commercial banks may be scarce or prohibitively expensive.

Because they are not-for-profit, credit unions tend to charge lower fees and interest rates on loans than commercial banks while paying higher interest rates on savings and investment accounts.

The services offered at large credit unions can be as comprehensive as those at large banks. At smaller credit unions, however, services and hours may be more limited, and a few deposits may not be insured.

Assets in most credit unions are insured by the National Credit Union Share Insurance Fund on the same terms that deposits in national and state banks are insured by the Federal Deposit Insurance Corporation (FDIC).

Creditor

A person or company who provides credit to another person or company functions as a creditor.

For example, if you take a mortgage or car loan at your bank, then the bank is your creditor. But if you buy a bond, you are the creditor because the money you pay to buy the bond is actually a loan to the issuer.

Crossed market

A market in a particular stock or option is described as crossed when a bid to buy that stock or option is higher than the offer to sell it, or when an offer to sell is lower than a bid to buy.

A crossed market reverses the normal relationship of a stock quotation in which the bid price is always lower than the ask price. It's illegal for market makers to cross a market deliberately.

A crossed market may occur when investors place after-hours orders electronically for execution at opening, or when investors trade directly through an electronic communications network (ECN).

NASD has introduced a set of pre-opening procedures for market makers on the Nasdaq Stock Market. They help prevent the confusion and potential inequalities in pricing that a crossed market can produce.

Cumulative voting

With this method of voting for a corporation's board of directors, you may cast the total number of votes you're entitled to any way you choose. For example, you can either split your votes equally among the nominees, or you can cast all of them for a single candidate.

Generally, you receive one vote for each share of company stock you own times the number of directors to be elected.

Cumulative voting is designed to give individual stockholders greater influence in shaping the board. They can designate all their votes for a single candidate who represents their interests instead of spreading their votes equally among the candidates, as is the case with statutory voting.

Currency fluctuation

A currency has value, or worth, in relation to other currencies, and those values change constantly.

For example, if demand for a particular currency is high because investors want to invest in that country's stock market or buy exports, the price of its currency will increase. Just the opposite will happen if that country suffers an economic slowdown, or investors lose confidence in its markets.

While some currencies fluctuate freely against each other, such as the Japanese yen and the US dollar, others are pegged, or linked. They may be pegged to the value of another currency, such as the US dollar or the euro, or to a basket, or weighted average, of currencies.

Currency swap

In a currency swap, the parties to the contract exchange the principal of two different currencies immediately, so that each party has the use of the different currency. They also make interest payments to each other on the principal during the contract term.

In many cases, one of the parties pays a fixed interest rate and the other pays a floating interest rate, but both could pay fixed or floating rates. When the contract ends, the parties re-exchange the principal amount of the swap.

Originally, currency swaps were used to give each party access to enough foreign currency to make purchases in foreign markets. Increasingly, parties arrange currency swaps as a way to enter new capital markets or to provide predictable revenue streams in another currency.

Currency trading

The global currency market, where roughly $1.9 trillion a day changes hands, is by far the largest financial market in the world.

Banks, other financial institutions, and multinational corporations buy and sell currencies in enormous quantities to handle the demands of international trade. In some cases, traders seek profits from minor fluctuations in exchange rates or speculate on currency fluctuations.

Current return

Current return, also called current yield, is the amount of interest you earn on a bond in any given year, expressed as a percent of the current market price.

The current return will, in most cases, not be the same as the coupon rate, or the interest rate the bond pays calculated as a percentage of its par value.

For example, if the par, or face value, of a bond is $1,000 and the coupon rate is 5%, then the interest payments, or annual income, from the bond is $50 per year. If, however, the bond is trading at $900, then that $50 annual income is actually a current return of 5.6%.

The current return does not take capital gains or losses into account, so it is not a reflection of the total return on your bond investment.

Current yield

Current yield is a measure of your rate of return on an investment, expressed as a percentage. With a bond, current yield is calculated by dividing the interest you collect by the current market price.

For example, if a bond paying 5% interest, or $50, is selling for $900, the current yield is 5.6%. If the market price is $1,200, the current yield is 4.2%. And if bond is selling exactly at par, or $1,000, the current yield is 5%, the same as the coupon rate.

If you own a stock, its current yield is the annual dividend divided by its market price.

Custodial account

If you want to make investments on a minor's behalf, or transfer property you own to that person, you can open a custodial account with a bank, brokerage firm, mutual fund company, or insurance company.

You name an adult custodian for the account—either yourself or someone else—who is responsible for managing the account until the child reaches the age of majority.

That age may be 18, 21, or 25 depending on the state and the type of account you choose. At majority, the child has the legal right to control the account and use the assets as he or she chooses.

There may be some tax advantages in transferring assets to a minor. If the child is under 18, investment earnings above a specific level that Congress sets each year are taxed at the parents' marginal tax rate.

But if the child is 18 or older, all investment earnings are taxed at the child's rate—again, typically the lowest rate. In addition, gifts you make to the account are no longer part of your estate, which may reduce vulnerability to estate taxes. However, it's wise to review your plans with your legal and tax advisers.

One drawback of a custodial account is that the assets are considered the property of the child, and may reduce the amount of financial aid the child qualifies for when he or she enrolls in a college or university.

Custodian

A custodian is legally responsible for ensuring that an item or person is safe and secure. In investment terms, a custodian is the financial services company that maintains electronic records of financial assets or has physical possession of specific securities.

The custodian's client may be another institution, such as a mutual fund, a corporation, or an individual. For example, with an individual retirement account (IRA), the custodian is the bank, brokerage firm, or other financial services company that holds your account.

Similarly, the Depository Trust Company, a subsidiary of the Depository Trust and Clearing Corporation (DTCC), is the custodian of millions of stock certificates held in its vaults.

Cyclical stock

Cyclical stocks tend to rise in value during an upturn in the economy and fall during a downturn. They usually include stock in industries that flourish in good times, including airlines, automobiles, and travel and leisure.

In contrast, stock in industries that provide necessities such as food, electricity, gas, and healthcare products tend to be more price-stable, as do companies that provide services that reduce the expenses of other companies. Those stocks are sometimes called countercyclicals.

Daily trading limit

The daily trading limit is the most that the price of a futures contract can rise or fall in a single session before trading in that contract is stopped for the day.

Trading limits are designed to protect investors from wild price fluctuations and the potential for major losses. They're comparable to the circuit breakers established by stock exchanges to suspend trading when prices fall by a specific percentage.

Date of maturity

The date of maturity, or maturity date, is the day on which a bond's term ends, and its issuer repays the principal and makes the final interest payment.

When the phrase is used in connection with mortgages or other personal loans, the date of maturity is the day your last payment is due and your debt is repaid.

Day order

A day order is an instruction you give to your broker to buy or sell a security at the market price or at a particular price you name before the end of the trading day. The order expires if it isn't filled.

In contrast, a good 'til canceled (GTC) order remains open on the broker's books until it's filled, you cancel it, or the brokerage firm's time limit for GTCs expires.

Day trader

When you continuously buy and sell investments within a very short time, perhaps a few minutes or hours, and rarely hold them overnight, you're considered a day trader.

The strategy is to take advantage of rapid price changes to make money quickly.

The risk is that as a day trader you can lose substantial amounts of money since no one can predict how or when prices will change. That risk is compounded by the fact that technology does not always keep pace with investors' orders, so if you authorize a sell at one price, the price it's actually executed at may be higher or lower, wiping out potential profit.

In addition, you pay transaction costs on each buy and sell order. Your gains must be large enough to offset those costs if you're going to come out ahead.

Dealer

Dealers, or principals, buy and sell securities for their own accounts, adding liquidity to the marketplace and seeking to profit from the spread between the prices at which they buy and sell.

In the over-the-counter market, in most cases, it is dealers—also called market makers—who provide the bid and ask quotes you see when you look up the price of a security.

Those dealers are willing to commit their capital to specific securities and are ready to trade the securities at the quoted prices.

Death benefit

A death benefit is money your beneficiary collects from your life insurance policy if you die while the policy is still in force.

In most cases, the beneficiary receives the face value of the policy as a lump sum. However, the death benefit is reduced by the amount of any unpaid loans you've taken against the policy.

Some retirement plans, including Social Security, also provide a one-time death benefit to your beneficiary at the time of your death.

Debenture

A debenture is an unsecured bond. Most bonds issued by corporations are debentures, which are backed by their reputation rather than by any collateral, such as the company's buildings or its inventory.

Although debentures sound riskier than secured bonds, they aren't when they're issued by well-established companies with good credit ratings.

Debit

A debit is the opposite of a credit. A debit may be an account entry representing money you owe a lender or money that has been taken from your account.

For example, your bank debits your checking account for the amount of a check you've written, and your broker debits your investment account for the cost of a security you've purchased.

Similarly, a debit card authorizes the bank to take money out of your bank account electronically, either as cash or as an on-the-spot payment to a merchant. That's different from a credit card, which authorizes you to borrow the money from the card issuer.

Debit balance

A debit balance is what you owe. It's entered as accounts receivable on the books of the lender and appears on your account statement as a liability.

For example, if you have a margin account and borrow money to buy stock, your monthly brokerage statement will show a debit balance for the amount of the margin loan.

Debit card

A debit card—sometimes called a cash plus card—allows you to make point-of-sale (POS) purchases by swiping the card through the same type of machine you use to make credit card purchases.

Sometimes you authorize a debit card transaction with your personal identification number (PIN). Other times, you sign a receipt just as you would if you were charging the purchase to your credit card. You can also use the card to make ATM withdrawals.

When you use a debit card, the amount of your purchase is debited, or subtracted, from your account at the time of the transaction and transferred electronically to the seller's account.

You have some of the same protections against loss with a debit card as you do with a credit card, but there is one important difference. While $50 is the most you can ever be responsible for if your credit card is lost or stolen, you could lose much more with a lost or stolen debit card if you don't report what has happened within two days of discovering it.

If you delay reporting a missing card, you could lose up to $500. And if you wait more than 60 days after receiving a bank statement that includes a fraudulent use of your card, you could lose everything in your account including your overdraft line of credit. You can find the specific rules on the Federal Trade Commission website at www.ftc.gov.

In addition, if you purchase defective merchandise with a debit card, there are no refunds. Most credit card issuers do not, generally speaking, make you pay for defective products.

Debt

A debt is an obligation to repay an amount you owe. Debt securities, such as bonds or commercial paper, are forms of debt that bind the issuer, such as a corporation, bank, or government, to repay the security holder. Debts are also known as liabilities.

Debt security

Debt securities are interest-paying bonds, notes, bills, or money market instruments that are issued by governments or corporations.

Some debt securities pay a fixed rate of interest over a fixed time period in exchange for the use of the principal. In that case, that principal, or par value, is repaid at maturity.

Some are pass-through securities, with principal and interest repaid over the term of the loan. Still other issues are sold at discount, with interest included in the amount paid at maturity.

US Treasury bills, corporate bonds, commercial paper, and mortgage-backed bonds are all examples of debt securities.

Debt-to-equity ratio

A company's debt-to-equity ratio indicates the extent to which the company is leveraged, or financed by credit. A higher ratio is a sign of greater leverage.

You find a company's debt-to-equity ratio by dividing its total long-term debt by its total assets minus its total debt. You can find these figures in the company's income statement, which is provided in its annual report.

Average ratios vary significantly from one industry to another, so what is high for one company may be normal for another company in a different industry.

From an investor's perspective, the higher the ratio, the greater the risk you take in investing in the company. But your potential return may be greater as well if the company uses the debt to expand its sales and earnings.

Decimal pricing

US stocks, derivatives linked to stocks, and some bonds trade in decimals, or dollars and cents. That means that the spread between the bid and ask prices can be as small as one cent.

The switch to decimal stock trading, which was completed in 2001, was the final stage of a conversion from trading in eighths, or increments of 12.5 cents.

Trading in eighths originated in the 16th century, when North American settlers cut European coins into eight pieces to use as currency. In an intermediary phase during the 1990s, trading was handled in sixteenths, or increments of 6.25 cents.

Decliner

Stocks that have dropped, or fallen, in value over a particular period are described as decliners. If more stocks decline than advance, or go up in value, over the course of a trading day, the financial press reports that decliners led advancers.

The indexes that track the market may decline as well. If decliners dominate for a period of time, the market may also be described as bearish.

Decreasing term insurance

With a decreasing term life insurance policy, the amount of the death benefit decreases each year of the fixed term—such as 20 years—although the premium remains the same.

This type of insurance tends to be an economical way to protect your beneficiaries should you die unexpectedly during a period when you have substantial financial responsibilities.

For example, young parents with a large mortgage might consider decreasing term policies to help insulate each other against the responsibility of meeting their financial obligations should something happen to one of them.

Deductible

A deductible is the dollar amount you must pay for healthcare, damage to your property, or any other insurable claim before your insurance company begins to cover the cost of the bill.

For example, if you have a health insurance policy with an annual $300 deductible, you have to spend $300 of your own money before your insurer will pay whatever portion of the rest of the year's bills it has agreed to cover.

However, in some types of policies, the deductible is per event, not per year. Generally speaking, the higher the deductible you agree to pay, the lower your insurance premiums tend to be. However, the deductible for certain coverage is fixed by the insurance provider. That's the case with Original Medicare.

Deduction

A deduction is an amount you can subtract from your gross income or adjusted gross income to lower your taxable income when you file your income tax return.

Certain deductions, such as money contributed to a traditional IRA or interest payments on a college loan, are available only to taxpayers who qualify for these deductions based on specific expenditures or income limits, or both.

Other deductions are more widely available. For example, you can take a standard deduction, an amount that's fixed each year. And if your expenses for certain things, such as home mortgage interest, real estate taxes, and state and local income taxes, total more than the standard deduction, it may pay for you to itemize deductions instead.

However, if your adjusted gross income is above the limit Congress sets for the year, you may lose some of or all these deductions.

Deed

A deed is a written document that transfers ownership of land or other real estate from the owner, also known as the grantor, to the buyer, or grantee.

The form a deed takes varies from place to place, but the overall structure and the provisions it contains are the same. The description of the property being transferred is always included.

When you use a mortgage to purchase the property that's being transferred by deed, you may receive the deed at the time of purchase, with the lender holding a lien on the property. Or the deed may belong to the lender until you have paid off the mortgage.

In either case, a deed's creation must be witnessed and should be recorded with the appropriate local authority to ensure its validity.

Deep discount bond

Deep discount bonds are originally issued with a par value, or face value, of $1,000. But they decline in value by at least 20%—to a market value of $800 or less—typically because interest rates have increased.

They may also decline if people believe the company may have difficulty making the interest payment or repaying the principal. Either way, investors will no longer pay full price for the bond.

Deep discount bonds are different from original issue discount bonds, which are sold at less than par value and accumulate interest until maturity, when they can be redeemed for par value. Zero-coupon bonds are an example of original issue discount bonds.

Deep discount brokerage firm

A financial services company that offers rock-bottom rates for large-volume securities transactions is sometimes described as a deep discount firm.

However, online brokerage firms or electronic communications networks (ECNs) may offer investors cheaper prices for even small-volume trades.

Default

If a person or institution responsible for repaying a loan or making an interest payment fails to meet that obligation on time, that person or institution is in default.

If you are in default, you may lose any property that you put up as collateral to get the loan. For example, if you fail to repay your car loan, your lender may repossess the car.

Defaulting has a negative impact on your credit history and your credit score, which generally makes it difficult to borrow again in the future. In fact, failure to pay on time is the single most important contributor to a poor credit history.

A bond issuer who defaults may not pay interest when it comes due or repay the principal at maturity, or both.

Defensive security

Defensive securities tend to remain more stable in value than the overall market, especially when prices in general are falling.

Defensive securities include stocks in companies whose products or services are always in demand and are not as price-sensitive to changes in the economy as other stocks. Some defensive securities could be stock in food, pharmaceuticals, and utilities companies.

Defensive securities are also known as countercyclicals.

Deferred annuity

A deferred annuity contract allows you to accumulate tax-deferred earnings during the term of the contract and sometimes add assets to your contract over time. In contrast, an immediate annuity starts paying you income right after you buy.

Your deferred annuity earnings can be either fixed or variable, depending on the way your money is invested.

Deferred annuities are designed primarily as retirement savings accounts, so you may owe a penalty if you withdraw principal, earnings, or both before you reach age 59½.

Defined benefit plan

A defined benefit plan—popularly known as a pension—provides a specific benefit for retired employees, either as a lump sum or as income for the rest of their lives. Sometimes the employee's spouse receives the benefit for life as well.

The pension amount usually depends on the employee's age at retirement, final salary, and the number of years on the job. All the details are spelled out in the plan.

However, an employer may end its defined benefit plan or replace this traditional source of retirement income with defined contribution or cash balance plans.

Defined contribution plan

In a defined contribution retirement plan, the benefits—that is, what you can expect to accumulate and ultimately withdraw from the plan—are not pre-determined, as they are with a defined benefit plan.

Instead, the retirement income you receive will depend on how much is contributed to the plan, how it is invested, and what the return on the investment is.

One advantage of defined contribution plans, such as 401(k)s, 403(b)s, 457s, and profit-sharing plans, is that you often have some control over how your retirement dollars are invested. Your choice may include stock or bond mutual funds, annuities, guaranteed investment contracts (GICs), company stock, cash equivalents, or a combination of these choices.

An added benefit is that, if you switch jobs, you can take your accumulated retirement assets with you, either rolling them into an IRA or a new employer's plan if the plan accepts transfers.

Deflation

Deflation, the opposite of inflation, is a gradual drop in the cost of goods and services, usually caused by a surplus of goods and a shortage of cash.

Although deflation seems to increase your buying power in its early stages, it is generally considered a negative economic trend. That's because it is typically accompanied by rising unemployment, falling production, and limited investment.

Delivery date

The delivery date, also known as the settlement date, is the day on which a stock, option, or bond trade must be settled, or finalized.

For stocks, the delivery date is three business days after the trade date, or T + 3. For listed options and government securities, it's one day after the trade date, or T + 1.

If you're the seller, your brokerage firm must turn over the security by the delivery date or transfer the record of ownership to the account of another of its clients who has purchased the security. That process is called netting.

If you're the buyer, you must provide payment by the delivery date so that the transaction can be finalized. You may pay through a margin or money market account with the brokerage firm, by check or electronic transfer, or by instructing your broker to sell other investments.

Delta

The relationship between an option's price and the price of the underlying stock or futures contract is called its delta.

If the delta is 1, for example, the relationship of the prices is 1 to 1. That means there's a $1 change in the option price for every $1 change in the price of the underlying instrument.

With a call option, an increase in the price of an underlying instrument typically results in an increase in the price of the option. An increase in a put option's price is usually triggered by a decrease in the price of the underlying instrument, since investors buy put options expecting its price to fall.

Department of Veterans Affairs (VA) mortgage

Department of Veterans Affairs (VA) mortgages enable qualifying veterans or their surviving spouses to borrow up to the annual federal limit in order to buy conventional homes, mobile homes, and condominiums with little or no down payment.

The VA guarantees repayment of the loans. This federal guarantee means that banks and thrift institutions can afford to provide 30-year VA mortgages on favorable terms even during periods when borrowing in general is expensive.

Interest rates on these mortgages, formerly fixed by the Department of Housing and Urban Development (HUD), are now set by the VA itself. For more information, call the VA's local toll-free number listed in your phone book.

Depositary bank

A US bank that holds American depositary shares (ADSs), or shares of corporations based outside the United States, and sells American depositary receipts (ADRs) to US investors is called a depositary bank.

Each ADR represents a specific number of ADSs, based on the bank's agreement with the issuing corporation. The depositary bank ensures that investors receive dividends and capital gains and handles tax payments that may be due in the country where the share-issuing company is headquartered.

Depository Trust and Clearing Corporation (DTCC)

The DTCC is the world's largest securities depository, holding trillions of dollars in assets for the members of the financial industry that own the corporation. It is also a national clearinghouse for the settlement of corporate and municipal securities transactions.

The DTCC, a member of the Federal Reserve System, was created in 1999 as a holding company. It has two primary subsidiaries, the Depository Trust Company (DTC) and the National Securities Clearing Corporation (NSCC).

It is also the holding company for the Emerging Market Clearing Corporation (EMCC) and the Fixed Income Clearing Corporation (FICC).

The FICC was formed as a merger of the Government Security Clearing Corporation (GSCC) and the Mortgage Backed Security Clearing Corporation (MBSCC).

Depreciation

Certain assets, such as buildings and equipment, depreciate, or decline in value, over time.

You can amortize, or write off, the cost of such an asset over its estimated useful life, thereby reducing your taxable income without reducing the cash you have on hand.

Depression

A depression is a severe and prolonged downturn in the economy. Prices fall, reducing purchasing power. There tends to be high unemployment, lower productivity, shrinking wages, and general economic pessimism.

Since the Great Depression following the stock market crash of 1929, the governments and central banks of industrialized countries have carefully monitored their economies. They adjust their economic policies to try to prevent another financial crisis of this magnitude.

Derivative

Derivatives are financial products, such as futures contracts, options, and mortgage-backed securities. Most of derivatives' value is based on the value of an underlying security, commodity, or other financial instrument.

For example, the changing value of a crude oil futures contract depends primarily on the upward or downward movement of oil prices.

An equity option's value is determined by the relationship between its strike price and the value of the underlying stock, the time until expiration, and the stock's volatility.

Certain investors, called hedgers, are interested in the underlying instrument. For example, a baking company might buy wheat futures to help estimate the cost of producing its bread in the months to come.

Other investors, called speculators, are concerned with the profit to be made by buying and selling the contract at the most opportune time. Listed derivatives are traded on organized exchanges or markets. Other derivatives are traded over-the-counter (OTC) and in private transactions.

Devaluation

Devaluation is a deliberate decision by a government or central bank to reduce the value of its own currency in relation to the currencies of other countries.

Governments often opt for devaluation when there is a large current account deficit, which may occur when a country is importing far more than it is exporting.

When a nation devalues its currency, the goods it imports and the overseas debts it must repay become more expensive. But its exports become less expensive for overseas buyers. These competitive prices often stimulate higher sales and help to reduce the deficit.

DIAMONDs

A DIAMOND is an index-based unit investment trust (UIT) that holds the 30 stocks in the Dow Jones Industrial Average (DJIA). It's similar in structure

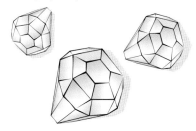

to an exchange traded fund (ETF).

Investors buy shares, or units, of the trust, which is listed on the American Stock Exchange (AMEX) as DIA. The share price changes throughout the day as investors buy and sell, just as share prices of stocks do.

That's in contrast to open-end mutual funds whose share prices change just once a day, when trading in their under-lying investments ends for the day.

Part of the appeal of DIAMOND shares is that the trust mirrors the performance of its benchmark index for dramatically less than the cost of buying shares in all 30 stocks in the DJIA.

A DIAMOND share trades at about 1/100 the value of the DJIA. So, for example, if the DJIA is at 11,500, shares in the trust will be priced around $115.

Diluted earnings per share

In addition to reporting earnings per share, corporations must report diluted earnings per share. This accounts for the possiblity that all outstanding warrants and stock options are exercised, and all convertible bonds and preferred shares are exchanged for common stock.

Diluted earnings actually report the smallest potential earnings per common share that a company could have based on its current earnings. In theory, at least, knowing the diluted earnings could

influence how much you would be willing to pay for the stock.

Dilution

Dilution occurs when a company issues additional shares of stock, and as a result the earnings per share and the book value per share decline.

This happens because earnings per share and book value per share are calculated by dividing the total earnings or book value by the number of existing shares.

The larger the number of shares, the lower the value of each share. Lower earnings per share may trigger a selloff in the stock, lowering its price. That's one reason a company may choose to issue bonds rather than new stock to raise additional capital.

Similarly, if companies merge or one buys another, earnings may be diluted if they don't increase proportionately with the combined number of shares in the newly created company.

Dilution can also occur if warrants and stock options on a stock are exercised, and if convertible bonds and preferred stock the company issued are converted to common stock.

Companies must report the worst-case potential for such dilution, or loss of value, to their shareholders as diluted earnings per share.

Direct deposit

Direct deposit is the electronic transfer of money from a payer, such as your employer or a government agency, directly into a bank account you designate.

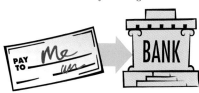

Direct deposit is faster and cheaper than sending a check and also more secure, which is why both payers and banks prefer this system. In fact, banks often provide free checking or other benefits if your paychecks are deposited directly.

Direct investment

You can make a direct investment in a company's stock through dividend reinvestment plans (DRIPs) and direct purchase plans (DPPs).

If a company in which you own stock offers a DRIP, you have the opportunity to reinvest cash dividends and capital gains distributions in more stock automatically each time they are paid.

In the case of DPPs, also known as direct stock purchase plans (DSPs), companies can sell their stock directly to investors without using a brokerage firm as intermediary.

Direct investment also refers to long-term investments in limited partnerships that invest in real estate, leased equipment, and energy exploration and development. In this type of investment, you become part owner of the hard assets of the enterprise.

You realize income from your investment by receiving a portion of the business's profits, for example, from rents, contractual leasing payments, or oil sales. In some cases you realize capital gains at the end of the investment term, if the business sells its assets.

These DPPs are largely nontraded and have no formal secondary markets. This means you will often have to hold the investment for terms of eight years or more, with no guarantee that any of the income or capital gains will materialize.

Many people make direct investments because there can be significant tax benefits, such as tax deferral and tax abatement, depending on the investment.

Direct purchase plan (DPP)

Some publicly held companies offer a direct purchase plan that lets you purchase their stock directly without using a broker.

You may pay a small commission or transaction fee—smaller than if you purchased the shares through a retail broker—although some DPPs charge no fee at all.

Direct purchase plans are similar to dividend reinvestment plans, or DRIPs, with the added benefit that you can make the initial purchase of the company's stock through the plan rather than having to purchase stock first, through a broker, in order to be eligible for a DRIP.

It's easy to open a DPP account, and because it lets you purchase fractional shares of the company's stock, you can decide whether to invest a lump sum or make small, regular purchases on a set schedule to build your investment. Your shares are registered on the company's books, and you can sell your shares through the plan as well.

Disclosure

A disclosure document explains how a financial product or offering works. It also details the terms to which you must agree in order to buy it or use it, and, in some cases, the risks you assume in making such a purchase.

For example, publicly traded companies must provide all available information that might influence your decision to invest in the stocks or bonds they issue. Mutual fund companies are required to disclose the risks and costs associated with buying shares in the fund.

Government regulatory agencies, such as the Securities and Exchange Commission (SEC), self-regulating organizations, state securities regulators, and NASD require such disclosures.

Similarly, federal and local governments require lenders to explain the costs of credit, and banks to explain the costs of opening and maintaining an account.

Despite the consumer benefits, disclosure information isn't always easily accessible. It may be expressed in confusing language, printed in tiny type, or so extensive that consumers choose to ignore it.

Discount

When bonds sell for less than their face value, they are said to be selling at a discount.

Bonds sell at a discount when the interest rate they pay is lower than the rate on more recently issued bonds or when the financial condition of the issuer weakens.

In the case of rising interest rates, demand for older, lower-paying bonds drops as investors put their money into newer, higher-paying alternatives, so the prices of the older bonds drop. If a rating agency reduces a bond's rating, the market price tends to drop because investors demand a higher yield for the additional risk they take in buying the bond.

Similarly, closed-end mutual funds may trade at a discount to their net asset value (NAV) as a result of weak investor demand or other market forces. Preferred stocks may also trade at a discount.

In contrast, certain bonds, called original issue discount bonds, or deep discount bonds, are issued at a discount to par value, or full face value, but worth par at maturity.

Discount brokerage firm

Discount brokerage firms charge lower commissions than full-service brokerage firms when they execute investors' buy and sell orders but may provide fewer services to their clients.

For example, they may not offer investment advice or maintain independent research departments.

Because of the information and online account access on most brokerage websites, differences between full-service and discount firms are less apparent to the average investor.

Discount point

Some lenders require you to prepay a portion of the interest due on your mortgage as a condition of approving the loan. They set the amount due at one or more discount points, with each discount point equal to 1% of the mortgage loan principal.

$$1 \text{ Point} = 1\% \text{ of loan amount}$$

For instance, if you must pay one point on a $100,000 mortgage, you owe $1,000.

From your perspective, the advantages of paying discount points are that your long-term interest rate is lowered slightly for each point you pay, and prepaid interest is tax deductible. The advantage, from the lenders' point of view, is that they collect some of their interest earnings up front.

Discount rate

The discount rate is the interest rate the Federal Reserve charges on loans it makes to banks and other financial institutions.

The discount rate becomes the base interest rate for most consumer borrowing as well. That's because a bank generally uses the discount rate as a benchmark for the interest it charges on the loans it makes.

For example, when the discount rate increases, the interest rate that lenders charge on home mortgages and other loans increases. And when the discount rate is lowered, the cost of consumer borrowing eventually decreases as well.

The term discount rate also applies to discounted instruments like US Treasury bills. In this case, the rate is used to identify the interest you will earn if you purchase at issue, hold the bill to maturity, and receive face value at maturity.

The interest is the difference between what you pay to purchase the bills and the amount you are repaid.

Discretionary account

A discretionary account is a type of brokerage account in which clients authorize their brokers to buy and sell securities on their behalf without prior consent for each transaction.

A client may set guidelines for the account, such as the types of securities the broker may purchase. However, the broker can buy and sell shares at his or her discretion.

Managed accounts—also called separate accounts and wrap accounts—are one type of discretionary account.

Disinflation

Disinflation is a slowdown in the rate of price increases that historically occurs during a recession, when the supply of goods is greater than the demand for them.

Unlike deflation, however, when prices for goods actually drop, disinflation prices do not usually fall, but the rate of inflation becomes negligible.

Dispute resolution

Dispute resolution—sometimes called alternative dispute resolution—refers to methods of resolving conflicts between parties or individuals that doesn't involve litigation.

Mediation and arbitration are two forms of dispute resolution that are frequently used when conflicts arise between investors and the brokers or investment advisers with whom they work.

If you have a conflict that you've been unable to resolve by talking with your broker and the firm, you can file a complaint with NASD or the New York Stock Exchange (NYSE), the self-regulatory body that regulates brokerage firms and uses mediators and arbitrators to help resolve disputes. If your conflict is with a registered investment adviser, you should contact the Securities and Exchange Commission (SEC).

Advocates of dispute resolution note that it tends to be quicker, cheaper, and less confrontational than litigation.

Distribution

A distribution is money a mutual fund pays its shareholders either from the dividends or interest it earns or from the capital gains it realizes on the sale of securities in its portfolio.

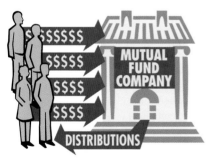

Unless you own the fund through a tax-deferred or tax-free account, you owe federal income tax on most distributions, the exception being interest income from municipal bond funds. That tax is due whether or not you reinvest the money to buy additional shares in the fund.

You'll owe tax at your regular rate on short-term gains and on income from interest. The tax on qualifying dividends

and long-term gains is calculated at your long-term capital gains rate. Your end-of-year statement will indicate which income belongs to each category.

The term distribution is also used to describe certain actions a corporation takes. For example, if a corporation spins off a subsidiary as a standalone company, it will issue shares in that subsidiary to current stockholders. That's considered a distribution. Corporate dividends may also be described as distributions.

Diversification

Diversification is an investment strategy in which you spread your investment dollars among different sectors, industries, and securities within a number of asset classes.

A well-diversified stock portfolio, for example, might include small-, medium-, and large-cap domestic stocks, stocks in six or more sectors or industries, and international stocks. The goal is to protect the value of your overall portfolio in case a single security or market sector takes a serious downturn.

Diversification can help insulate your portfolio against market and management risks without significantly reducing the level of return you want. But finding the diversification mix that's right for your portfolio depends on your age, your assets, your tolerance for risk, and your investment goals.

Dividend

Corporations may pay part of their earnings as dividends to you and other shareholders as a return on your investment. These dividends, which are often declared quarterly, are usually in the form of cash, but may be paid as additional shares or scrip.

Dividend payout ratio

You may be able to reinvest cash dividends automatically to buy additional shares if the corporation offers a dividend reinvestment program (DRIP).

Dividends are taxable unless you own the investment through a tax-deferred account, such as an employer sponsored retirement plan or individual retirement account. That applies whether you re-invest them or not.

However, dividends on most US and many international stocks are considered qualifying dividends. That means you owe tax at your long-term capital gains rate, provided you have owned the stocks the required length of time.

Dividends on real estate investment trusts (REITs), mutual savings banks, and certain other investments aren't considered qualifying and are taxed at your regular rate.

Dividend payout ratio

You can calculate a dividend payout ratio by dividing the dividend a company pays per share by the company's earnings per share. The normal range is 25% to 50% of earnings, though the average is higher in some sectors of the economy than in others.

Some analysts think that an unusually high ratio may indicate that a company is in financial trouble but doesn't want to alarm shareholders by reducing its dividend.

Dividend reinvestment plan (DRIP)

Many publicly held companies allow shareholders to reinvest dividends in company stock or buy additional shares through dividend reinvestment plans, or DRIPs.

Enrolling in a DRIP enables you to build your investment gradu-ally, taking advantage of dollar cost averaging and usually paying only a minimal transaction fee for each purchase.

Many DRIPs will also buy back shares at any time you want to sell, in most cases for a minimal sales charge.

One potential drawback of purchasing through a DRIP is that you accumulate shares at different prices over time, making it more difficult to determine your cost basis—especially if you want to sell some of but not all your holdings.

Dividend yield

If you own dividend-paying stocks, you figure the current dividend yield on your investment by dividing the dividend being paid on each share by the share's current market price.

For example, if a stock whose market price is $35 pays a dividend of 75 cents per share, the dividend yield is 2.14% ($0.75 ÷ $35 = .0214, or 2.14%).

Yields for all dividend-paying stocks are reported regularly in newspaper stock tables and on financial websites.

Dividend yield increases as the price per share drops and drops as the share price increases. But it does not tell you what you're earning based on your original investment or the income you can expect to earn in the future. However, some investors seeking current income or following a particular investment strategy look for high-yielding stocks.

Dogs of the Dow

If you follow a Dogs of the Dow investment strategy, you buy the ten highest-yielding stocks in the Dow Jones Industrial Average (DJIA) on the first of the year and hold them for a year.

According to this theory, the dogs will, over the year, produce a total return, or combination of dividends plus price appreciation, that's higher than the return on the DJIA as a whole. The increasing price is the result of demand for the high-yielding stock.

On the anniversary of your purchase, the stocks are no longer dogs because their higher prices reduce their current yield even if the dividend remains the same. So you sell them and buy the next batch of dogs.

Dollar cost averaging

Dollar cost averaging means adding a fixed amount of money on a regular schedule to an investment account, such as a mutual fund, retirement account, or a dividend reinvestment plan (DRIP).

Since the share price of the investment fluctuates, you buy fewer shares when the share price is higher and more shares when the price is lower.

The advantage of this type of formula investing, which is also sometimes called a constant dollar plan, is that, over time, the average price you pay per share is lower than the actual average price per share.

But to get the most from this approach, you have to invest regularly, including during prolonged downturns when the prices of the investment drop. Otherwise you are buying only at the higher prices.

Despite its advantages, dollar cost averaging does not guarantee a profit and doesn't protect you from losses in a falling market.

Domicile

Your domicile is your permanent residence, which you demonstrate by using it as your primary home, holding a driver's license using that address, and registering to vote in that district.

Your domicile affects your state and local income taxes, state estate and inheritance taxes, and certain other tax benefits or liabilities.

Domini Social Index 400

The Domini Social Index 400 is a market capitalization weighted index that tracks the performance of companies that meet a wide range of social and environmental standards.

For instance, the index screens out companies that manufacture or promote alcohol, tobacco, gambling, weapons, and nuclear power. It includes others that have outstanding records of social responsibility.

About half the stocks included in the Standard & Poor's 500 Index (S&P 500), on which the Domini Index is modeled, make the cut, including giants like Microsoft and Coca-Cola. The other stocks are selected based on the industries they

represent and their reputations for socially conscious business practices.

The index is considered a benchmark for measuring the effect that selecting socially responsible stocks has on a financial portfolio's performance. This practice is also called social screening.

Double bottom

Double bottom is a term that technical analysts use to describe a stock price pattern that, when depicted on a chart, shows two drops to the same dollar amount separated by a rebound.

For example, if a stock that had been trading at about $28 a share dropped to $18, rebounded to trade at about $22 for several weeks, and then dropped to $18 again, analysts would identify $18 as a double bottom.

An analyst observing this pattern might conclude that investors were comfortable paying $18 for the stock, and that the price might not drop below that level in the near term. In technical terms, the analyst would say that there was support for the price. However, there's no guarantee that it might not drop further and hit a new low.

Double top

Double top is a term that technical analysts use to describe a stock price pattern that, when depicted on a chart, shows two gains to the same dollar level separated by a price drop.

For example, if a stock that had been trading at about $28 a share rose to $35, dropped back to trade at about $28 for several weeks, and then rose to $35 again, analysts would identify $35 as a double top.

An analyst observing this pattern might conclude that investors were comfortable paying $35 for the stock, and that the price might not rise above that level in the near term. In technical terms, the analyst would say that there was resistance above that price. However, there's no way to predict whether the price would in fact remain at $35 or gain value and hit new a high.

Dow Jones 65 Composite Average

This composite of three Dow Jones averages tracks the stock performance of 65 companies in two major market sectors and the benchmark DJIA.

Those averages are the Dow Jones Industrial Average (DJIA), the Dow Jones Transportation Average, and the Dow Jones Utility Average.

Dow Jones Industrial Average (DJIA)

The Dow Jones Industrial Average (DJIA), sometimes referred to as the Dow, is the best-known and most widely followed market indicator in the world. It tracks the performance of 30 blue chip US stocks.

Though it is called an average, it actually functions more like an index. The DJIA is quoted in points, not dollars. It's computed by totaling the weighted prices of the 30 stocks and dividing by a number that is regularly adjusted for stock splits, spin-offs, and other changes in the stocks being tracked.

The companies that make up the DJIA are changed from time to time. For example, in 1999 Microsoft, Intel, SBC Communications, and Home Depot were added and four other companies were dropped. The changes are widely inter-preted as a reflection of the emerging or declining impact of a specific company or type of company on the economy as a whole.

Dow Jones Transportation Average

The Dow Jones Transportation Average tracks the performance of the stocks of 20 airlines, railroads, and trucking companies. It is one of the components of the Dow Jones 65 Composite Average.

Dow Jones Utility Average

The Dow Jones Utility Average tracks the performance of the stocks of 15 gas, electric, and power companies, and is one of the components of the Dow Jones 65 Composite Average.

Dow Jones Wilshire 5000 Index

The Dow Jones Wilshire 5000 is a market capitalization weighted index of approxi-mately 7,000 stocks.

It is the broadest US stock market index, tracking all the stocks traded on the New York Stock Exchange (NYSE), the American Stock Exchange (AMEX), the Nasdaq Stock Market (Nasdaq), and other US based stocks for which data is readily available.

The difference between the index's name (the 5000) and the number of stocks the index tracks at any one time occurs because the number of stocks being traded changes all the time.

Dow theory

Dow theory maintains that major market trends depend on how the Dow Jones Industrial Average (DJIA) and the Dow Jones Transportation Average behave.

They must move simultaneously in the same direction until they both hit a new high or a new low in order for a trend to continue.

Some experts discount the relevance of this approach as a useful guideline, arguing that waiting to invest until a trend is confirmed can mean losing out on potential growth.

Down payment

A down payment is the amount, usually stated as a percentage, of the total cost of a property that you pay in cash as part of a real estate transaction.

The down payment is the difference between the selling price and the amount of money you borrow to buy the property. For example, you might make a 10% down payment of $20,000 to buy a home selling for $200,000 and take a $180,000 mortgage.

With a conventional mortgage, you're usually expected to make a down payment of 10% to 20%. But you may qualify for a mortgage that requires a smaller down payment, perhaps as little as 3%.

The upside of needing to put down less money is that you may be able to buy sooner. But the downside is that your mortgage payments will be larger and you'll pay more interest, increasing the cost of buying.

Downtick

When a security sells at a lower price than its previous sale price, the drop in value is called a downtick. For example, if a stock that had been trading at 25 sells at 24.99 the next time it trades, the 1 cent drop is a downtick.

Durable power of attorney

You can grant a durable power of attorney to an agent of your choice, giving that person—called the attorney-in-fact—the right the make legal decisions for you if you aren't able to do so.

Your attorney-in-fact also has the right to buy and sell property on your behalf and to handle your financial affairs. You retain the right to revoke the power or name a new agent at any time.

An agent with durable power of attorney continues to have the power to act on your behalf if you become incompetent. However, not all states allow durable powers.

Duration

In simplified terms, a bond's duration measures the effect that each 1% change in interest rates will have on the bond's market value.

Unlike the maturity date, which tells you when the issuer has promised to repay your principal, duration, which takes the bond's interest payments into account, helps you to evaluate how volatile the bond's price will be over time.

Basically, the longer the duration—expressed in years—the more volatile the price. So a 1% change in interest rates will have less effect on the price of a bond with a duration of 2 than it will on the price of a bond with a duration of 5.

Dutch auction

A Dutch auction opens at the highest price and drops gradually until there's a buyer willing to pay the amount being asked. The transaction is completed at that price.

The only securities auctions in US markets that are conducted as Dutch auctions are the competitive bids for US Treasury bills, notes, and bonds.

In contrast, a conventional commercial auction begins with the lowest price, which gradually increases as potential buyers bid against each other. The selling price is determined when no bidder will top the last offer on the table.

A double-action auction—the system in place on US stock exchanges—features many buyers and sellers bidding against each other to close a sale at a mutually agreed-upon price.

Early withdrawal

If you withdraw assets from a fixed-term investment, such as a certificate of deposit (CD), before it matures, it is considered an early withdrawal.

Similarly, if you withdraw from a tax-deferred or tax-free retirement savings plan before you turn 59½, in most cases, it's considered early.

If you withdraw early, you usually have to pay a penalty imposed by the issuer (in the case of a CD) or the government (if it's an IRA or other tax-deferred or tax-free savings plan).

However, you may be able to use the money in your account without penalty under certain circumstances. For example, if you withdraw IRA assets to pay for higher education, to buy a first home, or for other qualified reasons, the penalty is waived. But taxes will still be due on the tax-deferred portion of the withdrawal.

Earned income

Earned income is pay you receive for work you perform, and includes salaries, wages, tips, and professional fees.

Your earned income is included in your gross income, along with unearned income from interest, dividends, and capital gains. If you have earned income, you're eligible to contribute to an individual retirement account (IRA).

Earned income credit (EIC)

The earned income tax credit (EIC) reduces the income tax that certain low-income taxpayers would otherwise owe. It's a refundable credit, so if the tax that's due is less than the amount of the credit, the difference is paid to the taxpayer as a refund.

To qualify for the EIC, a taxpayer must work, earn less than the government's ceiling for his or her filing status and family situation, meet a set of specific conditions, and file the required IRS schedules and forms.

Earnings

In the case of an individual, earnings include salary and other compensation for work you do, as well as interest, dividends, and capital gains from your investments.

From a corporate perspective, earnings are profits, or net income, after the company has paid income taxes and bond interest.

Earnings estimate

Professional stock analysts use mathematical models that weigh companies' financial data to predict their future earnings per share on a quarterly, annual, and long-term basis.

Investment research companies, such as Thomson Financial and Zacks, publish averages of analysts' estimates for specific companies. These averages are called consensus estimates.

Earnings momentum

When a company's earnings per share grow from year to year at an ever-increasing rate, that pattern is described as earnings momentum. One example might be a company whose earnings grow one year at 10%, the next year at 18%, and a third year at 25%.

In many cases, this momentum triggers an increase in the stock's share price as well, because investors identify the stock as one they expect to continue to grow and increase in value.

Earnings per share (EPS)

Earnings per share (EPS) is calculated by dividing a company's total earnings by the number of outstanding shares.

For example, if a company earns $100 million in a year and has 50 million outstanding shares, the earnings per share are $2.

Earnings per share can also be calculated on a fully diluted basis, by adding outstanding stock options, rights, and warrants to the outstanding shares.

The results report what EPS would be if all of those options, rights, and warrants were exercised and the company had to issue more shares to meet its obligations.

EARNINGS PER SHARE

$$\frac{\text{Total company earnings}}{\text{Number of outstanding shares}} = \text{EARNINGS PER SHARE}$$

for example

$$\frac{\$100,000,000}{50,000,000} = \$2 \text{ PER SHARE}$$

Earnings and other financial measures are provided on a per share basis to make it easier for you to analyze the information and compare the results to those of other investments.

Earnings surprise

When a company's earnings report either exceeds or fails to meet analysts' estimates, it's called an earnings surprise.

An upside surprise occurs when a company reports higher earnings than analysts predicted and usually triggers an increase in the stock price.

A negative surprise, on the other hand, occurs when a company fails to meet expectations and often causes the stock's price to fall. Companies try hard to avoid negative surprises since even a small deviation can create a big stir.

EBITDA

Earnings before interest, taxes, depreciation, and amortization are commonly shortened to EBITDA. EBITDA reports a company's profits before interest on debt and taxes owed or paid to the government are subtracted.

EBITDA is used to compare the profitability of a company with other companies of the same size in the same industry but which may have different levels of debt or different tax situations.

Economic cycle

An economic cycle is a period during which a country's economy moves from strength to weakness and back to strength.

This pattern repeats itself regularly, though not on a fixed schedule. The length of the cycle isn't predictable either and may be measured in months or in years.

The cycle is driven by many forces—including inflation, the money supply, domestic and international politics, and natural events.

In developed countries, the central bank uses its power to influence interest rates and the money supply to prevent dramatic peaks and deep troughs, smoothing the cycle's highs and lows.

This up and down pattern influences all aspects of economic life, including the financial markets. Certain investments or categories of investment that thrive in one phase of the cycle may lose value in another. As a result, in evaluating an investment, you may want to look at how it has fared through a full economic cycle.

Economic indicator

Economic indicators are statistical measurements of current business conditions.

Changes in leading indicators, including those that track factory orders, stock prices, the money supply, and consumer confidence, forecast short-term economic strength or weakness.

In contrast, lagging indicators, such as business spending, bank interest rates, and unemployment figures, move up or down in the wake of changes in the economy.

The Conference Board, a nonprofit business research firm, releases its weighted indexes of leading, lagging, and coincident indicators every month.

Though the individual components are also reported separately throughout the month, the indicators provide a snapshot of the economy's overall health.

Education savings account (ESA)

You can put up to $2,000 a year into a Coverdell education savings account (ESA) that you establish in the name of a minor child. The assets in the account can be invested any way you choose.

There is no limit to the number of accounts you can set up for different beneficiaries, but no more than a total of $2,000 can be contributed in a single beneficiary's name in any one year. If you choose, you may switch the beneficiary of an ESA to another member of the same extended family.

Your contribution is not tax deductible. But any earnings that accumulate in the account can be withdrawn tax free if they're used to pay qualified educational expenses for the beneficiary until he or she reaches age 30. The costs can be incurred at any level, from elementary school through a graduate degree, or at a qualified post-secondary technical or vocational school.

There are no restrictions on using ESA money in the same year the student uses other tax-free savings, or the student, parent, or guardian uses tax credits for educational expenses. But you can't take a credit for expenses you covered with tax-free withdrawals.

To qualify to make a full $2,000 contribution to an ESA, your modified adjusted gross income (MAGI) must be $95,000 or less, and your right to make any contribution at all is phased out if your MAGI is $110,000 if you're a single taxpayer. The comparable range if you're married and file a joint return is $190,000, phased out at $220,000.

Effective tax rate

Your effective tax rate is the rate you actually pay on all of your taxable income. You find your annual effective rate by dividing the tax you paid in the year by your taxable income for the year.

Your effective rate will always be lower than your marginal tax rate, which is the rate you pay on the income that falls into the highest tax bracket you reach.

For example, if you file your federal tax return as a single taxpayer, had taxable income of $75,000, and paid $15,332 in federal income taxes, your federal marginal tax rate would be 28% but your effective rate would be 20.4%. That lower rate reflects the fact that you paid tax on portions of your income at the 10%, 15%, and 25% rates, as well as the final portion at 28%.

Efficient market

When the information that investors need to make investment decisions is widely available, thoroughly analyzed, and regularly used, the result is an efficient market.

This is the case with securities traded on the major US stock markets. That means the price of a security is a clear indication of its value at the time it is traded.

Conversely, an inefficient market is one in which there is limited information available for making rational investment decisions and limited trading volume.

Efficient market theory

Proponents of the efficient market theory believe that a stock's current price accurately reflects what investors know about the stock.

They also maintain that you can't predict a stock's future price based on its past performance. Their conclusion, which is contested by other experts, is that it's not possible for an individual or institutional investor to outperform the market as a whole.

Index funds, which are designed to match, rather than beat, the performance of a particular market segment, are in part an outgrowth of efficient market theory.

Electronic benefits transfer (EBT)

Electronic benefits transfer, or EBT, is a system through which recipients of certain government benefits receive and spend funds electronically, using a plastic EBT card similar to a bank debit card.

Benefits are deposited electronically into the recipient's program account. The recipient can then use his or her EBT card to make purchases, which are debited from the account.

All states now use EBT in addition to traditional paper coupons to distribute food stamp benefits. Some states also use EBT to disburse benefits for other programs, including the US Department of Agriculture's Special Supplemental Nutrition Program for Women, Infants, and Children (WIC) and the Temporary Assistance to Needy Families (TANF) programs.

There are no fees when recipients use EBT cards for purchases, but fees may apply to cash withdrawals from ATMs or electronic balance inquiries.

Electronic bill payment

If you have an electronic bill payment arrangement with your bank, your bills are sent to an account you designate and the bank pays them automatically each month by deducting the money from that account and transferring it to your payees, either electronically or by check.

The advantage of using electronic payment is that your bills will be paid on time, though it is your responsibility to ensure that there is enough money on deposit to cover what's due.

When the payments are made to credit accounts with the same bank, you may be offered a slightly reduced interest rate for using the service.

However, you'll want to investigate whether there's an added fee for automatic payment and how much flexibility you have in determining how much of a bill's balance due is paid each month on credit accounts where you have the option to pay less than the full amount owed.

Electronic bill presentment

If you pay bills online, you may be able to take advantage of electronic bill presentment, a paper-free method of reporting your outstanding charges and the amount due.

The creditor may either email your monthly statement or notify you via email that the statement is ready for viewing at a secure website.

Electronic check conversion

Electronic check conversion is a payment process in which you give a payee a check, but the actual payment is processed as an electronic funds transfer.

The payment is automatically debited from your account using the account, routing information, and bank ID information on your check, which is either voided and returned to you or destroyed.

A business must notify you before it uses electronic check conversion to process your payment. Keep in mind that an electronic funds transfer will be completed much more quickly than a check, so it's important to have the funds available in your account before you authorize an electronic check conversion.

As with any other type of electronic funds transfer, you have the right to ask

your bank to investigate any errors or misuses.

Electronic communications network (ECN)

An ECN is an alternative securities trading system that collects, displays, and executes orders electronically without a middleman, such as a specialist or market maker.

Trading on an ECN allows institutional and individual investors to buy and sell anonymously. Further, ECNs facilitate extended, or after-hours, trading.

ECN trade execution can be faster and less expensive than trades handled through screen-based or traditional markets, though the volume is sometimes thin.

However, some ECNs have been approved for official stock exchange status, expanding the number of stocks that can be traded on their systems.

Electronic Data Gathering, Analysis, and Retrieval System (EDGAR)

EDGAR is an electronic database that contains all the corporate financial reports filed with the Securities and Exchange Commission (SEC).

Any company with more than $10 million in assets and over 500 shareholders, or that is listed on a major exchange in the United States or quoted on the Over the Counter Bulletin Board (OTCBB) is required to file prospectuses, an annual 10-K—or audited financial report—three unaudited 10-Qs, notices of insider trades, tender offers, and other detailed company information.

Smaller companies may file voluntarily. You can access all EDGAR filings free of charge on the SEC website (www.sec.gov).

Electronic funds transfer

Electronic funds transfer (EFT) is the means by which financial institutions exchange billions of dollars every day without the physical movement of any paper money. Money moves electronically from one bank account to another, usually within 24 hours of a scheduled payment.

The system covers all electronic credit and debit money transfers, including direct deposits—which occur when you authorize your employer or other payer to automatically deposit payroll into your bank account—debit card and ATM transactions, online bill payment, wire transfers, and debit transfers as well as automatic deductions from your accounts to make regular payments.

According to the US Department of the Treasury, it costs the federal government only 9 cents to issue an EFT payment as opposed to 86 cents to make a traditional check payment.

Elimination period

If you have disability insurance or long-term care insurance, there's a waiting period, called the elimination period, from the time you become disabled, or are certified in need of long-term care, and when you begin receiving benefits.

You often have a choice of elimination periods—such as 30, 60, or 90 days—when you purchase the insurance, though sometimes the payment gap is dictated by the terms of the policy.

In general, the shorter the elimination period the higher the premiums will be for comparable coverage.

Emergency fund

An emergency fund is designed to provide financial back-up for unexpected expenses or for a period when you aren't working and need income.

To create an emergency fund, you generally accumulate three to six months' worth of living expenses in a secure, liquid account so that the money is available if you need it.

EMERGENCY

It's a good idea to keep your emergency fund separate from other savings or investment accounts and replenish it if you withdraw. But you don't have to limit yourself to low-interest savings accounts, and might consider other liquid accounts, such as money market funds, that may pay higher interest.

If you're single or have sole responsibility for one or more dependents, you may want to consider an even bigger emergency fund, perhaps large enough to cover a year's worth of ordinary expenses.

Emerging market

Countries in the process of building market-based economies are broadly referred to as emerging markets. However, there are major differences among the countries included in this category.

Some emerging-market countries, including Russia, have only recently relaxed restrictions on a free-market economy. Others, including Indonesia, have opened their markets more widely to overseas investors, and still others, including Mexico, are expanding industrial production.

Their combined stock market capitalization is less than 3% of the worldwide total.

Emerging markets fund

Emerging markets mutual funds invest primarily in the securities of countries in the process of building a market-based economy.

Some funds specialize in the markets of a certain region, such as Latin America or Southeast Asia. Others invest in a global cross-section of countries and regions.

Employee Retirement Income Security Act (ERISA)

This comprehensive law, best known by the acronym ERISA, governs qualified retirement plans, including most private-company defined benefit and defined contribution plans, and protects the rights of the employees who participate in the plans.

ERISA also established individual retirement arrangements (IRAs), made it easier for self-employed people to set up retirement plans, and made employee stock ownership plans part of the tax code.

Among ERISA requirements are that plan participants receive a detailed document that explains how their plan operates, what employee rights are—including qualifying to participate and uniform vesting schedules—and what the grievance and appeals process is.

In addition, ERISA assigns fiduciary responsibility to those who sponsor, manage, and control plan assets. This means they must act in the best interests of the plan participants. ERISA rules do not apply to plans provided by federal, state, or local governments, church plans, or certain other plans.

ERISA has been amended several times since it was passed in 1974, making some provisions more flexible and others more restrictive. Among the changes were the Consolidated Omnibus Budget Reconciliation Act (COBRA), which provides continuing access to coverage, for a fee, when an employee leaves an employer who offers health insurance, and the Health Insurance Portability and Accountability Act (HIPAA), which protects access to health insurance coverage for employees and their families with pre-existing medical conditions when the employee leaves a job that provided coverage and moves to a new job where coverage is also offered.

Employee stock ownership plan (ESOP)

An ESOP is a trust to which a company contributes shares of newly issued stock, shares the company has held in reserve, or the cash to buy shares on the open market.

The shares go into individual accounts set up for employees who meet the plan's eligibility requirements.

An ESOP may be part of a 401(k) plan or separate from it. If it's linked, an employer's matching contribution may be shares added to the ESOP account rather than cash added to an investment account.

If you're part of an ESOP and you leave your job, you have the right to sell your shares on the open market if your employer is a public company.

If it's a privately held company, you have the right to sell them back at fair market value. The vast majority of ESOPs are offered by privately held companies.

Employer sponsored retirement plan

Employers may offer their employees either defined benefit or defined contribution retirement plans, or they may make both types of plans available.

Any employer may offer a defined benefit plan, but certain types of defined contribution plans are available only through specific categories of employers.

For example, 403(b) plans may be offered only by tax-exempt, nonprofit employers, and 457 plans only by state and municipal governments. SIMPLE plans, on the other hand, can only be offered by employers with fewer than 100 workers.

Corporate employers who contribute to a retirement plan can take a tax deduction for the amount of their contribution and may enjoy other tax benefits. However, the plan must meet certain Internal Revenue Service (IRS) guidelines.

Offering a retirement plan may also make the employer more attractive to potential employees. However, employers are not required to offer plans. If they do, they can make the plan as generous or as limited as they choose as long as the plan meets the government's non-discrimination guidelines.

Enhanced index fund

An enhanced index fund chooses selectively among the stocks in a particular index in order to produce a slightly higher return. By contrast, an index fund strives to mirror the performance of a particular index by owning all the stocks in the index.

The goal is to narrowly beat the index anywhere from a fraction of a percent to two percentage points, but not more. A wider spread would classify the enhanced fund as an actively managed mutual fund rather than an index fund.

Enhanced index fund managers may achieve higher returns by identifying the undervalued stocks in the index. Or they might adjust holdings to include a larger proportion of securities in higher performing sectors, or use other investment strategies, such as buying derivatives.

While enhanced index funds may expose you to the risk of greater losses than their plain-vanilla counterparts, they may also offer an opportunity for higher returns.

Equal Credit Opportunity Act (ECOA)

The Equal Credit Opportunity Act (ECOA) is designed to ensure that all qualified people have access to credit.

It forbids lenders from rejecting credit applicants on the basis of race, gender, marital status, age, or national origin and requires lenders to consider public assistance in the same light as other forms of income.

The act says that creditors must approve or reject your application within 30 days if you've filed a complete application, and, if you ask within 60 days, must provide an explanation for turning you down. The ECOA requires creditors to provide specific reasons for rejecting you and forbids indefinite or vague explanations.

If you feel you're being discriminated against and the lender does not respond to your complaints, you can contact the attorney general of your state or the government agency that oversees the creditor. By law, the creditor must provide that information. If you can't get the information from the creditor, you can contact the Federal Trade Commission at www.ftc.gov.

Equity

In the broadest sense, equity gives you ownership. If you own stock, you have equity in, or own a portion—however small—of the company that issued the stock.

House Valued at $300,000

$200,000 Outstanding mortgage

$100,000 Your equity

Having equity is the opposite of owning a bond or commercial paper, which is a debt the company must repay to you.

Equity also refers to the difference between an asset's current market value—the amount it could be sold for—and any debt or claim against it. For example, if you own a home currently valued at $300,000 but still owe $200,000 on your mortgage, your equity in the home is $100,000.

The same is true if you own stock in a margin account. The stock may be worth $50,000 in the marketplace, but if you have a loan balance of $20,000 in your margin account because you financed the purchase, your equity in the stock is $30,000.

Equity fund

Equity funds invest primarily in stock. The stock a fund buys—whether in small, up-and-coming companies or large, well-established firms—depends on the fund's investment objectives and management style.

The general approach may be implied by the fund's name or the category in which it places itself, such as large-cap growth or small-cap value. However, a fund's manager may have the flexibility to invest more broadly to meet the fund's objectives.

Equivalent taxable yield

While taxable bonds normally pay higher interest rates than tax-exempt bonds, they sometimes provide a lower overall yield.

EQUIVALENT TAXABLE YIELD

$$\frac{\text{Tax-exempt yield}}{100 - \text{your tax rate}} = \frac{\text{EQUIVALENT}}{\text{TAXABLE YIELD}}$$

Finding the equivalent taxable yield lets you determine the minimum interest rate a taxable bond must pay to equal the yield of a comparable tax-exempt bond. The formula for the equivalent taxable yield is tax-exempt interest rate ÷ (100 – your tax rate).

So, for example, if a municipal bond pays an annual interest rate of 7%, and your tax rate is 35%, the equivalent taxable yield would be 7 ÷ (100 – 35) = 10.8%. That means that in order to be as attractive an investment as the 7% municipal bond, a taxable bond would need to pay an annual interest rate of 10.8% or more.

Escrow

When someone else holds assets of yours until the terms of a contract or an agreement are fulfilled, your assets are said to be held in escrow. The assets could be money, securities, real estate, or a deed.

The person or organization that holds the assets is the escrow agent, and the account in which they are held is an escrow account.

For example, if you make a down payment on a home, the money is held in escrow until the sale is completed or the deal falls through.

Amounts you prepay to cover property taxes and insurance premiums as part of your regular mortgage payment are also held in escrow until those bills come due and are paid. In that case, you may earn interest on the amount in the escrow account.

Escrow agent
An escrow agent is the person or group that holds certain of your assets in an escrow account while you negotiate the final terms of a contract.

For example, if you are buying a home, the escrow agent would hold the down payment you make when your offer is accepted until the purchase is finalized.

Estate
Your estate is what you leave behind, financially speaking, when you die. To figure its worth, your assets are valued to determine your gross estate.

The assets may include cash, investments, retirement accounts, business interests, real estate, precious objects and antiques, and personal effects.

Then all your outstanding debts, which may include income taxes, loans, or other obligations, are paid, and those plus any costs of settling the estate are subtracted from the gross estate.

If the amount that's left is larger than the amount you can leave to your heirs tax free, you have a taxable estate, and federal estate taxes may be due. Depending on the state where you live and the size of your taxable estate, there may be additional state taxes as well.

After any taxes that may be due are paid, what remains is distributed among your heirs according to the terms of your will, the terms of any trusts you established, and the beneficiaries you named on certain accounts—or the rulings of a court, if you didn't leave a will.

Estate tax
Your estate owes federal estate tax on the value of your taxable estate if the estate is larger than the amount you are permitted to leave to your heirs tax free.

That amount, which is set by Congress, is $2 million for 2006, 2007, and 2008 and is scheduled to increase to $3.5 million in 2009.

Under current law, the estate tax will be eliminated in 2010. Without further Congressional action, the tax will be re-instated in 2011. However, modifications to the law may be made before that date.

If your estate may be vulnerable to these taxes, which are figured at a higher rate than income taxes, you may want to reduce its value. You could do this by using a number of tax planning strategies, including making nontaxable gifts and creating irrevocable trusts.

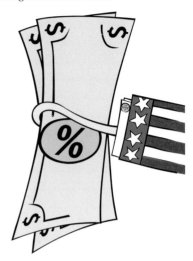

Further, if you're married to a US citizen and leave your entire estate to your spouse, there are no estate taxes, no matter how much the estate is worth. However, estate taxes may be due when your surviving spouse dies.

You may also face estate taxes in your state.

Euro
The euro is the common currency of the European Monetary Union (EMU). The national currencies of the participating countries were replaced with euro coins and bills on January 1, 2002.

Eurobond
A eurobond is an international bond sold outside the country in whose currency it is denominated, or issued.

For example, an Italian automobile company might sell eurobonds issued in US dollars to investors living in European countries.

Multinational companies and national governments, including governments of developing countries, use eurobonds to raise capital in international markets.

Eurocurrency
Eurocurrency is any major currency that is deposited by a national government or corporation based outside the country where the bank receiving the funds is located.

For example, Japanese yen deposited in a British bank by a Japanese car manufacturer is considered eurocurrency.

Eurocurrency is used in international trade and to make international loans.

Eurodollar

Eurodollars are US currency deposited in banks outside the United States but not always in Europe. Certain debt securities are issued in eurodollars and pay interest in US dollars into non-US bank accounts. Eurodollars are a form of eurocurrency.

European Central Bank (ECB)

The European Central Bank is the central bank of the European Monetary Union (EMU), whose member countries use the euro as their currency.

The ECB, which is based in Frankfurt, Germany, issues currency, sets interest rates, and oversees other aspects of monetary policy for the EMU.

The EMU's National Central Banks (such as the Banque de France and the Deutsche Bundesbank), together with the ECB, form the European System of Central Banks. They play an important role in implementing monetary policy, conducting foreign exchange operations, and maintaining the foreign reserves of member states.

European-style option

A listed option that you can exercise only on the last trading day before the expiration date is called a European-style option whether it trades on a US exchange, a European exchange, or elsewhere in the world.

For example, many index options listed on various US exchanges are European-style options. In contrast, you can exercise an American-style option at any point between the day you purchase it and its expiration date.

All equity options are American style, no matter where the exchange on which they trade is located.

Ex-dividend

You must own a security by the record date the company sets to be entitled to the dividend it will pay on the payable date.

The period between those dates—anywhere from a week to a month or more—during which new investors in the security are not entitled to that dividend is called the ex-dividend period.

On the day the ex-dividend period begins, which is the first trade date that will settle after the record date, the stock is said to go ex-dividend.

Generally, the price of a stock rises in relation to the amount of the anticipated dividend as the ex-dividend date approaches. It drops back on the first day of the ex-dividend period to reflect the amount that is being paid out as dividend.

Excess contribution

An excess contribution occurs when the salary deferrals or matching contributions of highly compensated employees are higher than the amounts permitted by federal law.

If that happens, the company must pay out those amounts to the employees involved before the end of the following tax year or face penalties.

Excess contributions are different from excess deferrals, also called after-tax contributions, which employees may legally make to their employer sponsored retirement plans.

Exchange

Traditionally, an exchange has been a physical location for trading securities. Trading is handled, at least in part, by an open outcry or dual auction system.

Two examples in the United States are the New York Stock Exchange (NYSE), which has the largest trading floor in the world, and the Chicago Board Options Exchange (CBOE).

However, the definition is evolving. Traditional exchanges handle an increasing number of trades electronically, off the floor. Nasdaq and other totally electronic securities markets, without trading floors, have exchange status.

As a result, the terms exchange and market are being used interchangeably to mean any environment in which listed products are traded.

The term exchange also refers to the act of moving assets from one fund to another in the same fund family or from one variable annuity subaccount to another offered through the same contract.

Exchange rate

The exchange rate is the price at which the currency of one country can be converted to the currency of another. Although some exchange rates are fixed by agreement, most fluctuate or float from day to day.

Daily exchange rates are listed in the financial sections of newspapers and can also be found on financial websites.

Exchange traded notes

Exchange traded notes (ETNs) are debt securities issued by a financial institution, listed on a stock exchange, and traded in the secondary market.

Unlike regular bonds, there are no periodic interest payments, and your principal isn't protected. So you could lose some of or all the amount you invest.

You can sell your ETN in the secondary market at its current price or hold it until maturity, though that may be 30 years in the future.

The price in the secondary market is determined by supply and demand, the current performance of the index, and the credit rating of the ETN issuer. At maturity, the issuer pays a return linked to the performance of the market index, such as a commodity index, to which the ETN is linked, minus the issuer's annual fee.

Exchange traded fund (ETF)

Exchange traded funds (ETFs) are listed on a stock exchange and trade like stock. You can use traditional stock trading techniques, such as stop orders, limit orders, margin purchases, and short sales when you buy or sell ETFs.

But ETFs also resemble mutual funds in some ways. For example, you buy shares of the fund, which in turn owns a portfolio of stocks.

Each ETF has a net asset value (NAV), which is determined by the total market capitalization of the stocks in the portfolio, plus dividends but minus expenses, divided by the number of shares issued by the fund.

ETF prices change throughout the trading day, in response to supply and demand, rather than just at the end of the trading day as open-end mutual fund prices do.

The market price and the NAV are rarely the same, but the differences are typically small. That's due to a unique process that allows institutional investors to buy or redeem large blocks of shares at the NAV with in-kind baskets of the fund's stocks.

Exclusion

Medical services that insurance companies do not pay for are called exclusions. A typical exclusion is a wartime injury or a self-inflicted wound.

But coverage for certain pre-existing conditions, or health problems you had before you were covered by the policy, may also be excluded on some policies.

Executor/Executrix

When you die, your executor administers your estate and follows the directions provided in your will. Among the executor's duties are collecting and valuing your assets, paying taxes and debts out of those assets, and distributing the remaining assets to your heirs.

You may want to appoint a family member or close friend as executor. Or you may choose a professional, such as a lawyer or bank trust officer.

What some people do is name a professional and a friend or family member to work together, especially if the estate is large or there are potential complications.

Executors are entitled to be paid for their work, which ends when your estate is settled, usually anywhere from one to three years after your death. Professional executors always charge, while friends and family may or may not.

Exemption

An exemption is a fixed dollar amount that you can subtract from your adjusted gross income to reduce your taxable income. The per-person exemption amount is set by Congress each year, and typically increases from year to year.

If you're over 65 or blind, you qualify for an additional exemption. Taxpayers whose adjusted gross income is higher than the government limit may not qualify for an exemption.

Exercise

When you act on a buying or selling opportunity that you have been granted under the terms of a contract, you are said to exercise a right.

Contracts may include the right to exchange stock options for stock, buy stock at a specific price, or buy or sell the security or product underlying an option at a specific exercise price.

For example, if you buy a call option giving you the right to buy stock at $50 a share, and the market price jumps to $60 a share, you'd likely exercise your option to buy at the lower price.

Exercise price

An option's exercise price, also called the strike price, is the price at which you can buy or sell the stock or other financial product that underlies that option.

The exercise price is set by the exchange on which the option trades and remains constant for the life of the option.

However, the market value of the underlying investment rises and falls continuously during the period in response to market demand.

Expense ratio

An expense ratio is the percentage of a mutual fund's or variable annuity's total assets deducted to cover operating and management expenses.

HOW EXPENSE RATIOS WORK

$$\frac{\text{Value of your shares} \times \text{Expense ratio}}{\text{YEARLY FEES}}$$

for example

$$\frac{\$150{,}000 \text{ Value} \times 1.25\% \text{ Expense ratio}}{\$1{,}875 \text{ YEARLY FEES}}$$

Those expenses include employee salaries, custodial and transfer fees, distribution, marketing, and other costs of offering the fund or contract. However, they don't cover trading costs or commissions.

For example, if you own shares in a fund with a 1.25% expense ratio, your annual share is $1.25 for every $100 in your account, or $12.50 on an account valued at $1,000.

Expense ratios vary from one fund company to another and among different types of funds. Typically, international equity funds have among the highest expense ratios, and index funds among the lowest. Similar differences in expense ratios are characteristic of different variable annuity investment accounts.

Expiration cycle

Equity and index options expire on a predictable four-month schedule, two of which are determined by the expiration cycle to which the underlying instrument has been randomly assigned and two by when you purchase the option.

There are three expiration cycles, one beginning in January, one in February, and one in March. Each cycle includes four months, and an option always expires in two of those months. The other two expiration months are the month in which it is purchased and the following month.

For example, if you purchase an option on an equity assigned to Cycle 1, which includes January, April, July, and October, between January 1 and the third Friday in January you have a choice of contracts expiring in January and in February—because they are the current month and the following one—or in April or July—because they are the next two months in Cycle 1.

Similarly, if you purchased an option on the same equity in April, you'd also have a choice of four expiration dates: April and May—the current and following months—and then July and October, the next two months in Cycle 1.

Expiration date

The expiration date is the day on which an options contract expires and becomes worthless. Listed options always expire on the Saturday following the third Friday of their expiration month.

For example, if you hold an American-style September equity option, you can exercise it any time before the end of trading on the third Friday in September, or whatever cutoff time your brokerage firm sets. In contrast, European-style options can be exercised only at expiration, usually on Friday.

Under specific circumstances, listed options will be exercised automatically at expiration unless the owner gives instructions not to exercise them.

Unlike the standard term of a listed option, the expiration date of an over-the-counter option is negotiated at the time of the trade.

Face value

Face value, or par value, is the dollar value of a bond or note, generally $1,000.

That is the amount the issuer has borrowed, usually the amount you pay to buy the bond at the time it is issued, and the amount you are repaid at maturity, provided the issuer doesn't default.

However, bonds may trade at a discount, which is less than face value, or at a premium, which is more than face value, in the secondary market. That's the bond's market value, and it changes regularly, based on supply and demand.

The death benefit of a life insurance policy which is the amount the beneficiary receives when the insured person dies. It's also known as the policy's face value.

FACT Act (Fair and Accurate Credit Transactions Act)

Designed to help consumers check their credit reports for accuracy and detect identity theft early, the FACT Act gives every consumer the right to request a free report from each of the three major credit bureaus—Equifax, Experian, and TransUnion—once a year.

To obtain your free reports, you must request them through the Annual Credit Report Request Service (www.annualcreditreport.com or 877–322–8228).

If you request your credit report directly from one of the three credit reporting agencies or through another service, you'll pay a fee.

Most experts recommend staggering your requests for the free reports—for instance, ordering one in January, the second in May, and the third in September—so that you can keep an eye on your credit throughout the year.

It's also a good idea to check your report at least two months before you anticipate applying for a major loan or a job, so you can notify the credit bureau if you find any inaccuracies.

You're also entitled to a free report directly from the credit reporting bureaus if you've recently been denied credit, have been turned down for a job, are on public assistance, or have reason to suspect that you're a victim of credit fraud or identity theft.

Fair Housing Act

The Fair Housing Act makes it illegal to discriminate, in any phase of selling or renting real estate, against anyone on the basis of race, color, religion, sex, handicap, family status, or national origin.

However, there are exceptions for religious organizations and private clubs if those organizations are providing rooms for the convenience of their members on a noncommercial basis.

If you feel you are the victim of housing discrimination, you can file a complaint with the US Department of Housing and Urban Development (HUD) or file a suit in federal or state court.

Fair market value

Fair market value is the price you would have to pay to buy a particular asset or service on the open market.

The concept of fair market value assumes that both buyer and seller are reasonably well informed of market conditions. It also assumes that neither is under undue pressure to buy or sell, and that neither intends to defraud the other.

Fallen angel

Corporate or municipal bonds that were investment-grade when they were issued but have been downgraded are called fallen angels. Bonds are downgraded by a rating service, such as Moody's Investors Service or Standard & Poor's (S&P). Downgrading may occur if the issuer's financial situation weakens, or if the rating service anticipates financial problems that could lead to default.

The term fallen angel is sometimes used more generically, to refer to stocks or other securities that are out of favor with investors.

Family of funds

Many large mutual fund companies offer a variety of stock, bond, and money market funds with different investment strategies and objectives. Together, these funds make up a family of funds.

If you own one fund in a family, you can usually transfer assets to another fund in the same family without sales charges. The transaction is known as an exchange.

But unless the funds are in a tax-deferred or tax-free retirement or education savings plan, you'll owe capital gains taxes on increases in value of the fund you're selling.

Investing in a family of funds can make diversification and asset allocation easier, provided there are funds within the family that meet your investment criteria. Investing in a family of funds can also simplify recordkeeping.

However, the advantages of consolidating your assets within one fund family are being challenged by the proliferation of fund networks. Fund networks, sometimes called fund supermarkets, make it easy to spread your investments among several fund families.

Fannie Mae

Fannie Mae has a dual role in the US mortgage market.

FannieMae

Specifically, the corporation buys mortgages that meet its standards from mortgage lenders around the country. It then packages those loans as debt securities, which it offers for sale, providing the investment marketplace with interest-paying bonds.

The money Fannie Mae raises by selling these bonds pays for purchasing more mortgages. Lenders use the money they realize from selling mortgages to Fannie Mae to make additional loans, making it possible for more potential homeowners to borrow at affordable rates.

Because lenders want to ensure their mortgage loans are eligible for purchase, most adopt Fannie Mae guidelines in evaluating mortgage applicants.

Fannie Mae is described as a quasi-government agency because of its special relationship with the federal government. It's also a shareholder-owned corporation whose shares trade on the New York Stock Exchange (NYSE).

Fast market

A fast market is one with heavy trading and rapidly changing prices in some but not necessarily all of the securities listed on an exchange or market.

In this volatile environment, which might be triggered by events such as an initial public offering (IPO) that attracts an unusually high level of attention or an unexpectedly negative earnings report, the rush of business may substantially delay execution times.

The probable result is that you end up paying much more or selling for much less than you anticipated if you gave a market or stop order.

While choosing not to trade in a fast market is one way to reduce your risk, you might also protect yourself while seeking potential profit by giving your broker limit or stop-limit orders. That way, you have the possibility of buying or selling within a price range that's acceptable to you, but are less exposed to the frenzy of the marketplace.

The term fast market is also used to describe a marketplace—typically an electronic one—where trades are executed rapidly.

Federal Deposit Insurance Corporation (FDIC)

The Federal Deposit Insurance Corportion (FDIC) insures deposits in banks and thrift institutions, assuring bank customers that their savings and checking accounts are safe.

Currently, the coverage limits are $100,000 per depositor per bank for individual, joint, and trust accounts, and $250,000 for self-directed retirement accounts. Business accounts are also insured up to $100,000.

FDIC

You qualify for more than $100,000 coverage at a single bank, provided your assets are in these different types of accounts.

For example, you are insured for up to a total of $100,000 in all accounts registered in your own name and for another $100,000 representing your share of jointly held accounts. In addition, your individual retirement account (IRA) is insured up to $250,000 if the money is invested in bank products, such as certificates of deposit (CDs).

However, if you purchase mutual funds, annuities, or other investment products through your bank, those assets are not insured by the FDIC even if they carry the bank name.

The FDIC, which is an independent agency of the federal government, also regulates more than 5,000 state chartered banks that are not members of the Federal Reserve System.

Federal funds

When banks have more cash than they're required to in their reserve accounts, they can deposit the money in a Federal Reserve bank or lend it to another bank overnight.

That money is called federal funds, and the interest rate at which the banks lend to each other is called the federal funds rate.

The term also describes money the Federal Reserve uses to buy government securities when it wants to take money out of circulation. It might do this to tighten the money supply in the hope of forestalling an increase in inflation.

Federal Housing Administration (FHA)

The Federal Housing Administration (FHA) was established by the federal government in 1937 to make home ownership possible for more people and to administer the home loan insurance program. It was consolidated into the Department of Housing and Urban Development (HUD) in 1965.

Among its other responsibilities, the FHA sets credit standards and loan limits, monitors loan quality and availability, and insures lenders against mortgage losses. That insurance, for which borrowers pay a mortgage insurance premium, encourages qualifying lenders to make FHA loans.

Federal Housing Administration mortgage

Federal Housing Administration (FHA) mortgages, which are offered by private lenders, resemble conventional mortgages in many ways, but there are some significant differences.

An FHA mortgage is government insured, so lenders are protected against default. That insurance, for which borrowers pay a mortgage insurance premium, encourages qualifying lenders to make FHA loans.

The buyer's closing costs are limited and the required down payment is lower. There is a price ceiling on the amount a homebuyer can borrow with an FHA mortgage, based on the state and county where the property is located.

Furthermore, people who may not qualify for a conventional mortgage because of previous credit problems may qualify for an FHA loan.

These mortgages are assumable, which means a new buyer can take over the payments without having to secure a new loan.

Federal Insurance Contributions Act (FICA)

The Federal Insurance Contribution Act (FICA) is the federal law that requires employers to withhold 6.2% from their employees' paychecks, up to an annual earnings cap.

Employers must match employee withholding and deposit the combined amount in designated government accounts.

These taxes provide a variety of benefits to qualifying workers and their families through the program known as Social Security. Retirement income is the largest benefit that FICA withholding supports, but the money also funds disability insurance and survivor benefits.

Under this act, an additional 1.45% is withheld, and matched by the employer, to pay for Medicare, which provides health insurance for qualifying disabled workers and people 65 and older. There's no earnings cap for this tax.

If you're self-employed, you pay FICA taxes as both employer and employee, or 15.3%.

Federal Open Market Committee (FOMC)

The Open Market Committee (FOMC) of the Federal Reserve Board meets eight times a year to evaluate the threat of inflation or recession.

Based on its findings, the 12-member FOMC determines whether to change the discount rate or alter the money supply to curb or stimulate economic growth.

For example, the FOMC may raise the discount rate, which the Federal Reserve charges member banks to borrow, with the goal of tightening credit and limiting inflationary growth. It may lower rates to encourage borrowing and economic expansion. Or it may take no action.

Changes in the discount rate result in virtually immediate changes in the short-term rates that banks charge consumers—and each other—to borrow.

The Federal Reserve Bank of New York implements FOMC decisions to alter the money supply. It buys government securities to put more money into circulation and loosen credit or it sells securities to take money out of the market and tighten credit.

Federal Reserve Fedwire

Fedwire is an electronic transfer system owned and operated by the 12 Federal Reserve Banks that enables participants to move money from an account they maintain with the Federal Reserve to the account of another participant in real time during operating hours.

The payments are final and irrevocable, either when the amount is credited to the recipient's account or when the payment order is sent to the participant, whichever occurs first.

Fedwire, which operates on the Federal Reserve's national communications network (FEDNET), connects the Federal Reserve Banks, their branches, the US Department of the Treasury, banks that are members of the Federal Reserve and those that aren't, and branches or agencies of banks based abroad.

The system is used both to handle internal banking business, such as shifting balances to reflect money transferred by check, and to facilitate commercial transactions between bank clients.

Federal Reserve System

The Federal Reserve System, sometimes known as the Fed, is the central bank of the United States.

The Federal Reserve System, which was established in 1913 to stabilize the country's financial system, includes 12 regional Federal Reserve banks, 25 Federal Reserve branch banks, all national banks, and some state banks. Member banks must meet the Fed's financial standards.

Under the direction of a chairman, a seven-member Federal Reserve Board oversees the system and determines national monetary policy. Its goal is to keep the economy healthy and its currency stable.

The Fed's Open Market Committee (FOMC) sets the discount rate and establishes credit policies. The Federal Reserve Bank of New York puts those policies into action by buying and selling government securities.

Fee-for-service

When you're covered by fee-for-service health insurance, you pay your medical bills and file a claim for reimbursement from your insurance company.

Most fee-for-service plans pay a percentage—often 70% to 80%—of the amount they allow for each office visit or medical treatment. You pay the balance of the approved charge plus any amount that exceeds the approved charge.

Your share of the approved charge is called coinsurance.

If you are enrolled in Original Medicare, which is a fee-for-service plan, your healthcare provider will file the insurance claim on your behalf.

FICO score

Created by the Fair Isaac Corporation, FICO is the best-known credit scoring system in the United States.

Based on the information in your credit report, your FICO score is calculated using complex, proprietary formulas that weigh the amount of debt you carry relative to your available credit, the timeliness of your payments, the type of debt you carry, and a great many other factors to assign you a credit score between 300 and 850.

The top 20% of credit profiles receive a score over 780 and the lowest 20% receive scores under 620. Lenders use your credit score to assess your credit risk, or the likelihood that you will default on a loan and offer the best—or lowest—interest rates to credit applicants with the highest scores.

The Equal Credit Opportunity Act (ECOA) prohibits factors such as race, color, gender, religion, national origin, or marital status from being considered in any credit scoring system, including FICO.

Fiduciary

A fiduciary is an individual or organization legally responsible for managing assets on behalf of someone else, usually called the beneficiary. The assets must be managed in the best interests of the beneficiary, not for the personal gain of the fiduciary.

However, the concept of acting responsibly can be broadly interpreted, and may mean preserving principal to some fiduciaries and producing reasonable growth to others.

Executors, trustees, guardians, and agents with powers of attorney are examples of individuals with fiduciary responsibility. Firms known as registered investment advisers (RIAs) are also fiduciaries.

Fill or kill (FOK)

If an investor places an FOK order, it means the broker must cancel the order if it can't be filled immediately.

This type of order is typically used as part of a trading strategy requiring a series of transactions to occur simultaneously.

Finance charge

The finance charge, or total dollar amount you pay to borrow, includes the interest you pay plus any fees for arranging the loan.

A finance charge is expressed as an annual percentage rate (APR) of the amount you owe, which allows you to compare the costs of different loans.

The Truth-in-Lending Law requires your lender to disclose the APR you'll be paying and the way it is calculated before you agree to the terms of the loan.

Financial Accounting Standards Board (FASB)

The Financial Accounting Standards Board (FASB) is an independent, self-regulatory board that establishes and interprets generally accepted accounting principles (GAAP).

It operates under the principle that the economy and the financial services industry work smoothly when credible, concise, and clear financial information is available.

FASB

FASB periodically revises its rules to make sure corporations are following its principles. The corporations are supposed to fully account for different kinds of income, avoid shifting income from one period to another, and properly categorize their income.

Financial future

When a futures contract is linked to a financial product, such as a stock index, Treasury notes, or a currency, the contract is described as a financial future.

In most cases, the hedgers who use financial futures contracts are banks and other financial institutions that want to protect their portfolios against sudden changes in value.

The changing prices of a financial futures contract reflect the perception that investors have of what may happen to the market value of the underlying instrument.

For example, the price of a contract on Treasury notes changes in anticipation of a change in interest rates. Expected increases in the rate produce falling contract prices, while anticipated drops in the rate produce rising contract prices.

Financial institution

Any institution that collects money and puts it into assets such as stocks, bonds, bank deposits, or loans is considered a financial institution. There are two types of financial institutions: depository institutions and nondepository institutions.

Depository institutions, such as banks and credit unions, pay you interest on your deposits and use the deposits to make loans. Nondepository institutions, such as insurance companies, brokerage firms, and mutual fund companies, sell financial products.

Many financial institutions provide both depository and nondepository services.

Financial instrument

A financial instrument is a physical or electronic document that has intrinsic monetary value or transfers value. For example, cash is a financial instrument, as is a check.

Listed and unlisted securities, loans, insurance policies, interests in a partnership, and precious metals are also financial instruments. A contractual obligation is also a financial instrument as is a deed that records home ownership.

Financial plan

A financial plan is a document that describes your current financial status, your financial goals and when you want to achieve them, and strategies to meet those goals.

You can use your plan as a benchmark to measure the progress you're making and update your plan as your goals and time frame change.

Financial planners and other investment professionals can help you create a plan, identify appropriate investments and insurance, and monitor your portfolio. You may pay a one-time fee to have a plan created, or it may be included as part of a fee-based account with a stockbroker or investment adviser.

Financial planner

A financial planner evaluates your personal finances and helps you develop a financial plan to meet both your immediate needs and your long-term goals. Some, but not all, planners have credentials from professional organizations.

Some well-known credentials are Certified Financial Planner (CFP), Chartered Financial Consultant (ChFC),

Certified Investment Management Analyst (CIMA), and Personal Financial Specialist (PFS).

A PFS is a Certified Public Accountant (CPA) who has passed an exam on financial planning. Some planners are also licensed to sell certain investment or insurance products.

Fee-only financial planners charge by the hour or collect a flat fee for a specific service, but don't sell products or earn sales commissions. Other planners don't charge a fee but earn commissions on the products they sell to you. Still others both charge fees and earn commissions but may offset their fees by the amount of commission they earn.

Financial pyramid

Many investors structure their portfolios in the form of a financial pyramid. The base of the pyramid is made up of

nonvolatile, liquid assets.

The next level includes securities that provide both income and long-term capital growth. At the third level, a smaller portion of the portfolio is allocated to more volatile investments with higher potential returns and greater risk.

And at the top level, the smallest percentage of the overall portfolio is invested in ventures that have the highest potential return but also pose the greatest investment risk.

This strategic approach gives you the potential to realize significant returns if some of your speculative investments succeed without risking more than you can afford to lose.

Firm quote

A firm quote includes a bid and ask price at which a market maker is willing to trade a specific quantity—100 shares of stock, for example.

For example, a firm quote of 42.50/42.70 means that the market maker will pay $42.50 for 100 shares and is willing to sell them for $42.70. But those prices would not apply to trades larger than 100 shares. Then prices would have to be negotiated.

First dollar coverage

First dollar coverage means that your health insurance plan typically begins to pay its share of your covered services from the first service you receive in the plan network. In a fee-for-service plan, payments for covered services begin as soon as you have met the deductible.

Fixed annuity

A fixed annuity is a contract that allows you to accumulate earnings at a fixed rate during a build-up period.

You pay the required premium, either in a lump sum or in installments. The insurance company invests its assets, including your premium, so it will be able to pay the rate of return that it has promised to pay.

At a time you select, usually after you turn 59½, you can choose to convert your account value to retirement income.

Among the alternatives is receiving a fixed amount of income in regular payments for your lifetime or the lifetimes of yourself and a joint annuitant. That's called annuitization. Or, you may select some other payout method.

The contract issuer assumes the risk that you could outlive your life expectancy and therefore collect income over a longer period than it anticipated. You take the risk that the insurance company will be able to meet its obligations to pay.

Fixed-income investment

Fixed-income investments typically pay interest or dividends on a regular schedule and may promise to return your principal at maturity, though that promise is not guaranteed in most cases.

Among the examples are government, corporate, and municipal bonds, preferred stock, and guaranteed investment contracts (GICs).

The advantage of holding fixed-income securities in an investment portfolio is that they provide regular, predictable income.

But a potential disadvantage of holding them over an extended period, or to maturity in the case of bonds, is that they may not increase in value the way equity investments may. As a result, a portfolio overweighted with fixed-income investments may make you more vulnerable to inflation risk.

Fixed-rate mortgage

A fixed-rate mortgage is a long-term loan that you use to finance a real estate purchase, typically a home.

Your borrowing costs and monthly payments remain the same for the term of the loan, no matter what happens to market interest rates.

This predetermined expense is one of a fixed-rate loan's most attractive features, since you always know exactly what your mortgage will cost you.

If interest rates rise, a fixed-rate mortgage works in your favor. But if market rates drop, you have to refinance to get a lower rate and reduce your mortgage costs.

Typical terms for a fixed-rate mortgage are 15, 20, or 30 years, though you may be able to arrange a different length. With a hybrid mortgage, which begins as a fixed-rate loan and converts to an adjustable rate, the fixed-term portion is often seven or ten years.

Flat tax

A flat tax, also known as a regressive tax, applies to everyone at the same rate, as a sales tax does.

Advocates of a flat income tax for the United States say it's simpler and does away with the kinds of tax breaks that tend to favor the wealthy. Opponents say that middle-income taxpayers would carry too large a proportion of the total tax bill.

Flexible spending account (FSA)

Some employers offer flexible spending accounts (FSAs), sometimes called cafeteria plans, as part of their employee benefits package.

You contribute a percentage of your pretax salary, up to the limit your plan allows, which you can use to pay for qualifying expenses.

Qualifying expenses include medical costs that aren't covered by your health insurance, childcare, care for your elderly or disabled dependents, and life insurance.

The amount you put into the plan is not reported to the IRS as income, which means your taxable income is reduced.

However, you have to estimate correctly the amount you'll spend during the year when you arrange to have amounts deducted from your paycheck. Once you decide on the amount you are going to contribute to an FSA for a year, you cannot change it unless you have a qualifying event, such as marriage or divorce.

If you don't spend all that you had withheld within the year—or in some plans within the year plus a two-and-one-half month extension—you forfeit any amount that's left in your account.

In some plans you pay for the qualifying expenses and are reimbursed when you file a claim. In other plans, you use a debit card linked to your account to pay expenses directly from the account.

Float

In investment terms, a float is the number of outstanding shares a corporation has available for trading.

If there is a small float, stock prices tend to be volatile, since one large trade could significantly affect the availability and therefore the price of these stocks. If there is a large float, stock prices tend to be more stable.

In banking, the float refers to the time lag between your depositing a check in the bank and the day the funds become available for use. For example, if you deposit a check on Monday, and you can withdraw the cash on Friday, the float is four days and works to the bank's advantage.

Float is also the period that elapses from the time you write a check until it clears your account, which can work to your advantage. However, as checks are increasingly cleared electronically at the point of deposit, this float is disappearing.

In a credit account, float is the amount of time between the date you charge a purchase and the date the payment is due. If you have paid your previous bill in full and on time, you don't owe a finance charge on the amount of the purchase during the float.

Floating an issue

When a corporation or public agency offers new stocks or bonds to the public, making the offering is called floating an issue.

In the case of stocks, the securities may be an initial public offering (IPO) or additional issues of a company that has already gone public. In that case, they're called secondary offerings.

Floating rate

A debt security or corporate preferred stock whose interest rate is adjusted periodically to reflect changing money market rates is known as a floating rate instrument.

These securities, for example five-year notes, are initially offered with an interest rate that is slightly below the rate being paid on comparable fixed-rate securities.

But because the rate is adjusted from time to time, its market price generally remains very close to the offering price, or par.

When a nation's currency moves up and down in value against the currency of another nation, the relationship between the two is described as a floating exchange rate.

For example, the US dollar is worth more Japanese yen in some periods and less in others. That movement is usually the result of what's happening in the economy of each of the nations and in the economies of their trading partners.

A fixed exchange rate, on the other hand, means that two (or more) currencies, such as the US dollar and the Bermuda dollar, always have the same relative value.

Floating shares

Floating shares are shares of a public corporation that are available for trading in a stock market.

The number of floating shares may be smaller than the company's outstanding shares if founding partners, other groups with a controlling interest, or the company's pension fund, employee stock ownership plan (ESOP), or similar programs hold shares in their portfolios that they aren't interested in selling.

Some equity index providers, including Standard & Poor's, use floating shares rather than outstanding shares in calculating their market-capitalization weighted indexes on the grounds that a float-adjusted index is a more accurate reflection of market value.

Floor broker

Floor brokers at a securities or commodities exchange handle client orders to buy or sell through a process known as a double action auction, in which brokers bid against each other to secure the best price.

The orders these brokers execute are sent to the floor of the exchange from the trading department or order room of the brokerage firms they work for. When a transaction is completed, the floor broker relays that information back to the firm, and the client is notified.

Floor trader

Unlike floor brokers, who fill client orders, floor traders buy and sell stocks or commodities for their own accounts on the floor of an exchange.

Floor traders don't pay commissions, which means they can make a profit on even small price differences. But they must still abide by trading rules established by the exchange. One of those rules is that client orders take precedence over floor traders' orders.

Foreclosure

Foreclosure occurs when your lender repossesses your home because you have defaulted on your mortgage loan or home equity line of credit.

You default by failing to pay interest and repay the principal you owe on time. Foreclosed property is often sold at auction to allow the lender to recover some of or all the outstanding debt.

Foreign exchange (FOREX)

Any type of financial instrument that is used to make payments between countries is considered foreign exchange. The list of instruments includes electronic transactions, paper currency, checks, and signed, written orders called bills of exchange.

Large-scale currency trading, with minimums of $1 million, is also considered foreign exchange and can be handled as spot price transactions, forward contract transactions, or swap contracts.

Spot transactions close at the market price within two days, and the others are set to close at an agreed-upon price and an agreed-upon date in the future.

Form ADV

All investment advisory firms must register by filing a Form ADV either with the Securities and Exchange Commission if they manage $25 million or more in client assets or with the state securities regulator in the state where they principally work.

The form is divided into two sections. Part 1 provides information about past disciplinary actions, if any, against the adviser. Part 2 summarizes the adviser's background, investment strategies, services, and fees.

If an advisory firm is registered with the SEC, you can obtain copies of Form ADV at the SEC's Investment Adviser Public Disclosure (IAPD) website (www.adviserinfo.sec.gov).

Otherwise, you can request it directly from the adviser or your state securities regulator. You can find contact information on the website of the North American Securities Administrators Association (www.nasaa.org).

Formula investing

When you invest on a set schedule, you're using a technique known as formula investing. You're formula investing when you dollar cost average, or make investments to maintain a predetermined asset allocation.

One appeal of this approach, for investors who follow it, is that it eliminates having to agonize over when to buy or sell. It also encourages regular investing. But it does not guarantee your portfolio will grow in value or that you won't lose money.

Forward contract

A forward contract is similar to a futures contract in the sense that both types of contracts cover the delivery and payment for a specific commodity at a specific future date at a specific price.

The difference is that a futures contract has fixed terms, such as delivery date and quantity, and it's traded on a regulated futures exchange.

A forward contract is traded over the counter and all details of the contract are negotiated between the counterparties, or partners to the agreement.

The price specified in the forward contract for foreign currency, government securities, or other commodities may be higher or lower than the actual market price at the time of delivery, known as the spot price.

But the participants have locked in a price early specifically so they know what they will receive or pay for the product, eliminating market risk.

Forward price-to-earnings ratio

Stock analysts calculate a forward price-to-earnings ratio, or forward P/E, by dividing a stock's current price by estimated future earnings per share.

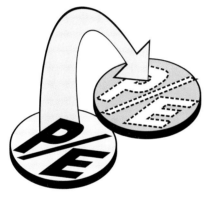

Some forward P/Es are calculated based on estimated earnings for the next four quarters. Others use actual earnings from the past two quarters with estimated earnings for the next two.

A forward P/E may help you evaluate the current price of a stock in relation to what you can reasonably expect to happen in the near future. In contrast, a trailing P/E is based exclusively on past performance.

For example, a stock whose price seems high in relation to the last year's earnings may seem more reasonably priced if earnings estimates are higher for the next year. On the other hand, the expectation of lower future earnings may make the current price higher than you are willing to pay.

Fourth market

Institutional investors, including mutual fund companies and pension funds, who trade large blocks of securities among themselves are operating in what's called the fourth market.

Usually, the transactions are handled through electronic communications networks (ECNs).

Among the appeals of using an ECN are reduced trading costs, the ability to trade after hours, and the fact that offers to buy and sell are matched anonymously.

Fractional share

If you reinvest your dividends or invest a fixed dollar amount in a stock dividend reinvestment plan (DRIP) or mutual fund, the amount may not be enough to buy a full share.

Alternately, there may be money left over after buying one or more full shares. The excess amount buys a fractional share, a unit that is less than one whole share.

In a DRIP, a fractional share gives you credit toward the purchase of a full share. With a mutual fund, in contrast, the fractional share is included in your account value.

Freddie Mac

Freddie Mac is a shareholder-owned corporation that was chartered in 1970 to increase the supply of mortgage money that lenders are able to make available to homebuyers.

To do its job, Freddie Mac buys mortgages from banks and other lenders, packages them as securities, and sells the securities to investors. The money it raises by selling these bonds pays for purchasing the mortgages.

Lenders use the money they realize from selling mortgages to Freddie Mac to make additional loans. Lenders must be approved in order to participate in the program. Loans must meet Freddie Mac qualifications to be eligible for purchase.

FreddieMac

To facilitate the lending process, Freddie Mac provides lenders with an automated underwriting tool to help them evaluate mortgage applications.

Freddie Mac guarantees the securities it issues, but the bonds aren't federal debts and aren't federally guaranteed.

Like its sister corporation Fannie Mae, Freddie Mac shares are traded on the New York Stock Exchange (NYSE).

Free cash flow

A business's free cash flow statement may differ significantly from its cash flow statement. The cash flow statement generally represents earnings before interest, taxes, depreciation, and amortization (EBITDA).

Cash flow and EBITDA focus specifically on the profitability of the company's actual business operations, independent of outside factors such as debt and taxes. Free cash flow, however, reports the net movement of cash in and out of the company.

To determine free cash flow, equity analysts add up all a company's incoming cash and then subtract cash that a company pays out, including taxes and interest. The result tells you how much cash was left over or how short of cash the company was at the end of the fiscal period.

Front-end load

The load, or sales charge, that you pay when you purchase shares of a mutual fund or annuity is called a front-end load. Some mutual funds identify shares purchased with a front-end load as Class A shares.

The drawback of a front-end load is that a portion of your investment pays the sales charge rather than being invested. However, the annual asset-based fees on Class A shares tend to be lower than on shares with back-end or level loads.

In addition, if you pay a front-end load, you may qualify for breakpoints, or reduced sales charges, if the assets in your account reach a certain milestone, such as $25,000.

Front running

If you trade stock or other investments because you know that an upcoming transaction by a third party is likely to affect the market price of the investment, you're front running.

Because front running, sometimes known as forward trading, relies on information that isn't available to the general public, it's considered unethical in certain circumstances.

One example is a broker-dealer who trades at a better price for a personal account than for a client's account.

Full faith and credit

Federal and municipal governments can promise repayment of debt securities they issue because they can raise money through taxes, borrowing, and other sources of revenue. That power is described as full faith and credit.

Full-service brokerage firm

Full-service brokerage firms usually offer their clients a range of services in addition to executing their buy and sell orders.

These firms usually have full-time research departments and investment analysts who provide information the firm's brokers share with clients.

In addition, some employees of the firm may be qualified to provide investment advice, develop financial plans, or design strategies for meeting financial goals.

Full-service firms tend to charge higher commissions and fees than discount brokerage firms or firms that operate only online. However, some full-service firms offer online services and reduce their fees for transactions handled though a client's online account.

Fund family

A fund family, or family of funds, is a group of mutual funds controlled by a single investment company, bank, or other financial institution.

The various funds within the family have different investment objectives, such as growth or income. If you invest in several funds in a family, you can transfer assets from one fund to another by phone or online.

If it's a family of load funds, there may or may not be a sales charge for the transfer. If it's a no-load fund, no sales charges apply.

You will owe capital gains taxes on any profit you realize from selling fund shares that have increased in value even if the money is reinvested in another fund. The only way you'll avoid taxes is if you own the funds in a tax-deferred or tax-free account.

However, if the shares have lost value when you sell, you'll have a capital loss.

Fund network

Fund networks, sometimes called fund supermarkets, offer access to thousands of different mutual funds from many of the major fund families.

Investing through a fund network can make it easier to diversify your portfolio, or put your assets into a variety of investments, since you have access to all the funds through one account.

And you can usually—although not always—transfer assets from one fund family in the network to another without an exchange fee although sales charges may apply with some funds.

In addition, capital gains taxes may be due if you're investing through a taxable account and the shares of the fund you're leaving have increased in value.

Fund of funds (FOF)

A fund of funds is a pooled investment, such as a mutual fund or a hedge fund, whose underlying investments are other funds rather than individual securities.

Despite some major differences, what all funds of funds have in common is an emphasis on diversification for its potential to reduce risk without significantly reducing return.

They're also designed to simplify the investment process by offering one-stop shopping.

Many mutual fund FOFs are asset allocation funds and typically include both stock and bond funds in a particular combination that the FOF manager has chosen to meet a specific objective. A mutual fund FOF may select all its funds from a single fund family or it may choose funds offered by different investment companies.

A hedge fund FOF, which owns stakes in other hedge funds, allows investors to commit substantially less money to gain exposure to this investment category than it would cost to invest in even one fund.

A major drawback with all funds of funds is that the fees tend to be higher than you would pay owning the underlying funds directly.

Fundamental analysis

Fundamental analysis is one of two main methods for analyzing a stock's potential return.

Fundamental analysis involves assessing a corporation's financial history and current standing, including earnings, sales, and management. It also involves gauging the strength of the corporation's products or services in the marketplace.

A fundamental analyst uses these details as well as the current state of the economy to assess whether the stock is likely to increase or decrease in value in the short- and long-term and whether the stock's current price is an accurate reflection of its value.

Fungible

When two or more things are interchangeable, can be substituted for each other, or are of equal value, they are described as fungible.

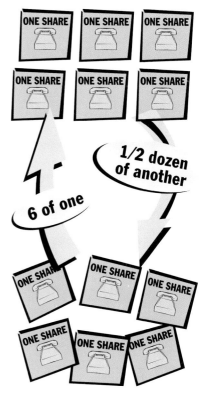

For example, shares of common stock issued by the same company are fungible at any point in time since they have the same value no matter who owns them.

Forms of money, such as dollar bills or euros, are fungible since each can be exchanged or substituted for another of the same currency.

Similarly, put and call futures contracts on the same commodity that expire on the same date are fungible since a contract to buy—a call—can offset, or neutralize, a futures contract to sell—a put.

On the other hand, multiple classes of the same stock may not be fungible. For example, in some markets citizens of the country are eligible to buy one class of stock and noncitizens a different class. Typically, the shares have different prices and may not be exchanged for each other.

Futures Commission Merchant (FCM)

A futures commission merchant (FCM) is a person or a firm that acts as an agent to execute buy or sell orders for futures contracts or commodity options.

You may open an account directly with an FCM or place your orders through an introducing broker or commodity trading adviser.

Futures contract

Futures contracts, when they trade on regulated futures exchanges, obligate you to buy or sell a specified quantity of the underlying product for a specific price on a specific date.

The underlying product could be a commodity, stock index, security, or currency.

Because all the terms of a listed futures contract are structured by the exchange, you can offset your contract and get out of your obligation by buying or selling an opposing contract before the settlement date.

Futures contracts provide some investors, called hedgers, a measure of protection from price volatility on the open market.

For example, wine manufacturers are protected when a bad crop pushes grape prices up on the spot market if they hold a futures contract to buy the grapes at a lower price. Grape growers are also protected if prices drop dramatically—if,

for example, there's a surplus caused by a bumper crop—provided they have a contract to sell at a higher price.

Unlike hedgers, speculators use futures contracts to seek profits on price changes. For example, speculators can make (or lose) money, no matter what happens to the grapes, depending on what they paid for the futures contract and what they must pay to offset it.

Futures exchange

Traditionally, futures contracts and options on those contracts have been bought and sold on a futures exchange, or trading floor, in a defined physical space.

In the United States, for example, there are futures exchanges in Chicago, Kansas City, Minneapolis, and New York.

As electronic trading of these products expands, however, buying and selling doesn't always occur on the floor of an exchange. So the term is also used to describe the activity of trading futures contacts.

Gainer

Stocks that increase in value over the course of the trading day are described as gainers or advancers.

Those that increase the most in relation to their opening price are called percentage gainers, or percentage winners. Those that go up the greatest number of points are called net gainers, or dollar winners.

On a day that the stock market indexes go up, there are typically more gainers than there are losers or laggards—stocks that have lost value. And on a day where there's little change, there are likely to be similar numbers of gainers and losers.

General account

A general account is a deposit account. In the insurance industry, a general account is the account into which all incoming funds, except those designated for a separate account, are deposited.

Deposits to a general account include premiums for life insurance and fixed annuities, plus assets in the fixed port-folios of variable annuities.

Assets in a general account can be used to cover company expenses and are vulnerable to creditors' claims. In fact, this account can be sued to pay the firm's obligations. That's one reason that contract holders are cautioned that payouts are subject to the insurer's ability to pay its claims.

The Federal Reserve considers brokerage firms' margin accounts that are governed by Regulation T as general accounts. The Fed requires that all margin transactions made on behalf of clients be conducted through the clients' individual general accounts.

General Agreement on Tariffs and Trade (GATT)

A General Agreement on Tariffs and Trade was signed in 1947 to provide an international forum to encourage free trade, reduce tariffs, and provide a mechanism for resolving trade disputes.

GATT

The Uruguay Round Agreements Act was ratified by Congress in 1994 to foster trade by cutting international tariffs, standardizing copyright and patent protection, and liberalizing trade legislation.

General obligation (GO) bond

State and local governments issue general obligation (GO) municipal bonds and pay the interest and repay the principal from general revenues.

GO bonds are considered somewhat less risky, and so pay slightly lower rates, than the same municipality's revenue bonds, which are backed by income from a specific project or agency.

A municipality's general revenues come from the taxes it is able to raise and money it can borrow. Those powers are sometimes described as its full faith and credit.

Gift tax

A gift tax is a tax on the combined total value of the taxable gifts you make that exceed your lifetime federal tax-exempt limit of $1 million. The tax is figured as a percentage of the value of your gifts over that amount.

For example, if during your lifetime you make taxable gifts of money and property valued at $1.2 million, you will owe federal gift tax on $200,000. You might also owe state gift tax, depending on where you live.

However, you can make annual tax-free gifts to as many individuals and nonprofit institutions as you like. As long as the value of the gifts to each individual is less than the annual limit set by Congress, that amount doesn't count against your lifetime tax-free limits.

Gifts to nonprofits are not taxed and don't count against your lifetime limit either.

If you're married, you can give your spouse gifts of any value at anytime, totally tax free, provided he or she is a US citizen. There are limits on spousal gifts when the spouse is not a citizen.

You are not required to report the tax-free gifts on your tax return, but you must report taxable gifts whose value exceeds the annual tax-free limit on IRS Form 709 for the year you make them. The tax becomes due when the cumulative total exceeds $1 million.

However, the law setting the $1 million limit is set to expire at the end of 2010. Unless Congress acts before that date, the lifetime tax-exempt limit will fall back to $675,000.

Gilt-edged security

When the term gilt-edged is applied to bonds, it's the equivalent of describing a stock as a blue chip.

Both terms mean that the issuing corporation has a long, strong record for meeting its financial obligations to its investors. That includes making interest and dividend payments on time and redeeming bonds on schedule.

Global depositary receipt (GDR)

To raise money in more than one market, some corporations use global depositary receipts (GDRs) to sell their stock on markets in countries other than the one where they have their headquarters.

The GDRs are issued in the currency of the country where the stock is trading. For example, a Mexican company might offer GDRs priced in pounds in London and in yen in Tokyo.

Individual investors in the countries where the GDRs are issued buy them to diversify into international markets. GDRs let you do this without having to deal with currency conversion and other complications of overseas investing.

However, since GDRs are frequently offered by newer or less-known companies, the prices are often volatile and the stocks may be thinly traded. That makes buying GDRs riskier than buying domestic stocks.

Global fund

Global, or world, mutual funds invest in US securities as well as those of other countries. In that way, they differ from international funds, which invest only in non-US markets.

Although global funds may keep as much as 75% of their assets invested in the United States, fund managers are able to take advantage of opportunities they see in various overseas markets.

Go long

When you go long, you buy a security or other financial product that you intend to hold for a period of time or one that you expect to increase in value so that you can sell it at a profit.

For example, if you're buying and selling options or futures contracts, you go long when you enter a contract to buy the underlying instrument. In the case of stock, you go long when you buy shares to hold in your portfolio, at least for the next term.

Go public

A corporation goes public when it issues shares of its stock in the open market for the first time, in what is known as an initial public offering (IPO).

That means that at least some of the shares will be held by members of the public rather than exclusively by the investors who founded and funded the corporation initially or the current owners or management.

Go short

When you enter a futures contract that commits you to sell or deliver the underlying product, you go short or have a short position.

You're also going short when you write an options contract, giving the buyer the right to exercise the contract. With stocks, you go short when you borrow shares of stock through your broker and sell them at their current market price.

Gold standard

The gold standard is a monetary system that measures the relative value of a currency against a specific amount of gold.

It was developed in England in the early 18th century when the scientist Sir Isaac Newton was Master of the English Mint. By the late 19th century, the gold standard was used throughout the world.

The United States was on the gold standard until 1971, when it stopped redeeming its paper currency for gold.

Good 'til canceled (GTC)

If you want to buy or sell a security at a specific price, you can ask your broker to issue a good 'til canceled (GTC) order. When the security reaches the price you've indicated, the trade will be executed.

This order stays in effect until it is filled, you cancel it, or the brokerage firm's time limit on GTC orders expires.

A GTC, also called an open order, is the opposite of a day order, which is automatically canceled at the end of the trading day if it isn't filled.

In addition, some firms offer good through month (GTM) or good through week (GTW) orders.

Good faith deposit

A good faith deposit is a sum of money provided by a buyer to a seller, which demonstrates the buyer's intention to purchase.

For instance, if you've decided on a home you want to buy, you generally make a good faith deposit to support your bid.

A good faith deposit, also called a binder or earnest money, is usually a fixed amount that's standard in the community where you're buying. It's different from a down payment. That's a larger cash payment, figured as a percentage of the purchase price, which you make when you sign the contract to purchase the property.

If you and the seller can't agree on the terms of the sale, you generally get your good faith deposit back.

Good faith estimate

A good faith estimate is a written summary provided by your mortgage lender. It shows the amount you can expect to pay at your real estate closing to cover all the fees and expenses that are part of arranging your mortgage loan.

It includes, among other things, the title search and title insurance, lawyers' fees, transfer taxes, and filing fees. The total amount of a good faith estimate is in addition to the down payment you will make.

Good will

When the term good will is used in connection with evaluating a company, it covers the intangible value of its reputation, its satisfied clients, and its productive work force. Those factors are all considered evidence of the corporation's potential to produce strong earnings.

Government bond

The term government bond is used to describe the debt securities issued by the federal government, such as US Treasury bills, notes, and bonds. They're also known as government obligations.

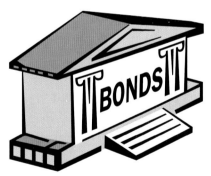

You can buy and sell these issues directly using a Treasury Direct account or through a broker.

Treasurys are backed by the full faith and credit of the US government, and the interest they pay is exempt from state and local, though not federal, income taxes. The cash raised by the sale of Treasurys is used to finance a variety of government activities.

Debt instruments issued by government agencies are also described as government bonds, or government securities, though they are not backed by the government's ability to collect taxes to pay them off.

For example, bonds issued by the Government National Mortgage Association (Ginnie Mae) and the Tennessee Valley Authority (TVA) are government bonds.

Government National Mortgage Association (Ginnie Mae)

The Government National Mortgage Association, known as Ginnie Mae, guarantees mortgage-backed securities issued by approved private institutions and marketed to investors through brokerage firms.

The agency's dual mission is to provide affordable mortgage funding while creating high-quality investment securities that offer safety, liquidity, and an attractive yield.

Ginnie Mae securities are backed by mortgages that are insured by either the Federal Housing Administration (FHA) or the Rural Housing Service (RHS), or guaranteed by the Department of Veterans Affairs (VA).

Ginnie Mae securities are sold in large denominations—usually $25,000. But you can buy Ginnie Mae mutual funds, which allow you to invest more modest amounts.

Ginnie Mae is an agency of the US Department of Housing and Urban Development (HUD).

Grace period

A grace period is the number of days between the date a credit card issuer calculates your new balance and the date your payment is due.

In most cases, if you have paid the previous balance in full and on time, and you haven't taken any cash withdrawals, no finance charges are added to the amount of your purchases.

If you generally pay the entire balance due on time, you may want to choose a card with a longer rather than a shorter grace period, assuming the other terms are comparable. That gives you more time to be sure your payments arrive on time.

However, a minority of credit arrangements include a minimum finance charge, even if you do pay on time. Other lenders

go back two billing cycles and will add finance charges if you have not paid the full amount due each time.

The grace period on a student loan allows you to defer repayment so that the first installment isn't due until six or nine months after you graduate or are no longer enrolled at least half time. The timing depends on the type of loan.

You also have a grace period in which to pay the premium on an insurance policy before the policy is cancelled. It's usually one month after the due date.

Green fund

A mutual fund that selects investments based on a commitment to environmental principles may be described as a green fund.

Not all green funds stress exactly the same values. A fund that seeks environmentally friendly businesses—say those that use alternative fuels—may not be concerned about what those companies manufacture.

Another fund may avoid any company in what it considers an unacceptable industry, despite the company's individual environmental record. In every case, the fund's approach is described in its prospectus.

Green shoe clause

A green shoe clause allows the group of investment banks that underwrite an initial public offering (IPO) to buy and offer for sale 15% more shares at the same offering price than the issuing company originally planned to sell.

The clause is activated if demand for shares is more enthusiastic than anticipated and the stock is trading in the secondary market above the offering price.

But if demand is weak, and the stock price falls below the offering price, the syndicate doesn't exercise its option for more shares.

This contract provision, which may be acted on for up to 30 days after the IPO, gets its name from the Green Shoe Company, which was the first to agree to sell extra shares when it went public in 1960.

Gross domestic product (GDP)

The total value of all the goods and services produced within a country's borders is described as its gross domestic product.

When that figure is adjusted for inflation, it is called the real gross domestic product, and it's generally used to measure the growth of the country's economy.

In the United States, the GDP is calculated and released quarterly by the Department of Commerce.

Gross margin

Gross margin is the percentage by which profits exceed production costs. To find gross margin you divide sales minus production costs by sales.

For example, if you want to calculate your gross margin on selling handmade scarves, you need to know how much you spent creating the scarves, and what you collected by selling them.

If you sold 10 scarves at $15 a piece, and spent $8 per scarf to make them, your gross margin would be 46.7%, or $150 in sales minus $80 in production costs divided by $150. Gross margin is not the same as gross profit, which is simply sales minus costs. In this example, it's $70, or $150 minus $80.

If you're doing research on a company you're considering as an investment, you can look at the gross margin to help you see how efficiently it uses its resources.

If the company has a higher gross margin than its competition, it can command higher prices or spend less on production. That might mean it can allocate more resources to developing new products or pursuing other projects.

Gross national product (GNP)

The gross national product is a measure of a country's economic output—the total value of all the goods and services that it produces in a particular year. The GNP is similar to the gross domestic product (GDP), but not exactly the same.

Unlike the GDP, the GNP includes the income generated by investments owned outside the country by its citizens, and excludes any income earned on domestic soil by noncitizens or organizations based elsewhere.

Gross spread

In an initial public offering (IPO), the gross spread is the difference between what the underwriters pay the issuing company per share and the per share price that investors pay. It's usually about 7%.

For example, if a stock is to be offered to the public at $10 a share, the underwriters may pay the issuing company around $9.30 per share. With millions of shares being sold, the 70 cents per share adds up to millions of dollars for the investment bank.

Growth

Growth is an increase in the value of an investment over time. Unlike investments that produce income, those that are designed for growth don't necessarily provide you with a regular source of cash.

A growth company is more likely to reinvest its profits to build its business. If the company prospers, however, its stock typically increases in value.

Stocks, stock mutual funds, and real estate may all be classified as growth investments, but some stocks and mutual funds emphasize growth more than others.

Growth and income fund

Growth and income mutual funds invest in securities that provide, as their name suggests, a combination of growth and income.

This type of fund generally funnels assets into common stocks of well-established companies that pay regular dividends and increase in value at a regular, if modest, rate. The balance of the fund's portfolio is in high-rated bonds and preferred stock.

Growth rate

A growth rate measures the percentage increase in the value of a variety of markets, companies, or operations.

For example, a stock research firm typically tracks the rate at which a company's sales and earnings have grown as one of the factors in evaluating whether to recommend that investors purchase, hold, or sell its shares.

Similarly, the rate at which the gross domestic product grows is a measure of the strength of the US economy.

If you want to compare the vigor of entities or elements of different sizes, it's more accurate to look at growth rate than it is to look at the actual numerical change in value. For example, an emerging market might be growing at a much faster rate than a developed one even though the size of those economies is vastly different.

Guaranteed investment contract (GIC)

A guaranteed investment contract, or GIC (pronounced gick), promises to preserve your principal and to provide a fixed rate of return when you begin to withdraw from the contract, typically after you retire.

You can invest in a GIC through a salary reduction plan, such as a 401(k) or 403(b) sponsored by your employer, provided that investment option is offered.

Because of their fixed rates, GICs are vulnerable to inflation. And you may have to pay a penalty if you decide to change from a GIC to a different investment.

Insurance companies that offer GICs assume the risk that the rate they earn on their investments will outperform the rates they've guaranteed on the GICs.

Guaranteed renewable policy

Your insurance company can't cancel a guaranteed renewable life insurance policy as long as you pay the premium on time.

With this type of policy, your payments can be increased only if they're raised for everyone with the same policy. Today, all newly issued policies are guaranteed renewable.

Guarantor

If lenders are concerned about your income, your credit history, or other risk factors when you apply for a loan, they may require a guarantor, or cosigner.

The guarantor signs the loan with you and agrees to pay your debt if you default. For example, lenders may fear that your income may not be high enough to meet your payments if you encounter any unexpected financial setbacks.

Laws governing who may serve as a guarantor vary from state to state. Some states require that your guarantor be a resident of the state where you're obtaining the loan, while others will accept guarantors from out of state as well.

Guardian

A guardian is someone you designate to be legally responsible for your minor children or other dependents who are unable to take care of themselves if you are unavailable to provide for their care.

You may name the guardian in your will or while you are still alive. In most cases, a guardian makes both personal and financial decisions for his or her ward.

However, you may name two guardians with different areas of responsibility— perhaps one for financial matters if you have a substantial estate. If you become disabled or otherwise unable to manage your own affairs, the appropriate court in your state may name a guardian to manage your affairs.

Haircut

A haircut, in the financial industry, is a percentage discount that's applied informally to the market value of a stock or the face value of a bond in an attempt to account for the risk of loss that the investment poses.

So, for example, a stock with a market value of $30 may get a haircut of 20%, to $24, when an analyst or money manager tries to anticipate what is likely to happen to the price.

Similarly, when a broker-dealer calculates its net capital to meet the 15:1 ratio of debt to liquid capital permissible under Securities and Exchange Commission (SEC) rules, it typically gives volatile securities in its portfolio a haircut to reduce the potential for being in violation.

The only securities that consistently escape a haircut are US government bonds because they are considered free of default risk.

Hard assets

Hard assets are the tangible property of a company or partnership, such as the buildings, furniture, real estate, and other equipment it owns.

When you make a direct investment in hard assets, as you do when you invest in a direct participation program (DPP), you have an ownership interest in the actual assets rather than in shares of the corporation.

The profit, if any, that you realize from hard assets is dependent on their ability to produce revenue, as a rental property or a leased airplane might.

Hardship withdrawal

A hardship withdrawal, also known as a hardship distribution, occurs when you take money out of your 401(k) or other qualified retirement savings plan to cover pressing financial needs.

You must qualify to withdraw by meeting the conditions your plan imposes in keeping with Internal Revenue Service (IRS) guidelines. For example, you may have to demonstrate how urgent the situation is and prove you have no other resources.

Some allowances are purchasing your primary home, covering out-of-pocket medical expenses for yourself or a dependent, and paying college tuition for yourself or a dependent.

However, if you're younger than 59½, you must pay a 10% penalty plus income tax on the amount you withdraw. You also may not be permitted to contribute to the plan again for six months.

Head of household

Head of household is an IRS filing status that you can use if you are unmarried or considered unmarried on the last day of a tax year and provide at least half the cost of maintaining a home for one or more qualifying dependents.

That may be your child, grandchild, or other relative who lives in that home for more than half the year, or a parent whether or not he or she lives in your home.

The advantage of filing as head of household is that you can take a higher standard deduction than if you filed as a single taxpayer and you owe less federal income tax than you would as a single, assuming all other details were the same.

Filing as head of household also means you qualify for certain deductions and credits that would not be available to you if you used the married filing separate returns status.

Health insurance

Health insurance covers some of or all the cost of treating an insured person's illnesses or injuries. In some cases, it pays for preventive care, such as annual physicals and diagnostic tests.

You may have health insurance as an employee benefit from your job or, if you qualify, through the federal government's Medicare or Medicaid programs.

You may also buy individual health insurance directly from an insurance company or be eligible through a plan offered by a group to which you belong. As you do with other insurance contracts, you pay premiums to purchase coverage and the insurer pays some of or all your healthcare costs, based on the terms of your contract.

Some health insurance requires that you meet an annual deductible before the insurer begins to pay. There may also be coinsurance, which is your share, on a percentage basis, of each bill, or a copayment, which is a fixed dollar amount, for each visit.

Health insurance varies significantly from plan to plan and contract to contract. Generally, most plans cover hospitalization, doctors' visits, and other skilled care. Some plans also cover some combination of prescription drugs, rehabilitation, dental care, and innovative therapies or complementary forms of treatment for serious illnesses.

Health savings account (HSA)

A health savings account is designed to accumulate tax-free assets to pay current and future healthcare expenses. To open an HSA, you must have a qualifying high deductible health plan (HDHP) either through your employer or as an individual.

If you have an employer's plan, your contributions to the HSA are made with pretax income, and your employer may contribute as well. If you have an individual plan, you may deduct your contributions in calculating your adjusted gross income (AGI).

Congress sets an annual limit on the amount you can contribute to an HSA, which you set up with a financial institution such as a bank, brokerage firm, insurance company, or mutual fund company that offers these accounts.

No tax is due on money you withdraw from the HSA to pay qualified medical expenses such as doctor's visits, hospital care, eyeglasses, dental care, and medications for yourself, your spouse, and your dependants.

Any money that's left over in your HSA at the end of the year is rolled over and continues to accumulate tax-free earnings, which you can use for future healthcare costs.

Once you're 65, you can use the money in the HSA for non-medical expenses without paying a penalty, but you'll owe income taxes on those withdrawals. If you are younger than 65, you can also spend from your HSA on non-medical expenses, but you'll owe income taxes plus a 10% tax penalty on the amount you take out.

Hedge fund

Hedge funds are private investment partnerships open to institutions and wealthy individual investors. These funds pursue returns through a number of alternative investment strategies.

Those might include holding both long and short positions, investing in derivatives, using arbitrage, and speculating on mergers and acquisitions. Some hedge funds use leverage, which means investing borrowed money to boost returns.

Because of the substantial risks associated with hedge funds, securities laws limit participation to accredited investors whose assets meet or exceed Securities and Exchange Commission (SEC) guidelines.

Hedger

Hedgers in the futures market try to offset potential price changes in the spot market by buying or selling a futures contract.

In general, they are either producers or users of the commodity or financial product underlying that contract. Their goal is to protect their profit or limit their expenses.

For example, a cereal manufacturer may want to hedge against rising wheat prices by buying a futures contract that promises delivery of September wheat at a specified price.

If, in August, the crop is destroyed, and the spot price increases, the manufacturer can take delivery of the wheat at the contract price, which will probably be lower than the market price. Or the manufacturer can trade the contract for more than the purchase price and use the extra cash to offset the higher spot price of wheat.

Hedging

Hedging is an investment technique designed to offset a potential loss on one investment by purchasing a second investment that you expect to perform in the opposite way.

For example, you might sell short one stock, expecting its price to drop. At the same time, you might buy a call option on the same stock as insurance against a large increase in value.

High deductible health plan (HDHP)

A high deductible health plan (HDHP) requires substantially higher than average out-of-pocket expenses before the insurance company will start paying for your medical expenses.

However, the premiums for an HDHP are generally lower than the premiums for traditional fee-for-service, participating provider organization (PPO), or a health maintenance organization (HMO) plan.

The HDHP may also pay a larger percentage of your expenses once you have satisfied the deductible. If you have an HDHP, you may be eligible for a health savings account (HSA), which allows you to make tax-free withdrawals to pay for medical care that's not covered by your plan.

Money you put in an HSA or that an employer contributes to your account and that you don't spend for qualified expenses can be rolled over and used in later years.

High-yield bond

High-yield bonds are bonds whose ratings from independent rating services are below investment grade.

As a result, to attract investors, issuers of high-yield bonds must pay a higher rate of interest than the rates that issuers of higher-rated bonds with the same maturity are paying. The higher rate translates to more income, which is the higher yield.

High-yield bonds may also be described, somewhat more graphically, as junk bonds.

Highly compensated employees

Highly compensated employees are people whose on-the-job earnings are higher than the level the government has established to differentiate this category of worker.

In 2007, that amount is $100,000. It is increased from time to time to reflect the impact of inflation.

The major consequence of being a member of this group is that the percentage of earnings that highly compensated employees may contribute to their 401(k) or similar plan is determined by the contribution rates of other plan participants who earn less.

If lower-paid employees contribute an average of 2% or less, higher-paid employees may contribute up to twice that percentage.

If the average is 3% to 8%, higher-paid employees may contribute two percentage points more than the average. And if the average is 8% or higher, the maximum for highly compensated employees is 1.25 times that average.

Hold

A securities analyst's recommendation to hold appears to take a middle ground between encouraging investors to buy and suggesting that they sell.

However, in an environment where an analyst makes very few sell recommendations, you may interpret that person's hold as an indication that it is time to sell.

Hold is also half of the investment strategy known as buy-and-hold. In this context, it means to keep a security in your portfolio over an extended period, perhaps ten years or more.

The logic is that if you purchase an investment with long-term potential and keep it through short-term ups and downs in the marketplace, you increase the potential for building portfolio value.

Holding company

By acquiring enough voting stock in another company, a holding company, also called a parent company, can exert control over the way the target company is run without actually owning it outright.

The advantages of this approach, provided that the holding company owns at least 80% of the voting shares, are that it receives tax-free dividends if the subsidiary prospers and can write off some of the operating losses if the subsidiary falters.

Because of its shareholder status, however, the holding company is insulated to some extent from the target company's liabilities.

Holding period

A holding period is the length of time you keep an investment.

In some cases, a specific holding period is required in order to qualify for some benefit. For example, you must hold US savings bonds for a minimum of five years to collect the full amount of interest that has accrued.

Home equity line of credit (HELOC)

Sometimes referred to as a HELOC, a home equity line of credit lets you borrow against the equity you've built in your home, usually by using a debit card or writing checks against your available balance.

Your credit line, or limit, is fixed, but you can draw against it up to that limit rather than receive the entire loan

amount as a lump sum. Whatever you borrow reduces your available balance until you repay it. Then you can borrow it again.

Home equity lines of credit have variable interest rates. The terms of repayment vary and are spelled out in your agreement.

In some cases, you begin to repay principal and interest as soon as you borrow. In others, you pay interest only and make a one-time full payment of principal at some set date. Or you may make interest-only payments for a specific period, and then begin to repay principal as well.

HELOC

It's important to keep in mind that because your home serves as collateral for the line of credit, your home could be at risk if you default, or fall behind on repayment.

Home equity loan

A home equity loan, sometimes called a second mortgage, is secured by the equity in your home.

You receive the loan principal, minus fees for arranging the loan, in a lump sum. You then make monthly repayments over the term of the agreement, just as you do with your first, or primary, mortgage.

The interest rates on home equity loans are generally lower than the rates on unsecured loans. However, when you borrow against your equity you run the risk of foreclosure if you default on the loan, even if you have continued to make the required payments on your first mortgage.

Homeowners insurance

Homeowners insurance is a contract between an insurance company and a homeowner to cover certain types of damage to the property and its contents, theft of personal possessions, and liability in case of lawsuits based on incidents or events that occur on the property.

To obtain the insurance, which is based on the value of the home and what is covered in the policy, you pay a premium set by the insurance company.

For each claim there's generally a deductible—a dollar amount—that you must pay before the insurer is responsible for its share. If you have a mortgage loan, your lender will require you to have enough homeowners insurance to cover the amount you owe on the loan.

Homeowners insurance policies vary substantially from contract to contract and from insurer to insurer as well as from region to region. Almost all policies have exclusions, which are causes of loss that are not covered. All the coverage and exclusions of a particular policy are spelled out in the terms and conditions.

Hope scholarship credit

You may qualify for a Hope scholarship tax credit for money you spend on qualified educational expenses for yourself, your spouse, or a dependent child.

To qualify, the student must be enrolled at least halftime in the first or second year of a qualified higher education institution pursuing a degree or other credential.

Qualified institutions include liberal arts colleges, universities, and vocational, trade, or technical schools. If two qualifying students are enrolled at the same time, you may take two Hope tax credits.

To qualify for this credit, your modified adjusted gross income must fall within the annual limits that Congress sets. Those amounts tend to increase slightly each year.

If you claim the credit while you're taking withdrawals from tax-free college savings plans such as a Section 529 plan or an education savings account (ESA),

you'll have to plan carefully. Your withdrawals will lose their qualified status and be subject to tax and penalty if you use them to pay for the same expenses for which you claim the tax credit.

You can't take the credit, either, if you claim a tuition and fees deduction in calculating your adjusted gross income.

Hot issue

If a newly issued security rises steeply in price after its initial public offering (IPO) because of intense investor demand, it is considered a hot issue.

Hybrid annuity

With a hybrid annuity, you allocate part of your annuity's assets to providing fixed income payments and part to making variable income payments.

For example, you could buy a hybrid immediate annuity with a lump sum of $50,000, and allocate $35,000 to fixed payments and $15,000 to variable payments.

The fixed portion would lock in a specific yearly income, while income from the variable portion would depend on the performance of the underlying investments you selected.

This approach allows you to combine the advantages of both types of annuities—regular income from the fixed and growth potential from the variable—in a single package.

Hybrid mortgage

Sometimes called an intermediate ARM, a fixed-period ARM, or a multiyear mortgage, a hybrid mortgage combines aspects of fixed-rate and adjustable-rate mortgages.

The initial rate is fixed for a specific period—usually three, five, seven, or ten years—and then is adjusted to market rates. The adjustment may be a one-time change, or more typically, a change that occurs regularly over the balance of the loan term, usually once a year.

In many cases, the interest rate changes on a hybrid mortgage are capped, which can help protect you if market rates rise sharply.

One advantage of the hybrid mortgage is that the interest rate for the fixed-rate portion is usually lower than with a 30-year fixed-rate mortgage. The lower rate also means it's easier to qualify for a mortgage, since the monthly payment will be lower.

And if you move or refinance before the interest rate is adjusted—the typical mortgage lasts only seven years—you don't have to worry about rates going up.

However, some hybrid mortgages carry prepayment penalties if you refinance or pay off the loan early. While prepayment penalties are illegal in many states, they are legal in others.

Hypothecation

Hypothecation means pledging an asset as collateral for a loan.

If you use a margin account to buy on margin or sell short, for example, you pledge securities (stocks, bonds, or other financial instruments) as collateral for the debt. If the brokerage firm issues a margin call that you don't meet, it can sell those securities to cover its losses.

Similarly, if you arrange a mortgage on your home, you give the lender the right to sell your home if you fail to meet your obligation to make mortgage payments.

Hypothecation may make it easier for you to secure a loan, but you do run the risk of losing the asset if for some reason you default on your obligation to repay according the terms of the agreement.

Identity theft

Identity theft is the unauthorized use of your personal information, such as your name, address, Social Security number, or credit account information.

People usually steal your identity to make purchases or obtain credit, though they may also use the data to apply for a driver's license or other form of official identification.

Immediate annuity

You buy an immediate annuity contract with a lump-sum purchase. You begin receiving income from the annuity either right away or within 13 months.

A fixed immediate annuity guarantees the amount of income you'll receive in each payment, based on the claims paying ability of the insurance company selling the contract.

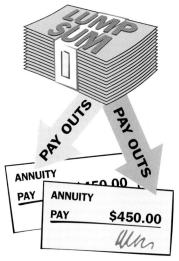

A variable immediate annuity pays income based on the performance of the annuity funds, or subaccounts, you select from those available through the contract.

Immediate annuities appeal to people who want to convert a sum of money to a source of regular income, either for them-

selves or for another person. One way they're frequently used is as a source of retirement income.

Imputed interest

Imputed interest is interest you are assumed to have collected even if that interest was not paid.

For example, you pay income tax on the imputed interest of a zero-coupon bond you hold in a taxable account even though the interest is not paid until the bond matures.

Similarly, you may be required to pay income tax on imputed interest if you make an interest-free loan, even if that loan is to your children or another member of your family. The government's position, in this case, is that you should have charged interest even though you didn't do so.

Incentive stock option (ISO)

Corporate executives may be granted incentive stock options (ISOs), also called qualifying stock options. These options aren't taxed when they're granted or exercised, but only when the underlying shares are sold.

If, after exercising the options, participating executives keep the shares for the required period, any earnings from selling the shares are taxed at the owner's long-term capital gains rate.

However, stock option transactions may make sellers vulnerable to the alternative minimum tax (AMT).

Income annuity

An income annuity, sometimes called an immediate annuity, pays an annual income, usually in monthly installments.

Your income is based on the annuity's price, your age (and your joint annuitant's age if you name one), the term length, and the specific details of the contract. It's also dependent on the annuity provider's ability to meet its obligations.

You might buy an income annuity with assets from your 401(k) plan, or your plan may buy an income annuity on your behalf. In that case, the annuity provider guarantees an income that will satisfy your minimum required distribution.

Income fund

Income funds are mutual funds whose investment objective is to produce current income rather than long-term growth, typically by investing in bonds or sometimes a combination of bonds and preferred stock.

Investors, especially those who have retired or are about to retire, may prefer income funds to potentially more volatile growth funds.

The amount of income a fund may generate is related to the risk posed by the investments that the fund makes and the return they generate.

A fund that buys lower-grade bonds may provide substantially more income than a fund buying investment-grade bonds. But the same fund may also put your principal, or investment amount, at substantial risk.

Income in respect of a decedent

Any income your beneficiary receives after your death that would have gone to you if you were still alive is described as income in respect of a decedent.

One example is the income your beneficiary gets as a minimum required distribution from your 401(k) or IRA. In this case, your beneficiary pays tax on that income at his or her ordinary rate, as you would have.

Income statement

An income statement, also called a profit and loss statement, shows the revenues from business operations, expenses of operating the business, and the resulting net profit or loss of a company over a specific period of time.

In assessing the overall financial condition of a company, you'll want to look at the income statement and the balance sheet together, as the income statement captures the company's operating performance and the balance sheet shows its net worth.

Income stock

Stock that pays income in the form of regular dividends over an extended period is often described as income stock.

The advantage of owning income stock is that it can supplement your budget or provide new capital to invest. Unless you own the stock in a tax-deferred or tax-free account, you'll owe income tax each year on the dividends you receive.

But dividends on qualifying stock, including most US stock and some international stock, are usually taxed at your lower long-term capital gains rate. Income stock is an important component of most equity income funds and growth and income funds.

Incorporation

When a business incorporates, it receives a state or federal charter to operate as a corporation. A corporation has a separate and distinct legal and tax identity from its owners.

In fact, in legal terms, a corporation is considered an individual—it can own property, earn income, pay taxes, incur liabilities, and be sued.

Incorporating can offer many advantages to a business, among them limiting the liability of the company's owners. This means that shareholders are not personally responsible for the company's debts. Another advantage is the ability to issue shares of stock and sell bonds, both ways to raise additional capital.

You know that a business is a corporation if it includes the word "Incorporated"—or the short form, "Inc."—in its official name.

Indemnity insurance

An indemnity insurance policy pays up to a fixed amount when you make a claim, often on a per-day basis.

The premiums on health insurance indemnity plans may be lower than on other heathcare plans, but the fixed payments may cover only a portion of your medical bills.

Some people use indemnity plans as supplements to, rather than substitutes for, more comprehensive health insurance. Others use low-cost indemnity plans for short-term coverage.

Indenture

An indenture is a written contract between a bond issuer and bond holder that is proof of the bond issuer's indebtedness and specifies the terms of the arrangement, including the maturity date, the interest rate, whether the bond is convertible to common stock, and, if so, the price or ratio of the conversion.

The indenture, which may be called a deed of trust, also includes whether the bond is callable—or can be redeemed by the issuer before it matures—what property, if any, is pledged as security, and any other terms.

Independent 401(k)

The independent 401(k)—also known as a solo 401(k), indy-k, or uni-k—is a variation of the 401(k) designed for people who are self-employed or operate a small business with a partner, spouse, or other immediate family members.

The annual contribution limit is the same as it is for other 401(k) plans, and catch-up contributions are allowed for participants 50 and older.

The plans are easier and less expensive to administer than traditional 401(k)s, and they have certain potential advantages over other retirement plans for small businesses as well, including high contribution limits, access to tax-free loans, and the ability to roll over savings from most other retirement plans.

Most business entities qualify to set up an independent 401(k), including partnerships, corporations, S-corporations, limited liability partnerships (LLPs), limited liability companies (LLCs), and sole proprietorships.

Index

An index reports changes up or down, usually expressed as points and as a percentage, in a specific financial market, in a number of related markets, or in an economy as a whole.

Each index—and there are a large number of them—measures the market or economy it tracks from a specific starting point. That point might be as recent as the previous day or many years in the past.

For those reasons, indexes are often used as performance benchmarks against which to measure the return of investments that resemble those tracked by the index.

A market index may be calculated arithmetically or geometrically. That's one reason two indexes tracking similar markets may report different results. Further, some indexes are weighted and others are not.

Weighting means giving more significance to some elements in the index than to others. For example, a market capitalization weighted index is more influenced by price changes in the stock of its largest companies than by price changes in the stock of its smaller companies.

Index fund

An index fund is designed to mirror the performance of a stock or bond index, such as Standard & Poor's 500 Index (S&P 500) or the Russell 2000 Index.

To achieve that goal, the fund purchases all the securities in the index, or a representative sample of them, and adds or sells investments only when the securities in the index change. Each index fund aims to keep pace with its underlying index, not outperform it.

This strategy can produce strong returns during a bull market, when the index reflects increasing prices. But it may produce disappointing returns during economic downturns, when an actively managed fund might take advantage of investment opportunities if they arise to outperform the index.

Because the typical index fund's portfolio is not actively managed, most index funds have lower-than-average management costs and smaller expense ratios. However, not all index funds tracking the same index provide the same level of performance, in large part because of different fee structures.

Index of Leading Economic Indicators

This monthly composite of ten economic measurements was developed to track and help forecast changing patterns in the economy. It is compiled by The Conference Board, a business research group.

The components are adjusted from time to time to help improve the accuracy of the index. In the past, it has successfully predicted major downturns, although it has also warned of some that did not materialize.

Consumer-related components include the number of building permits issued, manufacturers' new orders for consumer goods, and the index of consumer expectations.

Financial components include the S&P 500 Index of widely held stocks, the real money supply, and the interest rate spread.

Business-related components include the average work week in the manufacturing sector, average initial claims for unemployment benefits, non-defense plant and equipment orders, and vendor performance, which reflects how quickly companies receive deliveries from suppliers.

Index option

Index options are puts and calls on a stock index rather than on an individual stock. They give investors the opportunity to hedge their portfolios or speculate on gains or losses in a segment of the market.

For example, if you own a group of technology stocks but think technology stocks are going to fall, you might buy a put option on a technology index rather than selling short a number of different technology stocks.

If the value of the index does fall, you could exercise the option and collect cash to partially offset a drop in the value of your portfolio.

However, to use this strategy successfully, the index you choose must perform the way the portion of the portfolio you're trying to hedge performs.

And since changes in an index are difficult to predict, index options tend to be volatile. The more time there is until an index option expires, the more volatile the option tends to be.

Indexed annuity

An indexed annuity is a deferred annuity whose return is tied to the performance of a particular equity market index.

Your investment principal is usually protected against severe market downturns, in that you may have an annual return of 0% but not less than 0%.

However, earnings are generally capped at a fixed percentage, so any index gains that are above the cap are not reflected in your annual return.

Indexed annuity contracts generally require you to commit your assets for a particular term, such as 5, 10, or 15 years. Some but not all contracts limit your participation rate, which means that only a percentage of your premium has a potential to earn a rate higher than a guaranteed rate.

Individual retirement account

Individual retirement accounts are one of two types of individual retirement arrangements (IRAs) that provide tax ad-

vantages as you save for retirement. The other is an individual retirement annuity.

Both have the same annual contribution limits, catch-up provisions if you're 50 or older, and withdrawal requirements. In addition, both are available in three varieties: traditional deductible, traditional nondeductible, and Roth.

The primary difference between the two is in the investments you make with your contributions.

You open an individual retirement account with a financial services firm, such as a bank, brokerage firm, or investment company, as custodian. The accounts are self-directed, which means you can choose among the investments available through your custodian.

In common practice, however, perhaps because more people have individual retirement accounts, the acronym IRA tends to be used to refer to an account rather than annuity or arrangement.

Individual retirement annuity

An individual retirement annuity is one type of individual retirement arrangement.

It resembles the better-known individual retirement account in most ways, such as annual contribution limits, catch-up provisions if you're 50 or older, and withdrawal requirements.

In addition, the two share a common acronym—IRA—and come in three varieties: traditional nondeductible, traditional deductible, and Roth.

The key difference between the two is that with an individual retirement account you may invest your contributions in any of the alternatives available through your account custodian. With an individual retirement annuity, your money goes into either a fixed or variable annuity offered by the insurance company you have chosen as custodian.

Individual retirement arrangement (IRA)

Individual retirement arrangement (IRA)

An individual retirement arrangement (IRA), which may be set up as either an account or an annuity, allows people with earned income to contribute to a tax-deferred traditional IRA or a tax-free Roth IRA.

Your contribution can be as much as the annual cap, though it can't be more than you earn. The cap is $4,000 for 2007 and $5,000 for 2008. If you are 50 or older, you can make an additional catch-up contribution of $1,000 a year.

You can contribute to a traditional IRA regardless of your income, and you may qualify to deduct your contribution if your modified adjusted gross income is less than the ceiling for your tax filing status. You may also qualify if you're not eligible to participate in an employer sponsored plan where you work.

You qualify for a Roth if your modified adjusted gross income is less than the ceiling for your filing status.

If you open a traditional IRA, you usually can't withdraw without penalty before you turn 59½ and you must begin minimum required distributions (MRDs) by April 1 of the year following the year you turn 70½.

Income taxes figured at your regular rate are due on your earnings and on any contributions you deducted on your tax return in the year for which you made them.

With a Roth IRA your withdrawals are free of federal income tax provided you're at least 59½ and your account has been open at least five years. There are no required withdrawals.

Inefficient market

In an inefficient market, investors may not have enough information about the securities in that market to make informed decisions about what to buy or the price to pay.

Markets in emerging nations may be inefficient, since securities laws may not require issuing companies to disclose relevant information. In addition, few analysts follow the securities being traded there.

Similarly, there can be inefficient markets for stocks in new companies, particularly for new companies in new industries that aren't widely analyzed.

An inefficient market is the opposite of an efficient one, where enormous amounts of information are available for investors who choose to use it.

Inflation

Inflation is a persistent increase in prices, often triggered when demand for goods is greater than the available supply or when unemployment is low and workers can command higher salaries.

THE INFLATION CYCLE

1. Increasing demand boosts prices

3. Lower prices increase demand, and cycle begins again

2. Rising prices decrease demand, so prices drop

Moderate inflation typically accompanies economic growth. But the US Federal Reserve Bank and central banks in other nations try to keep inflation in check by decreasing the money supply, making it more difficult to borrow and thus slowing expansion.

Hyperinflation, when prices rise by 100% or more annually, can destroy economic, and sometimes political, stability by driving the price of necessities higher than people can afford.

Deflation, in contrast, is a widespread decline in prices that also has the potential to undermine the economy by stifling production and increasing unemployment.

Inflation rate

The inflation rate is a measure of changing prices, typically calculated on a month-to-month and year-to-year basis and expressed as a percentage.

For example, each month the Bureau of Labor Statistics calculates the inflation rate that affects average urban US consumers, based on the prices for about 80,000 widely used goods and services. That figure is reported as the Consumer Price Index (CPI).

Inflation-adjusted return

Inflation-adjusted return is what you earn on an investment after accounting for the impact of inflation.

For example, if you earn 7% on a bond during a period when the inflation rate averages 3%, your inflation-adjusted return is 4%.

Inflation-adjusted return is also known as real return.

Since inflation diminishes the buying power of your money, it's important that the rate of return on your overall investment portfolio be greater than the rate of inflation. That way, your money grows rather than shrinks in value over time.

Inflation-protected security (TIPS)

US Treasury inflation-protected securities (TIPS) adjust the principal twice a year to reflect inflation or deflation measured by the Consumer Price Index (CPI).

The interest rate is fixed and is paid twice a year on the adjusted principal. So if your principal is larger because of inflation you earn more interest. If it's lower because of deflation, you earn less.

You can buy TIPS with terms of 5, 10, or 20 years at issue using a Treasury Direct account or in the secondary market. At maturity you receive either the adjusted principal or par value, whichever is greater.

You owe federal income tax on the interest you earn and on inflation adjustments in each year they're added even though you don't receive the increases until the security matures. However, TIPS earnings are exempt from state and local income taxes.

These securities provide a safeguard against deflation as well as against inflation since they guarantee that you'll get back no less than par, or face value, at maturity.

Inherited IRA

An inherited IRA is an IRA that passes to a beneficiary at the death of the IRA owner. If you name your spouse as the beneficiary of your IRA, your spouse inherits the IRA at your death. At that point, it is your spouse's property.

But if you name anyone other than your spouse, that beneficiary inherits the rights to income from your IRA, which continues to be registered in your name, but not the IRA itself.

Initial public offering (IPO)

When a company reaches a certain stage in its growth, it may decide to issue stock, or go public, with an initial public offering (IPO). The goal may be to raise capital, to provide liquidity for the existing shareholders, or a number of other reasons.

Any company planning an IPO must register its offering with the Securities and Exchange Commission (SEC).

In most cases, the company works with an investment bank, which underwrites the offering. That means marketing the shares being offered to the public at a set price with the expectation of making a profit.

Insider trading

If managers of a publicly held company, members of its board of directors, or anyone who holds more than 10% of the company trades its shares, it's considered insider trading.

This type of trading is perfectly legal, provided it's based on information available to the public.

It's only illegal if the decision is based on knowledge of corporate developments, such as executive changes, earnings reports, or acquisitions or takeovers that haven't yet been made public.

It is also illegal for people who are not part of the company, but who gain access to private corporate information, to trade the company's stock based on this inside information. The list includes lawyers, investment bankers, journalists, or relatives of company officials.

Instinet

Instinet is the world's largest agency brokerage firm.

As an agency firm, it doesn't trade stock for its own account as traditional brokerage houses do. That way, it doesn't bid against the mutual funds, insurance companies, pension funds, and other institutional investors who are its primary clients.

Using Instinet's sophisticated electronic network, these investors can trade directly and anonymously with each other in more than 40 global markets. Or, using Instinet brokers, the investors can place orders on all US exchanges and many overseas exchanges, including those that aren't automated.

Institutional fund

An institutional fund is a mutual fund that's available to large investors, such as pension funds and not-for-profit organizations, with substantial amounts to invest.

Typical institutional funds have higher minimum investments but lower fees than the retail funds that are available to the general public.

Among the reasons institutional funds may cost less to operate is that they tend to have low turnover rates and their investors redeem shares less often than retail investors.

Institutional investor

Institutional investors buy and sell securities in large volume, typically 10,000 or more shares of stock, or bonds worth $200,000 or more, in a single transaction.

In most cases, the investors are organizations with large portfolios, such as mutual funds, banks, university endowment funds, insurance companies, pension funds, and labor unions.

Institutional investors may trade their own assets or assets that they are managing for other people.

Insufficient funds

If you don't have enough money available in your checking account to cover the checks you've written or electronic debits you've authorized, you have insufficient funds (ISF) or nonsufficient funds (NSF).

A check written against insufficient funds is informally called a returned check, a bounced check, or a bad check. If you write one, your account is considered overdrawn.

Unless you have overdraft protection, which is a line of credit linked to your checking account, your bank will charge you an NSF fee, usually $20 to $35 per check.

The check or an electronic copy is returned unpaid to the person who deposited it. The payee's bank may also charge a fee for depositing a check written against insufficient funds.

Insurance trust

You set up an insurance trust to own a life insurance policy on your life. When you die, the face value of the policy is paid to the trust.

That keeps the insurance payment out of your estate, while making money available to the beneficiary of the trust to pay any estate tax that may be due, or to use for any other purpose.

If you're married, you may set up an insurance trust to buy a second-to-die policy, which pays the face value of the policy at the death of the second spouse. That allows the first to die to leave all assets to the other, postponing potential estate tax until the survivor dies. At that point, the insurance benefit is available to pay any tax that might be due.

Insured bond

An insured bond is a municipal bond whose interest and principal payments are guaranteed by a triple-A rated bond insurer.

Insurance protects municipal bondholders against default by the issuer and protects bonds in case they're downgraded by ratings agencies, which can decrease market value.

Insured bonds generally offer a slightly lower rate of interest than uninsured bonds.

Integrated pension plan

In an integrated pension plan, your employer counts part of your Social Security benefit in the defined benefit pension you're entitled to and takes that amount out of your income.

You still collect from both sources, but you receive less from your employer than you would if your plan wasn't integrated.

There is some protection, though. By law, an employer using an integrated pension plan can't reduce your private pension by more than 50%.

Interest

Interest is what you pay to borrow money using a loan, credit card, or line of credit. It is calculated at either a fixed or variable rate that's expressed as a percentage of the amount you borrow, pegged to a specific time period.

For example, you may pay 1.2% interest monthly on the unpaid balance of your credit card.

Interest also refers to the income, figured as a percentage of principal, that you're paid for purchasing a bond, keeping money in a bank account, or making other interest-paying investments.

If it is simple interest, earnings are figured on the principal. If it is compound interest, the earnings are added to the principal to form a new base on which future income is calculated.

Interest is also a share or right in a property or asset. For example, if you are half-owner of a vacation home, you have a 50% interest.

Interest rate

Interest rate is the percentage of the face value of a bond or the balance in a deposit account that you receive as income on your investment.

INTEREST RATE	
Face value	$1,000
x Rate	x 6%
ANNUAL INTEREST	$60 PER YEAR

If you multiply the interest rate by the face value or balance, you find the annual amount you receive.

For example, if you buy a bond with a face value of $1,000 with a 6% interest rate, you'll receive $60 a year. Similarly, the percentage of principal you pay for the use of borrowed money is the loan's interest rate.

If there are no other costs associated with borrowing the money, the interest rate is the same as the annual percentage rate (APR).

Interest-only mortgage

With an interest-only mortgage loan, you pay only the interest portion of each scheduled payment for a fixed term, often five to seven years.

After that, your payments increase, often substantially, to cover the accumulated unpaid principal plus the balance of the loan and the interest.

Before the higher payments begin, you may renegotiate your loan at the current interest rate or pay off the outstanding balance. However, it's possible that interest rates may have risen, in which case you will end up paying a higher rate on the entire unpaid principal.

If you have regularly invested the principal you weren't repaying and realized a return higher than the loan's interest rate, you could come out ahead. However, many borrowers don't invest the savings.

One risk with interest-only loans is that you may not be able to meet the higher payments once full repayment begins, especially if the interest-only payments themselves were a stretch.

Interest-rate risk

Interest-rate risk describes the impact that a change in current interest rates is likely to have on the value of your investment portfolio.

INTEREST RATE

You face interest-rate risk when you own long-term bonds or bond mutual funds because their market value will drop if interest rates increase.

That loss of value occurs because investors will be able to buy bonds with a new, higher interest rate, so they won't pay full price for an older bond paying a lower interest rate.

Intermediate-term bond

Intermediate-term bonds mature in two to ten years from the date of issue. Typically, the interest on these bonds is greater than that on short-term bonds of similar quality but less than that on comparably rated long-term bonds.

Internalization

Intermediate-term bonds work well in an investment strategy known as laddering. Laddering involves buying bonds with different maturity dates so that portions of your fixed income portfolio mature in a stepped pattern over a number of years.

Internalization

Internalization occurs when a securities trade is executed within a brokerage firm rather than though an exchange. For example, if you give your broker an order to buy, the brokerage firm, acting as dealer, sells you shares it holds in its own account.

Similarly, if you give an order to sell, the firm buys your shares. The transaction is reported to the exchange or market where the stock is listed but the trade is settled within the firm.

Your broker might choose an internalized trade, sometimes called a principal transaction, because it results in the fastest trade at the best price.

The firm keeps the spread, which is the difference between the price the buyer pays and the amount the seller receives. But if the spread is smaller than it would be with a different execution, you, as buyer or seller, benefit.

Your broker may also execute your order by going directly to another firm. In that case, the transaction is reported to the appropriate market just as an internalized trade is, but the record-keeping and financial arrangements are handled between the firms.

International fund

This type of mutual fund invests in stocks, bonds, or cash equivalents that are traded in overseas markets, or in indexes that track international markets.

Like other funds, international funds have investment objectives and strategies, and pose some level of risk, such as the risk that currency fluctuations may greatly affect the fund's value.

Some international funds focus on countries with established economies, some on emerging markets, and some on a mix of the two.

US investors may buy funds that invest in other markets to diversify their portfolios, since owning a fund is usually simpler than investing in individual securities abroad.

A different group of funds, called global or world funds, also invest in overseas markets but typically keep a substantial portion of their portfolios in US securities.

International Monetary Fund (IMF)

The IMF was set up as a result of the United Nations Bretton Woods Agreement of 1944 to help stabilize world currencies, lower trade barriers, and help developing nations pay off debt.

The IMF's activities are funded by developed nations and are sometimes the subject of intense criticism, either by the nations the IMF is designed to help, the nations footing the bill, or both.

Intestate

A person who dies without a will is said to have died intestate.

In this case, the probate court in the person's home state—sometimes known as surrogate's court or orphan's court—determines who has the right to inherit the person's assets and who should be named guardian of any minor children.

The process, known as administration, can be time consuming and expensive, and the outcome may or may not reflect what the intestate person would have wanted.

In-the-money

An option is in-the-money at any point up to expiration if the exercise price is below the market price of a call option or above the market price of a put option. That means an in-the-money option has value.

For example, if you hold an equity call option with a strike price of 50, and the current market price of the stock is $52, the option is in-the-money.

As the option holder, you could buy the stock at $50 and either sell it at $52 or add it to your portfolio. Or, if you preferred, you could sell the option, potentially at a profit.

In-the-money options are generally among the most actively traded, especially as the expiration date approaches.

Intrinsic value

A company's intrinsic value, or underlying value, is used to calculate its projected worth.

You determine intrinsic value by subtracting long-term debt from anticipated future assets, including profits, the potential for increased efficiency, and the sale of new stock.

Another approach is to calculate intrinsic value by dividing the company's estimated future earnings by the number of its existing shares. This method weighs the current price of a stock against its future worth.

Critics of using intrinsic worth as a way to evaluate potential investments point out that all the numbers except debt are hypothetical.

The term is also used in options trading to indicate the amount by which an option is in-the-money. For example, an equity call option with a strike price of 35 has an intrinsic value of $4 if the market price of the underlying stock is $39. But if the market price drops to $34, the option has no intrinsic value.

Introducing broker (IB)
An introducing broker (IB) is a person or firm that takes orders to buy or sell futures contracts from clients and passes those orders to a futures commission merchant (FCM) for execution.

Payment is handled by the FCM, not the introducing broker. Guaranteed introducing brokers refer clients to just one futures commission merchant while independent introducing brokers can refer clients to any registered FCM.

Investment bank
An investment bank is a financial institution that helps companies take new bond or stock issues to market, usually acting as the intermediary between the issuer and investors.

Investment banks may underwrite the securities by buying all the available shares at a set price and then reselling them to the public. Or the banks may act as agents for the issuer and take a commission on the securities they sell.

Investment banks are also responsible for preparing the company prospectus, which presents important data about the company to potential investors.

In addition, investment banks handle the sales of large blocks of previously issued securities, including sales to institutional investors, such as mutual fund companies.

Unlike a commercial bank or a savings and loan company, an investment bank doesn't usually provide retail banking services to individuals.

Investment club
If you're part of an investment club, you and the other members jointly choose the invest-  ments the club makes and decide on the amount each of you will contribute to the club's account.

Among the reasons that clubs are popular are that they allow investors to commit only modest amounts, share in a diversified portfolio, and benefit from each other's research.

While clubs may establish themselves informally, many groups use the resources of BetterInvesting, an investor education membership organization.

Its website, www.betterinvesting.org, provides information on how to start an investment club and support services to existing clubs.

Investment company
An investment company is a firm that offers open-end funds, called mutual funds, closed-end funds, sometimes called investment trusts, or exchange traded funds to the public.

By describing a company offering the funds as an investment company, it's easier to distinguish the company from the funds that it offers.

For example, a single investment company might offer an aggressive-growth fund, a growth and income fund, a US Treasury bond fund, and a money market fund.

Or a closed-end investment company might offer an international fund focused on a single country, such as Ireland, or a region, such as Latin America.

Investment grade
When a bond is rated investment grade, its issuer is considered able to meet its obligations, exposing bondholders to minimal default risk.

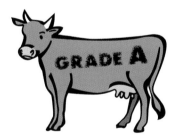

Most US corporate and municipal bonds are rated by independent services such as Moody's Investors Service and Standard & Poor's (S&P).

The ratings are based on a number of criteria, including the likelihood that the bond issuer will be able to make interest payments and repay the principal in full and on time.

The four categories of bonds rated BBB and higher by S&P or Baa and higher by Moody's are considered investment grade.

Investment horizon
Your investment horizon is the point in time when you hope to achieve a particular investment goal. That horizon,

sometimes called your time frame, may be fixed or flexible, depending on the nature of the goal and the investment decisions you take.

For example, paying for college is often a fixed goal because most students enroll the year they graduate from high school. Retirement may be a more flexible goal if you have the choice about when you will stop working.

The landscape can be more complicated if you have more than one investment goal, and therefore there's more than one horizon in the picture.

Investment income

Investment income—sometimes called unearned income—is the money that you collect from your investments.

It may include stock dividends, mutual fund distributions, and interest from CDs, interest-bearing bank accounts, bonds, and other debt instruments. You may also have rental income from real estate or other assets you own for investment purposes.

Capital gains you realize from selling investments for more than you paid to acquire them may also be considered investment income. Your net investment income is what you have left over after you subtract your investment expenses, such as fees and commissions.

Investment objective

An investment objective is a financial goal that helps determine the type of investments you make. For example, if you want a source of regular income, you might select a portfolio of high-rated bonds and dividend-paying stocks.

Each mutual fund describes its investment objective in its prospectus, along with the strategy the fund manager follows to meet that objective. Mutual fund investors often look for funds whose stated objectives are compatible with their own goals.

IRA rollover

If you move assets from an employer sponsored retirement plan to an IRA, you've completed an IRA rollover.

You owe no income tax on the money you move if you deposit the full amount into the new IRA within 60 days or arrange a direct transfer from the existing account to the new account.

If you're moving money from an employer's retirement plan to an IRA yourself, the plan administrator is required to withhold 20% of the total.

That amount is refunded after you file your income tax return, provided you've deposited the full amount into the new account on time, including the 20% that's been withheld. Any amount you don't deposit within the 60-day period is considered an early withdrawal and you'll have to pay tax on it.

You might also have to pay a penalty for early withdrawal if you're younger than 59½. But if you arrange a direct transfer from your plan to the rollover IRA nothing is withheld.

Irrevocable trust

An irrevocable trust is a legal agreement whose terms cannot be changed by the creator, or grantor, who establishes the trust, chooses a trustee, and names the beneficiary or beneficiaries.

The trust document names a trustee who is responsible for managing the assets in the best interests of the beneficiary or beneficiaries and carrying out the wishes the creator has expressed.

You typically use an irrevocable trust for the tax benefits it can provide by removing assets permanently from your estate.

In addition, through the terms of the trust you can exert continuing control over the way your property is distributed to your beneficiaries. Trusts have the additional advantages of being more difficult to contest than a will and more private.

If you establish an irrevocable trust while you're still alive, it's called a living or inter vivos trust. If you establish the trust in your will, so that it takes effect at the time of your death, it's called a testamentary trust.

Issue

When a corporation offers a stock or bond for sale, or a government offers a bond, the security is known as an issue, and the company or government is the issuer.

Issuer

An issuer is a corporation, government, agency, or investment trust that sells securities, such as stocks and bonds, to investors. Issuers may sell the securities through an underwriter as part of a public offering or as a private placement.

January effect

Each year, the stock market tends to increase slightly in value between December 31 and the end of the first week of January.

Known as the January effect, this rise starts when investors sell under-performing stocks at year-end to claim capital losses on their tax returns.

After the new tax year begins on January 1, the same investors tend to reinvest the money from those sales, heightening demand temporarily, and making the overall market rise slightly during that week.

Jumbo CD

Jumbo CDs are large-denomination certificates of deposit with balances of at least $100,000, and sometimes $1 million or more.

They tend to pay higher rates than smaller CDs and are purchased primarily by institutional investors. However, they're increasingly marketed to individual investors as low-risk, fixed-income assets.

Jumbo CDs may be negotiable or non-negotiable. Negotiable CDs may be traded in the secondary market and are often issued in bearer form, which means that physical possession of the paper document is the sole proof of ownership. The banks that sell bearer CDs keep no records of ownership.

Non-negotiable Jumbo CDs, like conventional CDs, remain on deposit in the bank that issued them and are held in the name of the purchaser.

These Jumbo CDs, like other bank deposits, are FDIC insured, up to $100,000 per depositor in different categories of taxable accounts in each bank and up to $250,000 if they are held in self-directed retirement accounts, such as an individual retirement account (IRA).

Junior security

In the world of bonds, the term junior means having less claim to repayment.

If you own a junior security and the issuing company goes out of business, you have less claim on any assets than an investor who owns a senior security issued by the same company.

But all bondholders, whether they own junior or senior securities, are senior to, or have a greater claim than, holders of preferred stock, who in turn are senior to holders of common stock.

Junk bond

Junk bonds carry a higher-than-average risk of default, which means that the bond issuer may not be able to meet interest payments or repay the loan when it matures.

Except for bonds that are already in default, junk bonds have the lowest ratings, usually Caa or CCC, assigned by rating services such as Moody's Investors Service and Standard & Poor's (S&P).

Issuers offset the higher risk of default on junk bonds by offering substantially higher interest rates than are being paid on investment-grade bonds. That's why junk bonds are also known, more positively, as high-yield bonds.

Keogh plan

A group of qualified retirement plans, including profit sharing plans, money purchase defined contribution plans, and a defined benefit plan, is available to self-employed people, small-business owners, and partners in companies that file an IRS Schedule K, among others.

Together these plans are sometimes described as Keogh plans in honor of Eugene Keogh, a US representative from Brooklyn, NY, who was a force behind their creation in 1963.

The employer, not the employee, makes the contributions to Keogh plans, but the employee typically chooses the way the contributions are invested.

Like other qualified plans, there are contribution limits, though they are substantially higher than with either 401(k)s or individual retirement plans,

and on a par with contribution limits for a simplified employee pension plan (SEP).

Any earnings in an employee's account accumulate tax deferred, and withdrawals from the account are taxed at regular income tax rates.

If you participate in a Keogh plan, a 10% federal tax penalty applies to withdrawals you take before you turn 59½, and minimum required distributions (MRD) must begin by April 1 of the year following the year that you turn 70½ unless you're still working. In that case, you can postpone MRDs until April 1 of the year following the year you actually retire.

The only exception—and it is more common here than in other retirement plans—is if you own more than 5% of the company. If you leave your job or retire, you can roll over your account value to an individual retirement account (IRA).

If you're eligible to establish a qualified retirement plan, a Keogh may be attractive because there are several ways to structure the plan, you may be able to shelter more money than with other plans by electing the defined benefit alternative, and you have more control in establishing which employees qualify for the plan.

But the reporting requirements can be complex, making it wise to have professional help in setting up and administering a plan.

Laddering

Laddering is an investment strategy that calls for establishing a pattern of rolling maturity dates for a portfolio of fixed-income investments. Your portfolio might include intermediate-term bonds or certificates of deposit (CDs).

For example, instead of buying one $15,000 CD with a three-year term, you buy three $5,000 CDs maturing one year apart. As each CD comes due, you can re-invest the principal to extend the pattern.

Or you could use the money for a preplanned purchase, have it available to take advantage of a new investment opportunity, or use it to cover unexpected expenses.

You can use laddering to pay for college expenses, with a series of zero coupon bonds coming due over four years, in time to pay tuition each year.

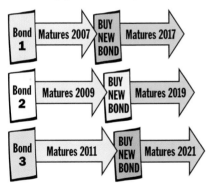

And if you ladder, you can avoid having to liquidate a large bond investment if you need just some of the money or to reinvest your entire principal at a time when interest rates may be low.

Lapse

A lapse causes a policy, right, or privilege to end because the person or institution that would benefit fails to live up to its terms or meet its conditions.

For example, if you have a subscription right to buy additional shares of a stock at a price below the public offering price, you must generally act before a certain date. If that date passes, your right is said to lapse.

Similarly, if you have a life insurance policy that requires you to pay annual premiums, the policy will lapse if you fail to pay the premiums in time.

Large-capitalization (large-cap) stock

The stock of companies with market capitalizations typically of $10 billion or more is known as large-cap stock. Market cap is figured by multiplying the number of either the outstanding or floating shares by the current share price.

Large-cap stock is generally considered less volatile than stock in smaller companies, in part because the bigger companies may have larger reserves to carry them through economic downturns.

However, market capitalization is always in flux. Today's large-cap stock can drop out of that category if the share price plunges either in a general market downturn or as a result of internal problems.

And the opposite is true as well. Many of the country's largest companies began life as start-ups.

Last trading day

The last trading day is the final day on which an order to buy or sell an options contract or futures contract can be executed.

In the case of an options contract, for example, the last trading day is usually the Friday before the third Saturday of the month in which the option expires, though a brokerage firm may set an earlier deadline for receiving orders.

If you don't act on an option you own before the final trading day, the option may simply expire, or if it is in-the-money it may be automatically executed on your behalf by your brokerage firm or the Options Clearing Corporation (OCC) unless you request that it not be.

But if a futures contract isn't offset, the contract seller is obligated to deliver the physical commodity or cash settlement to the contract buyer.

Lead underwriter

When a company wants to raise capital by selling securities to investors, it partners with an investment bank, known as the lead underwriter.

That bank has the primary responsibility for organizing and managing an initial public offering (IPO), a secondary stock offering, or a bond offering.

In the case of an IPO, the lead underwriter agrees to buy some or all the shares from the company and helps it determine an initial offering price for the security, create a prospectus, and organize a syndicate of other investment banks to help sell the securities to investors.

In return for assuming the financial risk of the IPO, the lead underwriter receives a fee, which is usually a percentage of the price of each share of the IPO.

Lease

A lease is a legal agreement that provides for the use of something—typically real estate or equipment—in exchange for payment.

Once a lease is signed, its terms, such as the rent, cannot be changed unless both parties agree. A lease is usually legally binding, which means you are held to its terms until it expires. If you break a lease, you could be held liable in court.

Level load

Some load mutual funds impose a recurring sales charge, called a level load, each year you own the fund rather than a sales charge to buy or sell shares.

The level-load rate is generally lower than the sales charge for front- or back-end loads. But the annual asset-based management fee on these funds is higher than for front-load funds.

This means the total amount you pay over time with a level load can be substantially more than a one-time sales charge, especially if you own the fund for a number of years.

If a fund company offers you a choice of the way you prefer to pay the load, level-load funds are generally identified as Class C shares. Front-end loads are Class A shares and back-end loads are Class B shares.

Level term insurance

With a level term life insurance policy, your annual premium remains the same for the term, which may be as long as 10 or 20 years.

The death benefit also remains the same. If the policy is guaranteed renewable, you can extend coverage for an additional term without having to qualify again, though the annual premium will increase because you're older.

Although the cost of insurance in the first few years will probably be higher for a level term than an increasing term policy, the total cost of a level term with the same benefit is usually less. As with all term policies, you don't build up a cash reserve and your coverage ends at the end of the term or at any time you stop making payments.

Level yield curve

A level yield curve results when the yield on short-term US Treasury issues is essentially the same as the yield on long-term Treasury bonds.

You create the curve by plotting a graph with yield on the vertical axis and maturity date on the horizontal axis and connecting the dots.

In most periods, the yield on long-term bonds is higher and the yield curve is positive because investors demand more for tying up their money for a longer period.

There are also times, when short-term T-bills yields are higher, that the pattern is reversed and the yield curve is negative, or inverted.

Leverage

Leverage is an investment technique in which you use a small amount of your own money to make an investment of much larger value. In that way, leverage gives you significant financial power.

For example, if you borrow 90% of the cost of a home, you are using the leverage to buy a much more expensive property than you could have afforded by paying cash.

If you sell the property for more than you borrowed, the profit is entirely yours. The reverse is also true. If you sell at a loss, the amount you borrowed is still due and the entire loss is yours.

Buying stock on margin is a type of leverage, as is buying a futures or options contract.

Leveraging can be risky if the underlying instrument doesn't perform as you anticipate. At the very least, you may lose your investment principal plus any money you borrowed to make the purchase.

A $3,700 investment buys a $37,000 contract

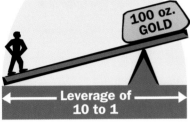

Leverage of 10 to 1

With some leveraged investments, you could be responsible for even larger losses if the value of the underlying product drops significantly.

Leveraged buyout

A leveraged buyout occurs when a group of investors using borrowed money, often raised with high yield bonds or other kinds of debt, takes control of a company.

These buyouts are usually hostile takeovers, and if they are successful, the investors will usually start to sell off assets to pay down the substantial debt they have incurred.

Liability

In personal finance, liabilities are the amounts you owe to creditors, or the people and organizations that lend you money. Typical liabilities include your mortgage, car and educational loans, and credit card debt.

When you figure your net worth, you subtract your liabilities, or what you owe, from your assets. The result is your net worth, or the cash value of what you own.

In business, liabilities refer to money a company owes its creditors and any claims against its assets.

Lien

A lien exists when you owe money to a lender on a particular vehicle or other asset, such as real estate, that has been used as collateral on a loan.

An asset on which there's a lien can't be sold until the lienholder has been repaid. When you own an asset on which there's a lien, you risk having it repossessed if you default and don't make the required payments in full and on time.

Lienholder

A lienholder is the bank, finance company, credit union, other financial institution, or individual with whom you signed an agreement to borrow money using a particular asset, such as a car, as collateral.

As long as there is a balance due on the loan, the lienholder must be repaid before you are free to sell the asset.

Life expectancy

Your life expectancy is the age to which you can expect to live. Actuarial tables establish your official life expectancy, which insurance companies use to evaluate the risk they take in selling you life insurance or an annuity contract.

The Internal Revenue Service (IRS) also uses life expectancy to determine the distribution period you must use to calculate minimum required distributions from your retirement savings plans or traditional IRAs.

However, your true life expectancy, based on your lifestyle, family history, and other factors, may be longer or shorter than your official life expectancy.

Life insurance

Life insurance is a contract you sign with an insurance company, obligating it to pay a death benefit of a certain value to the beneficiaries you name.

In most cases, the payment is made at the time of your death, but certain policies allow you to take a portion of the death benefit if you are terminally ill and need the money to pay for healthcare.

You may select either term or permanent insurance. With a term policy, you are insured for a specific period of time. When the term ends, you must renew the policy for another term or change your coverage. Otherwise, you're no longer insured. With a permanent policy, you can buy coverage for your lifetime.

You pay an annual premium, typically billed monthly or quarterly, for the coverage. The insurer sets the cost, based on your age, health, lifestyle, and other factors. With a permanent policy, your premium is fixed, but with a term policy it typically increases when you renew your coverage to reflect the fact that you're older.

Life settlement

If you are over age 70 and no longer need your life insurance policy, you may be able to sell it to a third party in what's called a life settlement.

You're paid a cash amount less than the death benefit but typically greater than the surrender value, and the party that buys your policy will get the death benefit when you die.

Similar to viatical settlements, in which terminally ill people may sell their life insurance policies, generally to use the cash to pay for healthcare, life settlements let you forgo a death benefit and use the cash in your policy while you're alive.

However, life settlements are for people who are healthy and expect to live more than a couple of years. Specific rules for life settlements are set by the state where a specific transaction takes place.

Some businesses specialize in buying life insurance policies from older or terminally ill individuals and reselling them as investments.

However, because these insurance arrangements are controversial and most investors understand them poorly, both people considering selling policies and people considering investing in them are advised to proceed with caution. For example, there may be complex estate-planning and tax consequences to life settlements.

Lifecycle fund

A lifecycle fund, which is a fund of funds, invests in individual mutual funds that a fund company puts together to help investors meet their objectives without having to select individual funds.

Some companies offer a set of lifecycle funds, each with a different level of risk and return, from conservative to aggressive. In that case, you may choose a lifecycle that's appropriate for reaching your goals within the time frame you've allowed.

The typical pattern is for younger investors to choose a more aggressive life-cycle fund and those nearing retirement to choose a more conservative fund.

With target date funds, which are a type of lifecycle fund, you choose a target retirement year, and the fund manager invests and reallocates your money more and more conservatively as you near retirement.

Lifeline account

A lifeline account is a basic checking account with low or no minimum deposit and balance requirements and very low or no monthly fees.

Most lifeline accounts, however, limit the number of checks that you can write and may otherwise restrict the banking services you receive.

Currently, certain states require banks to offer lifeline accounts, to ensure that lower-income people have access to banking services. However, you can find no-frills checking accounts in other states as well.

Lifetime learning credit

You may qualify to claim a lifetime learning tax credit of up to $2,000 each year for qualified higher educational expenses for yourself, your spouse, or a dependent if your family's modified adjusted gross income falls within the annual limits that Congress sets. Those amounts tend to increase slightly each year.

The education must be one or more courses but doesn't have to be part of a degree- or certificate-granting program, though the tax credit can be used for undergraduate, postgraduate, or professional studies.

Even if you are paying for more than one person's education, you can take only one lifetime learning credit per year.

If you claim the credit while you're taking withdrawals from tax-free college savings plans such as a Section 529 plan or an education savings account (ESA), you'll have to plan carefully. Your withdrawals will lose their qualified status and be subject to tax and penalty if you use them to pay for the same expenses for which you claim the tax credit.

You can't take the credit, though, if you claim a tuition and fees deduction in calculating your adjusted gross income or deduct the amount as a business expense.

Limit order

A limit order sets the maximum you will pay for a security or the minimum you are willing to accept on a particular transaction.

For example, if you place a limit order to buy a certain stock at $25 a share when its current market price is $28, your broker will not buy the stock until its share price reaches $25.

Similarly, if you give a limit order to sell at $25 when the stock is trading at $20, the order will be filled only if the price rises to $25.

A limit order differs from a market order, which is executed at the current price regardless of what that price is. It also differs from a stop order, which becomes a market order when the stop price is reached and the order is executed at the best available price.

Limit price

A limit price is the specific price at which you tell your stockbroker to execute a buy or sell order on a particular security.

If the transaction can be completed at that price, it goes through, but if that price is not available, no purchase or sale takes place.

The advantage of a limit order is that you won't pay more or sell for less than you want. Since your broker is monitoring the price, it is more likely that the trade will take place at the limit price than if you waited until the security reached that price to place your order.

The potential drawback of setting a limit price, which is also known as giving a limit order, is that the transaction may not take place in a fast market if the price of the security moves up or down quickly, passing the limit price.

Limited liability company (LLC)

Organizing a business enterprise as a limited liability company (LLC) under the laws of the state where it operates protects its owners or shareholders from personal responsibility for company debts that exceed the amount those owners or shareholders have invested.

In addition, an LLC's taxable income is divided proportionally among the owners,

who pay tax on their share of the income at their individual rates. The LLC itself owes no income tax.

The limited liability protection is similar to what limited partners in a partnership or investors in a traditional, or C, corporation enjoy.

The tax treatment is similar to that of a partnership or S corporation, another form of organization that's available for businesses with fewer than 75 employees. However, only some states allow businesses to use LLC incorporation.

Limited partner

A limited partner is a member of a partnership whose only financial risk is the amount he or she has invested.

In contrast, all the assets of the general partner or partners, including those held outside the partnership, could be vulnerable to claims brought by the partnership's creditors.

Limited partnership

A limited partnership is a financial affiliation that includes at least one general partner and a number of limited partners. The partnership invests in a venture, such as real estate development or oil exploration, for financial gain.

The arrangement can be public, which means you can buy into the partnership through a brokerage firm, or private.

What makes it a limited partnership is that everyone but the general partners has limited liability. The most the limited partners can lose is the amount they invest.

Line of credit

A line of credit, sometimes called a bank line, is the most you can borrow under a revolving credit arrangement with a credit card issuer, bank, or mortgage lender.

When you borrow against a line of credit, you pay interest on the amount of money you actually borrow, not on the available balance, or full amount you are able to borrow.

For example, if you have a $10,000 line of credit on a credit card, you may borrow as much or as little as you want up to that amount, and you pay interest only on the amount you have borrowed.

If you carry a balance of $3,000, you only pay interest on that amount, but there is still $7,000 available for you to borrow. Once you repay the amount you borrow, you can use it again.

A line of credit may be secured with collateral, or unsecured. A line of credit on a credit card is usually unsecured, for example. But if you have a home equity line of credit, your home serves as collateral against the amount you borrow.

Lipper, Inc.

Lipper provides financial data and performance analysis for more than 30,000 open- and closed-end mutual funds and variable annuities worldwide.

The company evaluates funds on the strength of their success in meeting their investment objectives and identifies the strongest funds in specific categories as Lipper Leaders.

The research company's mutual fund indexes are considered benchmarks for the various categories of funds.

Liquid asset

Liquid assets are accounts or securities that can be easily converted to cash at little or no loss of value.

These include cash, money in bank accounts, money market mutual funds, and US Treasury bills.

Actively traded stocks, bonds, and mutual funds are liquid in the sense that they are easy to sell, but the price is not guaranteed and could be less than the amount you paid to buy the asset.

In contrast, selling fixed assets, such as real estate, usually requires time and negotiation.

Liquidity

If you can convert an asset to cash easily and quickly, with little or no loss of value, the asset has liquidity. For example, you can typically redeem shares in a money market mutual fund at $1 a share.

Similarly, you can cash in a certificate of deposit (CD) for at least the amount you put into it, although you may forfeit some or all of the interest you had expected to earn if you liquidate before the end of the CD's term.

The term liquidity is sometimes used to describe investments you can buy or sell easily. For example, you could sell several hundred shares of a blue chip stock by simply calling your broker, something that might not be possible if you wanted to sell real estate or collectibles.

The difference between liquidating cash-equivalent investments and securities like stock and bonds, however, is that securities constantly fluctuate in value. So while you may be able to sell them readily, you might sell for less than you paid to buy them if you sold when the price was down.

Listed security

A listed security is a stock, bond, options contract, or similar product that is traded on an organized exchange.

Being listed has advantages, including being part of an orderly, regulated, and widely reported trading process that helps insure fairness and liquidity.

To be listed, the company issuing the security must meet the requirements of the exchange where it wishes to be traded. For example, to list a stock, the company typically must have a minimum market capitalization, a minimum number of existing shares, and a minimum per share price.

Listing requirement

Listing requirements are the standards a corporation must meet to have its stock or bonds traded on a particular exchange.

Exchanges set their own initial and continuing listing requirements. Among the listing criteria are a corporation's pretax earnings, a minimum market value, and a minimum number of existing shares.

Living will

A living will is a legal document that describes the type of medical treatment you want—or don't want—if you are terminally ill or unable to communicate your wishes.

Like wills that provide instructions about your assets, living wills must be signed and have two or more witnesses to be valid.

You can use a healthcare proxy or durable power of attorney for healthcare to authorize someone to act as your agent to ensure your wishes are followed. Because there are still unresolved questions about the extent of your agent's authority, it may be wise to get legal advice in preparing the documents.

Load

If you buy a mutual fund through a broker or other financial professional, you pay a sales charge or commission, also called a load.

If the charge is levied when you purchase the shares, it's called a front-end load. If you pay when you sell shares, it's called a back-end load or contingent deferred sales charge. And with a level load, you pay a percentage of your investment amount each year you own the fund.

Load fund

Some mutual funds charge a load, or sales commission, when you buy or sell shares or, in some cases, each year you own the fund. The charge is generally figured as a percentage of your investment amount.

Most load funds are sold by brokers or other investment professionals. The sales charge compensates them for their time.

In contrast, no-load funds, which don't have sales charges but may levy other fees, are usually sold directly to the public

by the investment company that offers the fund. Some companies offer both load and no-load versions of the same fund.

Loan note

A loan note is a promissory agreement describing the terms of a loan and committing the person or institution borrowing the money to live up to those terms.

For example, a mortgage loan note states the principal balance, the interest rate, the discount points, a payment schedule and due date, and any potential penalties for violating the repayment terms.

When the required repayment has been made, the agreement between the parties ends.

Lock-up period

A lock-up period is the time during which you cannot sell an investment that you own.

You are most likely to encounter a lock-up period if you acquire shares in an initial public offering (IPO) because you had a private equity investment in the company before it went public and receive shares in the IPO proportionate to your private equity ownership interest.

You may also have a lock-up period if you are an owner or an employee of the company and are granted shares.

The lock-up period may last as long as 180 days. In some cases, though, the lock-up period is graduated, meaning that after the initial 180 days you can sell an increasingly larger portion of your shares over the next two years.

After the lock-up period ends, you are free to sell all your shares if you wish.

Logarithmic scale

On a logarithmic scale or graph, comparable percentage changes in the value of an investment, index, or average appear to be similar. However, the actual underlying change in value may be significantly different.

For example, a stock whose price increases during the year from $25 to $50 a share has the same percentage change as a stock whose price increases from $100 to $200 a share.

On a logarithmic scale, it's irrelevant that the dollar value of the second stock is four times the value of the first.

Similarly, the percentage change in the Dow Jones Industrial Average (DJIA) as it rose from 1,000 to 2,000 is comparable to the percentage change when it moved from 4,000 to 8,000.

Long bond

Thirty-year bonds issued by the US Treasury are referred to as long bonds. The interest rate on the long bond is typically but not always higher than the rate on the Treasury's shorter term notes and bills.

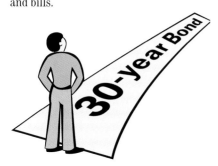

The rate on the most recently issued bond is the basis for pricing other long-term bonds and setting other financial benchmarks.

Long position

Having a long position in a stock means you own the security.

You have the right to collect the dividends or interest the security pays, the right to sell it or give it away when you wish, and the right to keep any profits if you do sell.

Similarly, you have a long position in an option when you hold the option, and you have the right to exercise it before expiration or sell it.

The term is also used to describe a position that's maintained by your brokerage firm or bank on your behalf. For example, if your firm holds stocks for you in street name, you are said to be long on their books.

Having a long position is the opposite of having a short position in a security. A short position means you have borrowed shares through your broker, sold them, and must return them, plus interest, at some point in the future.

Similarly, a short position in an option means that you have sold the option, giving the holder the right to exercise and committing yourself to fulfilling the terms should exercise occur and you're assigned to meet them.

Long-term capital gain (or loss)

When you sell a capital asset that you have owned for more than a year at a higher price than you paid to buy it, any profit on the sale is considered a long-term capital gain.

If you sell for less than you paid to purchase the asset, you have a long-term capital loss.

Unlike short-term gains, which are taxed at your income tax rate, most long-term gains on most investments, including real estate and securities, are taxed at rates lower than the rates on ordinary income. Currently, those rates are 15% if you're in the 25% tax bracket or higher, and 5% if you are in the 10% or 15% bracket.

You can deduct your long-term losses from your long-term gains, and your short-term losses from your short-term gains, to reduce the amount on which potential tax may be due. You may also be able to deduct up to $3,000 in accumulated long-term losses from your ordinary income and carry forward losses you can't use in one tax year to deduct in the next tax year.

Long-term care insurance

Long-term care insurance is a policy designed to cover at least some of your expenses if you have a chronic but not life-threatening illness, long-term disability, or you are unable to live independently because you can't perform a number of the activities of daily living.

Those activities typically include bathing, dressing, feeding yourself, taking medication, using the bathroom, and being able to move from a sitting to a standing position. Most contracts also cover cognitive impairments, such as Alzheimer's disease.

Under the terms of most long-term care contracts, you can be cared for in a nursing home or at home. The insurance pays for custodial rather than skilled care, which must be provided by licensed professionals. Skilled care is covered in part by Medicare and Medigap.

Every policy provides a specific daily or monthly benefit for up to a predetermined benefit period. Each policy also has an elimination period, which lasts from the day you become eligible until the day the insurer begins to pay. You generally can choose the benefit, benefit period, and elimination period that makes the most sense to you and that you can afford.

Long-term equity anticipation securities (LEAPS)

These long-term options on stocks have expiration dates of up to three years rather than the shorter terms of most stock options, which are never longer than nine months.

LEAPS

The benefit of LEAPS, from an investor's perspective, is that there's more time for the price movement you anticipate to occur.

However, LEAPS are available on fewer underlying stocks than standard options, and they are generally more expensive than the shorter term options on the same security.

Loose credit

In order to combat a sluggish economy, the Federal Reserve's Open Market Committee (FOMC) may institute a loose credit policy.

In that case, the Federal Reserve Bank of New York buys large quantities of Treasury securities in the open market, which gives banks additional money to lend at lower interest rates. This abundance, or looseness, of credit is intended to stimulate borrowing and invigorate the economy.

Tight money is the opposite of loose credit. It's the result of the Fed's decision to sell securities in the open market, which reduces bank reserves and makes borrowing more expensive. A tight money policy is designed to slow down a rapidly accelerating economy.

Loser

Stocks whose market prices drop the most during the trading day are described, rather bluntly, as losers.

The stocks that lose the most value relative to their opening price are called percentage losers, and the stocks that lose the greatest number of points are called net losers or dollar losers.

Each trading day, the number of losers is compared to the number of gainers, or stocks that have risen in value, to gauge the mood of the market. If there are more losers than gainers over a period of days, the market as a whole is in a slump.

Lump sum

A lump sum is an amount of money you pay or receive all at once rather than in increments over a period of time.

For example, you buy an immediate annuity with a single lump-sum payment. If you receive the face value of a life insurance policy when the insured person dies, or receive the full value of your retirement account, those payments are also lump sums.

Lump-sum distribution

When you retire, you may have the option of taking the value of your pension, salary reduction, or profit-sharing plan in different ways.

For example, you might be able to take your money in a series of regular lifetime payments, generally described as an annuity, or all at once, in what is known as a lump-sum distribution.

If you take the lump sum from a defined benefit pension plan, the employer follows specific regulatory rules to calculate how much you would have received over your estimated lifespan if you'd taken the pension as an annuity and then subtracts the amount the fund estimates it would have earned in interest on that amount during the payout period.

In contrast, when you take a lump-sum distribution from a defined contribution plan, such as a salary reduction or profit-sharing plan, you receive the amount that has accumulated in the plan.

You may or may not have the option to take a lump-sum distribution from these plans when you change jobs.

You can take a lump-sum distribution as cash, or you can roll over the distribution into an individual retirement arrangement (IRA). If you take the cash, you owe income tax on the full amount of the distribution, and you may owe an additional 10% penalty if you're younger than 59½.

If you roll over the lump sum into an IRA, the full amount continues to be tax deferred, and you can postpone paying income tax until you withdraw.

Make a market

A dealer who specializes in a specific security, such as a bond or stock, is said to make a market in that security. That means the dealer is ready to buy or sell at least one round lot of the security at its publicly quoted price.

Other broker-dealers turn to a market maker when they want to buy or sell that particular security either for their own account or for a client's account.

Electronic markets, such as Nasdaq, tend to have several market makers in a particular security. The overall effect of multiple market makers is greater liquidity in the marketplace and more competitive pricing.

Managed account

A managed account is a portfolio of stocks or bonds chosen and managed by a professional investment manager who makes the buy and sell decisions.

Each managed account has an investment objective, and each manager oversees multiple individual accounts invested in the same basic portfolio to meet the same objective.

While managed accounts resemble mutual funds in some ways, with a managed account you own individual securities rather than shares of a common fund.

You may also be able to request that the manager avoid certain investments, which you can't do with a mutual fund. And, through your broker, you might ask the manager to sell certain holdings in your account to realize capital gains or losses.

There are no phantom gains in managed accounts. Those gains can occur if a mutual fund realizes a profit from selling an investment and credits you with a capital gain even if there's no actual increase in your account value.

However, the minimum investment is usually substantially higher for a managed account—often $100,000. Plus the annual fees, which are included in the amount you pay the financial professional who recommends the account, may be higher than the fees on a mutual fund of similar value.

Management fee

A management fee is the percentage of your account value that an investment company or manager charges to handle your account.

Fees for passively managed index funds typically cost less than the fees for actively managed funds, though fees differ significantly from one fund company to another.

Margin

Margin is the minimum amount of collateral—in either cash or securities—you must have in your margin account to buy on margin, sell short, or invest in certain derivatives.

The initial margin requirement is set by federal law and varies from product to product. For example, to buy stock on margin, you must have at least 50% of the purchase price in your account.

After the initial transaction, maintenance rules set by the self-regulatory organizations, such as the New York Stock Exchange (NYSE) and NASD, apply.

Under those rules, you must have a minimum of 25% of the total market value of the margined investments in your account at all times. Individual firms may set their maintenance requirement higher—at 30% or 35%, for example.

If your equity in the account falls below the maintenance level, you'll receive a margin call for additional collateral to bring the account value back above the minimum level.

Margin account

Margin accounts are brokerage accounts that allow you a much wider range of transactions than cash accounts.

In a cash account you must pay for every purchase in full at the time of the transaction. In a margin account, you can buy on margin, sell short, and purchase certain types of derivative products.

Before you can open a margin account, however, you must satisfy the firm's requirements for margin transactions. You must also agree in writing to the terms of the account, and make a minimum deposit of at least $2,000 in cash or qualifying securities.

If you buy on margin or sell short, you pay interest on the cash or the value of the securities you borrow through your margin account and must eventually repay the loan.

Because both types of transactions use leverage, they offer the possibility of making a substantially larger profit than you could realize by using only your own money.

But because you must repay the loan plus interest even if you lose money on the investment, using a margin account also exposes you to more risk than a cash account.

Margin call

To protect the margin loans they make, brokers issue a margin call if your equity in your margin account falls below the required maintenance level of at least 25%.

If you get a margin call, you must deposit additional cash or securities to meet the call, bringing the balance of the account back up to the required level.

If you don't meet the call, securities in your account may be sold, and your broker repaid in full. For example, if you buy 1,000 shares on margin when they are selling at $10 a share, and the price falls to $7 a share, your equity would be $2,000 ($7,000 market value minus $5,000 loan is $2,000).

That's 28.6% of the market value. If your brokerage firm has a maintenance requirement of 30%, you would receive a margin call to bring your equity back to the required level—in this case $2,100, which is 30% of $7,000.

You might also get a margin call if you trade futures contracts and the value of your account drops below the required maintenance level. However, margin requirements for futures are different than for stock.

Margin requirement

The margin requirement is the minimum amount the Federal Reserve, in Regulation T, requires you to deposit in a margin account before you can trade through that account.

Currently this minimum, or initial margin, is $2,000, or 50% of the purchase price of securities you buy on margin, or 50% of the amount that you receive for selling securities short.

In addition, there's a minimum maintenance requirement, a minimum of 25% and often more, of the market value of the securities in the account. The maintenance requirement is set by the New York Stock Exchange (NYSE), NASD, and the individual brokerage firms.

Marginal tax rate

Because the US income tax system is progressive, your tax rate rises as your taxable income rises through two or more tax brackets.

Your marginal tax rate is the rate you pay on the taxable income that falls into the highest bracket you reach: 10%, 15%, 25%, 28%, 33%, or 35%.

For instance, if you have a taxable income that falls into three brackets, you would pay at the 10% rate on the first portion, the 15% rate on the next portion, and the 25% federal tax rate on only the third portion. Your marginal rate would be 25%.

However, your marginal tax rate is higher than your effective tax rate, which is the average rate you pay on your combined taxable income. That's because you're only paying tax at your marginal, or maximum, rate on the top portion of your income.

Keep in mind that your marginal tax rate applies only to tax on ordinary income and does not take into account other tax liabilities—such as realized long-term capital gains, which are taxed at your long capital gains rate, or tax credits for which you may be eligible, which may reduce the actual tax you pay.

Mark to the market

When an investment is marked to the market, its value is adjusted to reflect the current market price.

With mutual funds, for example, marking to the market means that a fund's net asset value (NAV) is recalculated each day based on the closing prices of the fund's underlying investments.

With a margin account to buy futures contracts, the value of the contracts in the account is recalculated at least once a day to determine whether it meets the firm's margin requirements.

If that value falls below the minimum specified, you get a margin call and must add assets to your account to return it to the required level.

Markdown

A markdown is the amount a broker-dealer earns on the sale of a fixed-income security and is the difference between the sales price and what the seller realizes on the sale.

The markdown may or may not appear in the commission column or be stated separately on a confirmation statement.

A markdown is determined, in part, by the demand for the security in the marketplace. A broker-dealer may charge a smaller markdown if the security can be resold at a favorable markup.

MARKDOWN

Market price
− Markdown
──────────
PRICE YOU GET

The term markdown also refers more generally to a reduced price on assets that a seller wants to unload and will sell at less than the original offering price.

Market

Traditionally, a securities market was a place—such as the New York Stock Exchange (NYSE)—where members met to buy and sell securities.

But in the age of electronic trading, the term market is used to describe the organized activity of buying and selling securities, even if those transactions do not occur at a specific location.

Market capitalization

Market capitalization is a measure of the value of a company, calculated by multiplying the number of either the outstanding shares or the floating shares by the current price per share.

For example, a company with 100 million shares of floating stock that has a current market value of $25 a share would have a market capitalization of $2.5 billion.

Outstanding shares include all the stock held by shareholders, while floating shares are those outstanding shares that actually are available to trade.

Market capitalization, or cap, is one of the criteria investors use to choose a varied portfolio of stocks, which are often categorized as small-, mid-, and large-cap.

Generally, large-cap stocks are considered the least volatile, and small caps the most volatile.

The term market capitalization is sometimes used interchangeably with market value, in explaining, for example, how a particular index is weighted or where a company stands in relation to other companies.

Market cycles

Market cycles are the recurrent patterns of expansion and contraction that characterize the securities and real estate markets.

While the pace of these recurrent cycles of gain and loss isn't predictable, certain economic conditions affect the markets in fairly reliable ways.

For instance, stock and real estate usually gain value when the economy is healthy and growing, whereas bonds often do well during periods of rising interest rates. And during times of economic uncertainty, investors often prefer to put their money into short-term cash equivalent investments, such as US Treasury bills.

The cyclical pattern in one type of asset sometimes works in opposition to what's occurring at the same time in another asset class or subclass. For example, when the stock market is gaining value, the bond market may be flat or falling, or vice versa. Similarly, sometimes large-company stocks increase in value faster than small caps, but sometimes the opposite is true.

But while the ups and downs of the markets are inevitable, it's also true that it's virtually impossible to pinpoint the peak of a rising market or the bottom of a falling market except in hindsight.

Market maker

A broker-dealer who is prepared to buy or sell a specific security—such as a bond or at least one round lot of a stock—at a publicly quoted price, is called a market maker in that security.

Other brokers buy or sell specific securities through market makers, who may maintain inventories of those securities.

There is often more than one market maker in a particular security, and they bid against each other, helping to keep the marketplace liquid.

The Nasdaq Stock Market and the corporate and municipal bond markets are market maker markets. In contrast, on the floor of the New York Stock Exchange (NYSE) there's a single specialist to handle transactions in each security.

Market order

When you tell your broker to buy or sell a security at the market, or current market price, you are giving a market order. The broker initiates the trade immediately.

The amount you pay or receive is determined by the number of shares and the current bid or ask price. Market orders, which account for the majority of trades, differ from limit orders to buy or sell, in which a price is specified.

Market price

A security's market price is the price at which it is currently trading in an orga-nized market.

A good indication of the market price of a stock selling on the New York Stock Exchange (NYSE) or the Nasdaq Stock Market is the last reported transaction price.

However, if you give a market order to buy securities, then market price means the current ask, or offer. If you give a market order to sell, market price means the current bid.

Market risk

Market risk, also known as systematic risk, is risk that results from the charac-teristic behavior of an entire market or asset class.

One example of this type of risk is that the market prices of existing bonds generally fall as interest rates rise because investors are not willing to pay par value to own a bond that pays less interest than other bonds available in the marketplace.

So if you wanted to sell your existing bonds, you would probably have to settle for less than you paid to buy them.

Asset allocation is generally considered an antidote for market risk, since if your portfolio includes multiple asset classes it tends to be less vulnerable to a downturn in any one class.

Market timing

Market timing means trying to anticipate the point at which a market has hit, or is about to hit, a high or low turning point, based on historical patterns, technical analysis, or other factors.

Market timers try to buy as the market turns up and sell before the market turns down. It's the anticipated change in direction rather than the amount of time that passes between those changes that's significant for these investors.

The term is sometimes used in a negative sense to refer to a trading strategy that aims for quick profits by taking advantage of short-term changes in securities' prices.

Market timers, sometimes known as day traders, trade electronically. They try to buy low and sell high by taking advantage of second-to-second or minute-to-minute changes in the financial marketplace. They base decisions on information such as a forecast on interest rates or a sell-off in a particular market sector.

Market value

The market value of a stock or bond is the current price at which that security is trading.

In a more general sense, if an item has not been priced for sale, its fair market value is the amount a buyer and seller agree upon. That's assuming that both know what the item is worth and neither is being forced to complete the transaction.

Markup

When you buy securities from a broker-dealer or market maker, you pay a markup. The markup is either a percentage of the selling price or a flat fee, over and above the amount it cost the broker-dealer to purchase the security.

The amount of this markup, or spread, is the broker-dealer's profit and depends in part on the demand for that security or others like it.

For example, if investors are buying up certain types of bonds, a broker-dealer may increase the markup for bonds in that category.

You might say that the broker-dealer acquires the security at wholesale price and sells it to you at retail price. The difference is the markup.

If the markup doesn't appear on the confirmation statement, you can ask the broker-dealer about the markup amount. Or you can compare the prices that different broker-dealers quote for the same security or the price being quoted for the security on the Internet. The differences in price generally reflect the differences in markups.

Matching contribution

A matching contribution is money your employer adds to your retirement savings account, such as a 401(k) or a SIMPLE.

It's usually a percentage of the amount you contribute up to a cap that the employer sets, such as 50% of your contribution up to 5% of your salary. The matching amount and any earnings are tax deferred until you withdraw them from your account.

In most plans, employers are not required to match contributions, but may do so if they wish. Employers also determine, within federal guidelines, how long you have to work for the company in order to be fully vested in the matching contributions.

Matrix trading

Matrix trading occurs when the yield spread between two categories of bonds with different levels of risk is temporarily inconsistent with what that spread would normally be, prompting traders to try to capitalize on an unusual situation by initiating a bond swap.

For example, such a swap might involve long-term corporate bonds with high ratings and those with low ratings or bonds with longer terms and those with shorter terms.

Maturity date

A bond or other loan that must be repaid comes due on its maturity date. On that date, the full face value of the bond (and sometimes the final interest payment) must be paid in full to the bondholder.

Certificates of deposit (CDs) also have maturity dates on which you may withdraw the principal and interest without penalty or roll over the money into a new CD.

Other debt instruments, such as mortgage-backed securities, pay back their principal over the life of the debt, similar to the way a mortgage is amortized, or paid down. While these instruments also have a maturity date, that date is when the last installment payment of the loan as well as the last interest payment is due.

Mediation

Mediation is an informal, voluntary method of resolving disputes, in which the parties in conflict meet with a trained, independent third party to come up with a solution that's satisfactory to everyone involved.

For example, if you have a problem with your broker that you can't resolve directly with the firm, you can file a request for mediation with NASD, which oversees brokerage firms and has over 900 trained mediators to help resolve disputes.

Mediation is considered less expensive, less formal, and less confrontational than arbitration or lawsuits. But both parties must agree to use the process.

While you may retain a legal adviser during mediation, any resolution will be crafted with your direct involvement, which is usually not the case with arbitration.

Also, unlike arbitration, mediation is nonbinding, which means that if you're not happy with the outcome, you can stop the process, and either drop the issue or move to more formal proceedings.

Medicaid

Medicaid is a federal government program run by the individual states. It's designed to provide assistance to people who can't afford skilled or custodial healthcare.

There are strict financial standards governing who qualifies for assistance, though there is significant variation from state to state in the way the program is managed.

Medicare

Medicare is a federal government insurance program designed to provide healthcare coverage for people 65 or older, certain disabled people, and people with chronic kidney disease.

Anyone who qualifies for Social Security is automatically eligible for Medicare at 65.

Part A, which covers hospital and certain other costs, is provided when you enroll. You can also sign up for Part B, which covers doctor visits and related costs, and Part D, which covers prescription medicines, at the same time.

You pay a separate premium for both Part B and Part D. The Part B premium is set annually and carries surcharges for people whose incomes are above the annual ceilings. Your Part D premium is determined by the private insurer plan you select. If you postpone applying for Parts B and D and don't have equivalent or better coverage—called creditable coverage—from another plan, you face a permanent surcharge when you do enroll.

You may also have a choice between Original Medicare, which is a fee-for-service plan run by the government, or a Medicare Advantage plan if one is available where you live. Medicare Advantage plans are private insurer plans.

Merger

When two or more companies consolidate by exchanging common stock, and the resulting single company replaces the old companies, the consolidation is described as a merger.

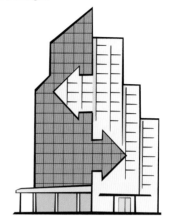

The shareholders of the old companies receive prorated shares in the new company. A merger is typically a tax-free transaction, meaning that shareholders owe no capital gains or lost taxes on the stock that is being exchanged.

A merger is different from an acquisition, in which one company purchases, or takes over, the assets of another. The acquiring company continues to function and the acquired company ceases to exist. Shareholders of the acquired company receive shares in the new company in exchange for their old shares.

Despite their differences, mergers and acquisitions are invariably linked, often simply described as M&As.

Micro-cap stock

A micro-cap stock is one with a smaller market capitalization—sometimes much smaller—than stocks described as small-caps. (Market capitalization is figured by multiplying the current market value by the number of outstanding shares.)

The cut-off for deciding that a stock belongs in one category or the other is arbitrary. However, the capitalization thresholds currently being suggested for micro-caps range from $50 million to $150 million.

Micro-caps are not only the smallest of the publicly traded corporations, but they are also the most volatile. That's partly because they often lack the reserves that may allow a larger company to weather rough periods.

And there are generally relatively few shares of a micro-cap company, so a large transaction may affect the stock's price quite a bit. In contrast, a similar transaction might not affect the stock price of a larger company that had many more shares in the market quite as much.

Mid-capitalization (mid-cap) stock

A mid-cap stock is one issued by a corporation whose market capitalization falls in a range between $2 billion and $10 billion, making it larger than a small-cap stock but smaller than a large-cap stock.

Market capitalization is figured by multiplying the number of either the outstanding or the floating shares by the current share price. Investors tend to buy mid-cap stocks for their growth potential. Their prices are typically lower than those of large-caps.

At the same time, these companies tend to be less volatile than small-caps, in part because they have more resources with which to weather an economic downturn.

Minimum finance charge

A minimum finance charge is a fee collected by a credit card issuer each billing period. It applies when the actual finance charge you owe isn't equal to or larger than this minimum.

For example, if the minimum finance charge is 50 cents, and you owe $5 in finance charges, the minimum would not apply. But if you had no other finance charges, you'd owe the 50 cents.

Not all issuers impose a minimum finance charge, so if you regularly pay your bill in full and on time, you may prefer an issuer who does not charge this fee.

Minimum required distribution (MRD)

A minimum required distribution is the smallest amount you must take each year from your retirement savings plan once you've reached the mandatory withdrawal age.

There are MRDs for 401(k) plans, 403(b) plans, and traditional IRAs, and the maximum age you can reach before they start is usually 70½. If you take less than the required minimum, you owe a 50% penalty on the amount you should have taken.

You calculate your MRD by dividing your account balance at the end of your plan's fiscal year—often December 31—by a distribution period based on your life expectancy. If your spouse is your beneficiary and more than ten years younger than you are, you can use a longer distribution period than you can in all other circumstances.

Minority interest

All shareholders whose combined shares represent less than half of the total outstanding shares issued by a corporation have a minority interest in that corporation.

In fact, in many cases, the combined holdings of the minority shareholders are considerably less than half of the total shares.

In another example, in a partnership, any partner who has a smaller percentage than another partner is said to have a minority interest. Under normal circumstances, it is difficult for those with a minority interest to have any real influence on corporate policy.

Modern portfolio theory

In making investment decisions, adherents of modern portfolio theory focus on potential return in relation to potential risk.

The strategy is to evaluate and select individual securities as part of an overall portfolio rather than solely for their own strengths or weaknesses as an investment.

Asset allocation is a primary tactic according to theory practitioners. That's because it allows investors to create portfolios to get the strongest possible return without assuming a greater level of risk than they are comfortable with.

Another tenet of portfolio theory is that investors must be rewarded, in terms of realizing a greater return, for assuming greater risk. Otherwise, there would be little motivation to make investments that might result in a loss of principal.

Modified adjusted gross income (MAGI)

Your modified adjusted gross income (MAGI) is your adjusted gross income (AGI) plus deductions, such as college loan interest and contributions to a deductible individual retirement account (IRA), which you may qualify to take if your MAGI is less than the annual ceilings set by Congress.

Other deductions, such as alimony, don't have income limits.

For example, suppose you're single, have a gross income of $51,000, and you're eligible to take a deduction for your IRA contribution of $4,000. Your AGI, when all deductions are taken, turns out to be $45,500. You then add the $4,000 back to find your MAGI of $49,500. Because your MAGI is less than the ceiling for deducting your full IRA contribution for your filing status, you can take the full deduction.

Momentum investing

A momentum investor focuses on stocks that are rising in value on increasing daily volume, and avoids stocks that are falling in price or that are perceived to be undervalued.

The logic is that when a pattern of growth has been established, it will continue to gain momentum and the growth will continue. Momentum investing is essentially the opposite of contrarian investing.

Monetary policy

A country's central bank is responsible for its monetary policy. In the United States, for example, the Federal Reserve aims to keep the economy growing but not allow it to become overheated.

In a sluggish economy, the Fed may lower the short-term interest rate to loosen credit and allow more cash to circulate in an attempt to stimulate expansion.

Or, if it fears the economy is growing too quickly, it may tighten credit by raising the short-term interest rate to reduce the money supply, in an attempt to rein in potential inflation.

In pursuit of its monetary policy, the Fed can also increase or decrease the money supply by buying or selling government securities.

To avoid a potential recession, for example, the Fed might increase its purchases of US Treasury notes and bonds from banks and brokerage firms, providing them with more money to lend.

Monetary reserve

A government's monetary reserve includes the foreign currency and precious metals that its central bank holds. That reserve enables the government to influence foreign exchange rates and to manage its transactions in the international marketplace.

For example, a country with a large reserve of US dollars is in a position to make significant investments in US markets.

Money factor

A money factor, also called a lease factor, is the finance charge you pay on an automobile lease. Unlike interest rates, which are expressed as a percentage of the amount borrowed, the money factor is usually stated as a decimal.

You can calculate the actual interest rate you're paying by multiplying the decimal by 24. So, for example, if you're quoted a money factor of 0.00297, the rate you're paying is 7.13% ($0.00297 \times 24 = 0.07128$).

You may find that the money factor is non-negotiable.

Money manager

Registered money managers are paid professionals who are responsible for handling the securities portfolios they oversee in the best interest of the institutions or individuals for whom they work. That obligation is known as fiduciary responsibility.

The specific decisions an individual money manager makes vary, depending on the portfolio in question. For example, pension funds, mutual funds, and insurance companies have money managers, as do endowments, managed accounts, and hedge funds.

The portfolio that the manager constructs and the amount and timing of the trading he or she authorizes are directly linked to the portfolio's investment objective and risk profile.

Money market

The money market isn't a place. It's the continual buying and selling of short-term liquid investments.

Those investments include Treasury bills, certificates of deposit (CDs), commercial paper, and other debt issued by corporations and governments. These investments are also known as money market instruments.

Money market account

Bank money market accounts normally pay interest at rates comparable to those offered by money market mutual funds or money market separate accounts offered under a variable annuity contract.

One appeal of money market accounts is that they have the added safety of Federal Deposit Insurance Corporation (FDIC) protection, up to the limit per depositor and account type.

One drawback may be that some banks reduce the interest they pay or impose fees if your balance falls below a specific amount.

Money market accounts may offer check writing and cash transfer privileges, although there are usually limits on the number of withdrawals or transfers you can make each month.

Money market fund

Money market mutual funds invest in stable, short-term debt securities, such as commercial paper, Treasury bills, and certificates of deposit (CDs), and other short-term instruments.

The fund's management tries to maintain the value of each share in the fund at $1.

Unlike bank money market accounts, money market mutual funds are not insured by the Federal Deposit Insurance Corporation (FDIC).

However, since they're considered securities at most brokerage firms, they may be insured by the Securities Investor Protection Corporation (SIPC) against the bankruptcy of the firm. In addition, some funds offer private insurance comparable to FDIC coverage.

Tax-free money market funds invest in short-term municipal bonds and other tax-exempt short-term debt. No federal income tax is due on income distributions from these funds, and in some cases no state income tax.

While taxable funds may offer a slightly higher yield than tax-free funds, you pay income tax on all earnings distributions.

Many money market funds offer check-writing privileges, which do not trigger capital gains or losses, as writing a check against the value of a stock or bond fund would.

Money order

A money order entitles the person named as payee on the order to receive the specific amount of cash shown on the order.

You can use money orders in place of checks if you don't have a checking account or if the payee requires a guaranteed form of payment. You can purchase money orders at banks, post office branches, credit unions, and other financial institutions.

You can use money orders to send money internationally as well as within the United States. The United States Postal Service (USPS) has agreements with 30 countries that allow recipients to cash USPS money orders in post offices in those countries.

Sellers sometimes impose a limit on the size of the money orders they sell, and they typically charge a fee for each order. However, those fees are less than for guaranteed bank checks. One drawback of a money order is that you have no proof that payment was received.

Money purchase plan

A money purchase plan is a defined contribution retirement plan that requires the employer to contribute a fixed percentage of each employee's salary every year the plan is in effect.

The contributions must be made regardless of how well the company does in a given year. In contrast, in profit-sharing plans, the employer's contribution is more flexible because it is based on annual profits.

However, some small-company employers or self-employed people create a paired plan that combines money purchase with profit sharing. Paired plans require them to add at least a minimum percentage of each employee's salary to the plan each year.

Money supply

The money supply is the total amount of liquid or near-liquid assets in the economy.

The Federal Reserve, or the Fed, manages the money supply, trying to prevent either recession or serious inflation by changing the amount of money in circulation.

The Fed increases the money supply by buying government bonds in the open market, and decreases the supply by selling these securities.

In addition, the Fed can adjust the reserves that banks must maintain, and increase or decrease the rate at which banks can borrow money. This fluctuation in rates gets passed along to consumers and investors as changes in short-term interest rates.

The money supply is grouped into four classes of assets, called money aggregates. The narrowest, called M1, includes currency and checking deposits. M2 includes M1, plus assets in money market accounts and small time deposits.

M3, also called broad money, includes M2, plus assets in large time deposits, eurodollars, and institution-only money market funds. The biggest group, L, includes M3, plus assets such as private holdings of US savings bonds, short-term US Treasury bills, and commercial paper.

Monte Carlo simulation

A Monte Carlo simulation can be used to analyze the return that an investment portfolio is capable of producing. It generates thousands of probable investment performance outcomes, called scenarios, that might occur in the future.

The simulation incorporates economic data such as a range of potential interest rates, inflation rates, tax rates, and so on. The data is combined in random order to account for the uncertainty and performance variation that's always present in financial markets.

Financial analysts may employ Monte Carlo simulations to project the probability of your retirement account investments producing the return you need to meet your long-term goals.

Moody's Investors Service, Inc.

Moody's is a financial services company best known for rating investments. Moody's rates bonds, common stock, commercial paper, municipal short-term bonds, preferred stocks, and annuity contracts.

Its bond rating system, which assigns a grade from Aaa through C3 based on the financial condition of the issuer, has become a world standard.

Morgan Stanley Capital International Indexes

These indexes are computed by Morgan Stanley Capital International Inc. (MSCI).

They track stocks traded in international stock markets, and are benchmarks for international stock investments and mutual fund portfolios.

The strong performance of the Europe and Australasia Far East Equity Index (EAFE) between 1982 and 1996 is often credited with generating increased US interest in investing overseas. The index was considered especially strong compared to the well-known Standard & Poor's 500 Index (S&P 500).

Morningstar, Inc.

Morningstar, Inc., offers a broad range of investment information, research, and analysis online, in software products, and in print.

For example, the company rates open- and closed-end mutual funds and variable annuities, as well as other investment products, using a system of one to five stars, with five being the highest rating.

The Morningstar system is a risk-adjusted rating that brings performance, or return, and risk together into one evaluation.

In addition, Morningstar produces analytical reports on the funds and variable annuities it rates, as well as on stocks sold in US and international markets.

Mortgage

A mortgage, or more precisely a mortgage loan, is a long-term loan used to finance the purchase of real estate.

As the borrower, or mortgager, you repay the lender, or mortgagee, the loan principal plus interest, gradually building your equity in the property.

The interest may be calculated at either a fixed or variable rate, and the term of the loan is typically between 10 and 30 years.

While the mortgage is in force, you have the use of the property, but not the title to it. When the loan is repaid in full, the property is yours. But if you default, or fail to repay the loan, the mortgagee may exercise its lien on the property and take possession of it.

Mortgage-backed security

Mortgage-backed securities are created when the sponsor buys up mortgages from lenders, pools them, and packages them for sale to the public, a process known as securitization.

The securities are available through publicly held corporations such as Fannie Mae and Freddie Mac or other financial institutions. Some of the securities are guaranteed by the Government National Mortgage Association, or Ginnie Mae.

The money raised by selling the bonds is used to buy additional mortgages, making more money available to lend.

The most common mortgage-backed securities, also known as pass-through securities, are self-amortizing, and pay interest and repay principal over the term of the security.

Mortgage-backed securities known as collateralized mortgage obligations (CMOs) or real estate mortgage investment conduits (REMICs) are structured differently. While a CMO or REMIC pays interest on a regular basis, the principal payments are structured in what are known as tranches and mature in sequence.

The principal is repaid to bondholders in the order in which the tranches are stacked, so the holders of the shortest-term tranche are paid principal first, the next shortest second, and so on.

You can buy individual mortgage-backed securities or select mutual funds, such as Ginnie Mae funds, that invest in mortgage-backed securities.

Moving average

A moving average of securities prices is an average that is recomputed regularly by adding the most recent price and dropping the oldest one.

For example, if you looked at a 365-day moving average on the morning of June 30, the most recent price would be for June 29, and the oldest one would be for June 30 of the previous year.

The next day, the most recent price would be for June 30, and the oldest one for the previous July 1.

Investors may use the moving average of an individual security over a shorter period, such as 5, 10, or 30 days, to determine a good time to buy or sell that security.

For example, you might decide that a stock that is trading above its 10-day moving average is a good buy or that it's time to sell when a stock is trading below its 10-day moving average. The longer the time span, the less volatile the average will be.

Multiple

A stock's multiple is its price-to-earnings ratio (P/E). It's figured by dividing the market price of the stock by the company's earnings.

The earnings could be the actual earnings for the past four quarters, called a trailing P/E. Or they might be the actual figures for the past two quarters plus an analyst's projection for the next two, called a forward P/E.

Investors use the multiple as a way to assess whether the price they are paying for the stock is justified by its earnings potential. The higher the multiple they are willing to accept, the higher their expectations for the stock.

However, some investors reject stocks with higher multiples, since it may be impossible for the stock to meet the market's expectations.

Municipal bond (muni)

Municipal bonds are debt securities issued by state or local governments or their agencies to finance general governmental activities or special projects.

For example, a state may float a bond to fund the construction of highways or college dormitories.

The interest a muni pays is usually exempt from federal income taxes, and is also exempt from state and local income taxes if you live in the state where it was issued.

However, any capital gains you realize from selling a muni are taxable, and some muni interest may be vulnerable to the alternative minimum tax (AMT).

Municipal bonds are issued by state and local governments

Munis generally pay interest at a lower rate than similarly rated corporate bonds of the same term. However, they appeal to investors in the highest tax brackets, who may benefit most from the tax-exempt income.

Municipal bond fund

Municipal bond funds invest in municipal bonds. Interest earnings from these funds are free from federal income tax but may be subject to the alternative minimum tax (AMT).

In addition, some mutual fund companies offer funds that invest exclusively in municipal bonds offered by a single state.

One advantage of muni bond funds is that buyers can invest a much smaller amount than they would need to buy a municipal bond on their own. Another advantage is that they pay income monthly rather than semiannually.

Mutual company

A mutual company is a privately held company owned by its policyholders, depositors, or other customers. A share of the profits is distributed as dividends, allocated in proportion to the amount of business each customer does with the company.

Insurance companies, federal savings and loan associations, and savings banks are examples of mutual companies, although each type operates somewhat differently.

Mutual fund

A mutual fund is a professionally managed investment product that sells shares to investors and pools the capital it raises to purchase investments.

A fund typically buys a diversified portfolio of stock, bonds, and money market securities, or a combination of stock and bonds, depending on the investment objectives of the fund. Mutual funds may also hold other investments, such as derivatives.

A fund that makes a continuous offering of its shares to the public and will buy any shares an investor wishes to redeem, or sell back, is known as an open-end fund. An open-end fund trades at net asset value (NAV).

The NAV is the value of the fund's portfolio plus money waiting to be invested, minus operating expenses, divided by the number of outstanding shares.

Load funds—those that charge upfront or back-end sales fees—are sold through brokers or financial advisers. No-load funds are sold directly to investors by the investment company offering the fund. These funds, which don't charge sales fees, may use 12b-1 fees to pass on the cost of providing shareholder services.

All mutual funds charge management fees, though at different rates, and they may also levy other fees and charges, which are reported as the fund's expense ratio. These costs plus the trading costs, which aren't included in the expense ratio, reduce the return you realize from investing in the fund.

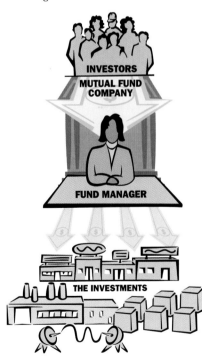

INVESTORS

MUTUAL FUND COMPANY

FUND MANAGER

THE INVESTMENTS

A fund that sells its shares to the public only until sales reach a predetermined level is known as a closed-end fund. The shares of a closed-end fund trade in the marketplace the way common stock does.

Naked option

When you write, or sell, a call option but don't own the underlying instrument, such as a stock in the case of an equity option, the option is described as naked.

Similarly, you write a naked put if you don't have enough cash on hand or in liquid investments to purchase the underlying instrument.

Because you collect a premium when you sell the option, you may make a profit if the underlying instrument performs as you expect, and the option isn't exercised.

The risk you run, however, is that the option holder will exercise the option. In the case of a call, you'll then have to buy the instrument at the market price in order to meet your obligation to sell. Or, if it's a put, you'll have to come up with the cash to purchase the instrument.

If that price of the underlying has moved in the opposite direction from the one you expected, meeting your obligation could result in a substantial net loss. Because of this risk, your brokerage firm may limit your right to write naked options or require that you write them in a margin account.

Named perils policy

A named perils policy is a standard homeowners insurance policy that offers limited protection for damage from fire and theft and other hazards specified in the policy.

NASD

NASD is the largest self-regulatory organization (SRO) in the United States.

Formerly known as the National Association of Securities Dealers, NASD regulates broker-dealer firms and licenses registered representatives—better known as stockbrokers—who make a business of trading securities.

In addition, NASD regulates trading in stocks, mutual funds, variable annuities, corporate bonds, and futures and options contracts on securities, and acts as regulator for a number of securities exchanges. NASD also reviews materials that investment companies provide to their clients and prospective clients to ensure those materials comply with the relevant guidelines.

Through its BrokerCheck database, NASD provides a resource for investors to check the credentials of people and firms with whom they're considering working. The NASD website also provides investor education and alerts on current issues of importance to investors.

Finally, NASD also resolves disputes between broker-dealers and their clients, through either mediation or arbitration. NASD disciplines firms and individuals who violate the rules.

Nasdaq Composite Index

The Nasdaq Composite Index tracks the prices of all the securities traded on the Nasdaq Stock Market.

That makes it a broader measure of market activity than the Dow Jones Industrial Average (DJIA) or Standard & Poor's 500 Index (S&P 500).

On the other hand, many computer, biotechnology, and telecommunications companies are listed on the Nasdaq. So the movement of the Index is heavily influenced by what's happening in those sectors.

The Index is market capitalization weighted, which means that companies whose market values are higher exert greater influence on the Index. Market capitalization, or value, is computed by multiplying the total number of existing shares by the most recent sales price.

So, for example, if a stock with 1 million shares increases $3 in value, it has a greater impact on the changing value of the Index than a stock that also increases $3 but has only 500,000 shares.

Nasdaq Stock Market

The Nasdaq Stock Market is the world's oldest and largest electronic stock market and is now a national securities exchange and an independent self-regulatory organization (SRO).

It has no central trading location or exchange floor. Instead it uses a fully automated, open market, multiple dealer trading system, with many market makers competing to handle transactions in each individual stock.

The most active stock market in the nation, Nasdaq handles more initial public offerings than any other US exchange. It lists many emerging companies as well as industry giants, especially in biotechnology, communications, financial services, media, retail, technology, and transportation.

National Association of Securities Dealers Automated Quotation System (NASDAQ)

NASDAQ is a computerized stock trading network that allows brokers to access price quotations for stocks being traded electronically or sold on the floor of a stock exchange.

National bank

All banks in the United States are chartered by either a state government or the federal government. Federally chartered banks, called national banks, are overseen by the Comptroller of the Currency of the US Department of the Treasury.

All national banks are members of the Federal Reserve System and deposits are insured by the Federal Deposit Insurance Corporation (FDIC).

The dual banking system of federal- and state-chartered banks can be traced to the National Banking Act of 1863. The act created the new federal bank system in an attempt to impose order on what had been a chaotic situation. State banks have survived, however, and the two banking systems coexist.

National Credit Union Administration (NCUA)

The National Credit Union Administration (NCUA) is an independent federal agency that authorizes the establishment and oversees the administration of most federal- and state-chartered credit unions in the United States.

The National Credit Union Share Insurance Fund arm of the agency insures credit union deposits, just as the Federal Deposit Insurance Corporation (FDIC) does bank deposits.

NCUA is funded by member credit unions and is backed by the full faith and credit of the federal government.

National debt

The total value of all outstanding Treasury bills, notes, and bonds that the federal government owes investors is referred to as the national debt.

The government holds some of this debt itself, in accounts such as the Social Security, Medicare, Unemployment Insurance, and Highway, Airport and Airway Trust Funds. The rest is held by individual and institutional investors, both domestic and international, or by overseas governments.

There is a debt ceiling imposed by Congress, but it is typically raised when outstanding debt approaches that level.

Interest on the national debt is a major item in the federal budget, but the national debt is not the same as the federal budget deficit. The deficit is the amount by which federal spending exceeds federal income in a fiscal year.

National Market System (NMS)

The National Market System (NMS) links all the major stock markets in the United States and was developed to foster competition among them.

Federal rules require these trading centers to ensure that transactions are executed at prices at least as good as protected quotations displayed at another center. A protected quotation is one that's immediately and automatically accessible.

Negative amortization

When your loan principal increases rather than decreases because your monthly payment isn't enough to cover the loan interest, that's called negative amortization.

This can happen if you have an adjustable-rate mortgage (ARM) that specifies a payment cap, or maximum rate increase, and the interest rate rises above the cap.

Negative amortization can also occur with mortgages that have no rate adjustment caps, or those that let you make very low initial payments that don't cover the loan interest.

The promise of low initial payments may make loans that could result in negative amortization attractive, but there are substantial risks. Eventually, your monthly payment will have to increase, sometimes sharply, to pay off the larger loan.

If interest rates have risen, you may not be able to refinance at a favorable rate. And if real estate prices fall, you could find yourself with a mortgage loan that is larger than the value of your home.

Negative yield curve

A negative, or inverted, yield curve results when the yield on short-term US Treasury issues is higher than the yield on long-term Treasury bonds.

You create the curve by plotting a graph with yield on the vertical axis and maturity date on the horizontal axis and connecting the dots. When the curve is negative the highest point is to the left.

A positive yield curve—one that's higher on the right—results when the yield on long-term bonds is higher than the yield on the short-term bills. A level curve results when the yields are essentially the same.

In most periods, the yield curve is positive because investors demand more for tying up their money for a longer period. But there are times, such as when interest rates seem to be on the upswing, that the pattern is reversed and the yield curve is negative.

Negotiable

A negotiable contract is one whose terms can be altered by agreement between the parties to the contract.

For example, when you negotiate the sale of your home, you might be willing to reduce the price, or you might be flexible about the closing date, generally in response to some concessions from the buyer.

Similarly, the interest rate on your mortgage or the number of points you pay might be negotiable with your lender.

A negotiable financial instrument or security is one that can be transferred easily from one party to another by endorsing and delivering the appropriate documentation.

Stock certificates are negotiable, for example, requiring the owner simply to sign the back and deliver the document to an agent. A check is also negotiable, transferring money from the writer to the payee on the basis of a signature and an endorsement.

Negotiable-order-of-withdrawal account

A negotiable-order-of-withdrawal (NOW) account is an interest-bearing checking account that pays interest on the balance, usually at a rate comparable to a money market account.

You may be required to maintain a fairly substantial minimum balance in a NOW account to avoid high fees or loss of interest, or both.

Net asset value (NAV)

The NAV is the dollar value of one share of a fund. It's calculated by totaling the value of all the fund's holdings plus money awaiting investment, subtracting operating expenses, and dividing by the number of outstanding shares.

A fund's NAV changes regularly, though day-to-day variations are usually small.

The NAV is the price per share an open-end mutual fund pays when you redeem, or sell back, your shares. With no-load mutual funds, the NAV and the offering price, or what you pay to buy a share, are the same. With front-load funds, the offering price is the sum of the NAV and the sales charge per share and is sometimes known as the maximum offering price (MOP).

NET ASSET VALUE (NAV)

$$\frac{\text{Value of funds holdings}}{\text{Outstanding shares}} = \frac{\text{NET ASSET}}{\text{VALUE}}$$

The NAV of an exchange traded fund (ETF) or a closed-end mutual fund may be higher or lower than the market price of a share of the fund. With an ETF, though, the difference is usually quite small because of a unique mechanism that allows institutional investors to buy or redeem large blocks of shares at the NAV with in-kind baskets of the fund's stocks.

Net change

The difference between the closing price of a stock, bond, or mutual fund, or the last price of a commodity contract, and the closing price on the previous day is reported as net change. It may also simply be referred to as change.

When a stock has gained in value, the positive net change is expressed with a plus sign and a number, such as +0.50, meaning that the price was up 50 cents from the previous trading day.

On days that a stock falls, the negative net change is expressed with a minus sign and a number, such as -1, meaning that the price was a dollar lower.

Net margin

A company's net margin, typically expressed as a percentage, is its net profit divided by its net sales. Net profit and net sales are the amounts the company has left after subtracting relevant expenses from gross profits and gross sales.

The higher the percentage, the more profitable the company is. Fundamental analysts use net margin, sometimes called net profit margin, as a way to assess how effective the company is in converting income to profit.

In general, a higher net margin is the result of an appropriate pricing structure and effective cost controls.

Net worth

A corporation's net worth is the retained earnings, or the amount left after dividends are paid, plus the money in its capital accounts, minus all its short- and long-term debt. Its net worth is reported in the corporation's 10-K filing and annual report.

Net worth may also be called shareholder equity, and it's one of the factors you consider in evaluating a company in which you're considering an investment.

To figure your own net worth, you add the value of the assets you own, including but not limited to cash, securities, personal property, real estate, and retirement accounts, and subtract your liabilities, or what you owe in loans and other obligations.

NET WORTH

$$\frac{\text{Value of assets}}{\text{- Liabilities}}$$
$$\text{NET WORTH}$$

If your assets are larger than your liabilities, you have a positive net worth. But if your liabilities are more than your assets, you have a negative net worth. When you apply for a loan, potential lenders are likely to ask for a statement of your net worth.

Netting

Netting is a process the National Securities Clearing Corporation (NSCC) uses to streamline securities transactions.

To net, the NSCC compares all the buy and sell orders for each individual security and matches purchases by clients of one brokerage firm with corresponding sales by other clients of the firm.

Those orders can be finalized internally by adjusting the firm's books to reflect changes in ownership.

The small percentage of trades that aren't netted require firms with net short positions, whose clients sold more than they purchased, to deliver the required securities to the NSCC, or more precisely have them debited from their Depository Trust Corporation (DTC) custodial account for delivery to the NSCC.

The NSCC credits those shares to the firms with a net long position, whose clients purchased more shares than they sold.

In the final step, the DTC nets the total costs of buying and selling throughout the trading day to limit the amount of money that must be exchanged among firms. Firms with a net debit wire payment to the DTC, and firms with a net credit receive funds.

New issue

When a stock or bond is offered for sale for the first time, it's considered a new issue.

New issues can be the result of an initial public offering (IPO), when a private company goes public, or they can be additional, or secondary, offerings from a company that's already public.

For example, a public company may sell bonds from time to time to raise capital. Each time a new bond is offered, it's considered a new issue.

New York Stock Exchange (NYSE)

The New York Stock Exchange (NYSE) is one of the two securities exchanges operated by the NYSE Group, Inc. It's the oldest securities exchange in the United States and the largest traditional exchange in the world.

Trading on the floor of the exchange is by double auction system, handled by floor brokers representing buyers and sellers, and by specialists—one for each listed security.

NYSEArca, the other NYSE Group exchange, is an all-electronic market, where trading is direct and anonymous.

New York Stock Exchange Composite Index

This New York Stock Exchange Composite Index measures the performance of the common stocks listed on the NYSE, including those of companies head-quartered in the United States and in other countries.

NYSE

The Index is market capitalization weighted, so that companies with the most shares and the highest prices have the greatest impact on the changing value of the Index.

Nikkei Stock Average

The Nikkei Stock Average, sometimes call the Nikkei Index or simply the Nikkei, is a price-weighted index of 225 blue chip stocks traded on the Tokyo Stock Exchange.

The Nikkei, which was introduced in 1950, is frequently described as the Japanese equivalent of the Dow Jones Industrial Average (DJIA).

No-load mutual fund

You buy a no-load mutual fund directly from the investment company that sponsors the fund. You pay no sales charge, or load, on the fund when you buy or sell shares.

No-load funds may charge a redemption fee if you sell before a certain time has elapsed in order to limit short-term turnover.

Some fund companies charge an annual fee, called a 12b-1 fee, to offset their marketing costs. Your share of this fee is a percentage of the value of your holdings in the fund.

You may also be able to buy no-load funds through a mutual fund network, sometimes known as a mutual fund super-market, typically sponsored by a discount brokerage firm. If you have an account with the firm, you can choose among no-load funds sponsored by a number of different investment companies.

Load funds and no-load funds making similar investments tend to produce almost equivalent total returns over the long term—say ten years or more. But it can take an investor nearly that long to offset the higher cost of buying load funds.

Nominal yield

Nominal yield is the annual income that you receive from a bond or other fixed-income security divided by the par value of the security.

The result, stated as a percentage, is the same as the rate of interest the security pays, also known as its coupon rate.

If you purchase the security in the secondary market, at a price above or below par, your actual yield will be more or less than the coupon rate.

So, for example, if you have $55 in annual income on a $1,000 bond, the nominal yield is 5.5%. But if you paid $975 for the bond in the marketplace, your actual yield is 5.64%. Similarly, if you had paid $1,050, your actual yield would be 5.23%.

Nominee name

Nominee name is the name that a brokerage firm uses to register ownership of stocks or bonds it holds for investors.

Holding stock in a single generic name, sometimes known as street name, makes it easier to transfer ownership when the securities are traded.

Nonbank banks

Nonbank banks, also called limited-service banks, offer some but not all the services of a traditional commercial bank.

They're typically owned by companies, including insurance companies, brokerage firms, and retail stores to provide financial services without being limited by the regulations that govern traditional banks, such as restrictions on interstate and branch banking.

Many nonbank banks are insured by the Federal Deposit Insurance Corporation (FDIC). Those banks are subject to the same reserve requirements and examinations as regular banks.

Opponents of nonbank banks believe they drain financial resources away from small towns to big cities in other states and undermine the nation's decentralized banking system.

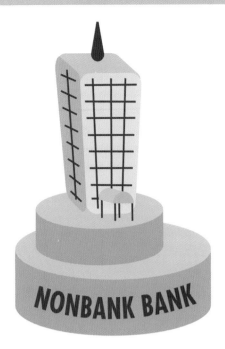

NONBANK BANK

Noncallable

When a bond is noncallable, the issuer cannot redeem it before the stated maturity date. Some bonds have call protection for their full term, and others for a fixed period—often ten years.

The appeal of a noncallable bond is that the issuer will pay interest at the stated coupon rate for the bond's full term. In contrast, if a bond is called, you receive a lump-sum repayment of principal, which you must reinvest.

Frequently, rates are lower at call that they were when the bond was issued, which means your reinvested principal will provide a smaller yield.

Noncompetitive bid

Investors who can't or don't wish to meet the minimum purchase requirements for competitive bidding on Treasury bills or notes may enter a noncompetitive bid.

You can invest as little as $1,000 or as much as $5 million in each new issue through Treasury Direct. Treasury Direct is a system that allows you to buy government securities without going through a bank or a brokerage firm.

The Treasury sells T-bills, for example, to all noncompetitive buyers whose bids arrive by the weekly deadline, for a price equal to what competitive bidders pay for that week's issue.

A noncompetitive bid may also be known as a noncompetitive tender.

Nondiscrimination rule

All qualified retirement plans, including 401(k) plans, must follow nondiscrimination rules. Among other things, the rules prevent highly paid employees from receiving more generous benefits than other employees.

However, employers may offer nonqualified plans to which antidiscrimination rules don't apply. Unlike contributions to qualified plans, contributions to nonqualified plans are not tax deductible.

Nonforfeiture clause

If there is a nonforfeiture clause in your insurance policy contract, and you have let the policy lapse because you haven't paid a premium that's due, you may qualify for the benefit named in the contract for a limited time, for a smaller benefit, or for a partial refund of your premium.

However, the added protection of adding a nonforfeiture clause generally increases the premium for the policy.

Nonprofit

Charitable, cultural, and educational organizations that exist for reasons other than providing a profit for their owners, directors, or members are nonprofit organizations.

501(c)(3)

However, these organizations can generate income to pay for their activities, salaries, and overhead by charging for services, making investments, and soliciting donations and memberships.

A nonprofit arts center, for instance, may charge patrons for tickets and event subscriptions.

Nonprofits incorporate in the states where they operate and are exempt from the state income taxes that for-profit corporations must pay. Some but not all qualify for federal tax-exempt status under section 501(c)(3) of the Internal Revenue Code.

Contributions to those qualifying organizations are tax deductible, though tax rules govern the percentage of your income you may deduct for gifts to different types of nonprofits.

In exchange for these tax benefits, nonprofits must comply with some of the same financial reporting rules that for-profit corporations follow.

For instance, nonprofits generally must follow corporate governance rules and make their financial reports available to the public.

Nonqualified annuity

An annuity you buy on your own, rather than through a qualified employer sponsored retirement plan or individual retirement arrangement, is a nonqualified annuity.

Nonqualified annuities aren't governed by the federal rules that apply to qualified contracts, such as annual contribution caps and mandatory withdrawals after you turn 70½.

While there may be a 10% tax penalty for withdrawals before you turn 59½, you can generally put up to $1 million in an annuity and postpone withdrawals until you're 75 or 80 or older. Those limits are set by the state where you purchase the contract or by the annuity company.

In other ways, though, qualified and nonqualified annuities are alike. You can choose between fixed or variable contracts, and the annuity can be either deferred or immediate.

Nonsystematic risk

Nonsystematic risk results from unpredictable factors, such as poor management decisions, successful competitive products, or suddenly obsolete technologies that may affect the securities issued by a particular company or group of similar companies.

Portfolio diversification, which means spreading your investment among a number of asset subclasses and individual issuers within those subclasses, can help counter nonsystematic risk.

Not-for-profit

A not-for-profit organization pays taxes and may make a profit, but those profits are not distributed to its owners or members.

Private clubs, sports organizations, political organizations, and advocacy groups are examples of not-for-profit institutions. Contributions to these not-for-profits are not tax deductible.

Until it became a publicly traded company in 2006, the New York Stock Exchange was a not-for-profit membership association.

Note

A note is a debt security that promises to pay interest during the term that the issuer has use of the money, and to  repay the principal on or before the maturity date.

For US Treasury securities, a note is an intermediate-term obligation—as opposed to a short-term bill or a long-term bond—that matures in two, three, five, or ten years from its issue date.

NYSE Arca

NYSE Arca, one of the two securities exchanges operated by the NYSE Group, Inc., is the first open, all-electronic stock exchange in the United States.

Trades are executed quickly—electronically and anonymously—on the US market trading center with the best available price. Among the securities traded on Arca are individual stocks, exchange-traded funds, and equity options.

NYSE Arca was formed by the merger of the NYSE and Archipelago Exchange, an electronic communications network (ECN), creating what is known as a hybrid market.

Odd lot

The purchase or sale of securities in quantities of fewer than the standard trading lot—100 shares of stock or $1,000 worth of bonds—is considered an odd lot.

At one time, trading an odd lot might have cost you a slightly higher commission, but in the electronic trading environment that's generally no longer the case.

Off-board

Transactions in New York Stock Exchange (NYSE) listed securities that aren't executed on a national exchange are known as off-board transactions.

Those trades may be handled through an electronic market, such as the Nasdaq Stock Market, through an electronic communications network (ECN), or internally at a brokerage firm. The term off-board derives from the fact that the NYSE is colloquially known as the Big Board.

Offer

The offer is the price at which someone who owns a security is willing to sell it. It's also known as the ask price, and is typically paired with the bid price, which is what someone who wants to buy the security is willing to pay. Together they constitute a quotation.

Offering date

The offering date is the first day on which a stock or bond is publicly available for purchase. For example, the first trading day of an initial public offering (IPO) is its offering date.

Offering price

A security's offering price is the price at which it is taken to market at the time of issue. It may also be called the public offering price.

For example, when a stock goes public in an initial public offering (IPO), the underwriter sets a price per share known as the offering price. Subsequent share offerings are also introduced at a specific price.

When the stock begins to trade, its market price may be higher or lower than the offering price. The same is true of bonds, where the offering price is usually the par, or face, value.

In the case of open-end mutual funds, the offering price is the price per share of the fund that you pay when you buy.

If it's a no-load fund or you buy shares with a back-end load or a level load, the offering price and the net asset value (NAV) are the same. If the shares have a front-end load, the sales charge is added to the NAV to arrive at the offering price.

Offset

You offset an options or futures position by taking a second position in a contract with identical terms, buying if you sold initially or selling if you bought initially.

With the offset, you neutralize any potential obligation you had to fulfill the terms of the contract, and you may make a profit or reduce a loss with the transaction.

For example, if you'd sold an equity call option that is close to being in-the-money, you might buy an off-setting call option. That neutralizes your obligation to deliver the underlying stock if the option you sold is exercised.

In a tax context, you can use capital losses to offset an equivalent dollar amount of capital gains, or up to $3,000 in capital losses to offset ordinary income. In either case, the offset allows you to reduce the tax you owe.

Further, banks have the right of offset if a borrower defaults on a loan. That right allows a bank to seize assets in the borrower's deposit accounts with the bank to reduce or eliminate any loss on the loan.

Offshore fund

An offshore fund is a mutual fund that's sponsored by a financial institution that's based outside the United States. Unless the fund meets all the regulatory requirements imposed on domestically sponsored funds, it can't be sold in the United States.

However, an offshore fund may be sponsored by an overseas branch of a US institution, may invest in US businesses, and may be denominated, or offered for sale, in US dollars. In total, there are approximately four times as many offshore funds as there are US-based funds.

Online brokerage firm

To buy and sell securities online, you set up an account with an online brokerage firm.

The firm executes your orders and confirms them electronically. When the markets are open, the turnaround may be very fast, but you can also give buy or sell orders at any time for execution when the markets open.

You may mail the firm checks to settle your transactions or transfer money electronically from your bank account.

Some online firms are divisions of traditional brokerage firms, while others operate exclusively in cyberspace. Most of them charge much smaller trading commissions than conventional firms.

Online firms usually provide extensive investment information, including regularly updated market news, on their websites, though they do not provide one-on-one consultations.

Online trading

If you trade online, you use a computer and an Internet connection to place your buy and sell orders with an online brokerage firm.

While the orders you give online are executed immediately while the markets are open, you also have the option of placing orders at your convenience, outside normal trading hours.

Open interest

Open interest is a record of the total number of open contracts in any particular commodity or options market on any given day.

You have an open interest when you enter a futures or options contract. The contract remains open until it expires, requires delivery or settlement, or you close it by selling it or buying an offsetting contract.

Open interest is not the same thing as trading volume, which records how many contracts have been opened or closed on a particular day.

Open market

In an open market, any investor with the money to pay for securities is able to buy those securities.

US markets, for example, are open to all buyers. In contrast, a closed market may restrict investment to citizens of the country where the market is located.

Closed markets may also limit the sale of securities to overseas investors, or forbid the sale of securities in specific industries to those investors.

In some countries, for example, overseas investors may not own more than 49% of any company. In others, overseas investors may not invest in banks or other financial services companies.

The term open market is also used to describe an environment in which interest rates move up and down in response to supply and demand.

The Federal Reserve's Open Market Committee assesses the state of the US economy on a regular schedule. It then instructs the Federal Reserve Bank of New York to buy or sell Treasury securities on the open market to help control the money supply.

Open order

An order that remains on the books until it is either executed or canceled is known as an open order, or a good til canceled order (GTC).

Open outcry

When exchange-based commodities traders shout out their buy and sell orders or use a combination of words and hand signals to negotiate an order, it's known as open outcry.

When someone who shouts an offer to buy and someone who shouts an order to sell name the same price, a deal is struck, and the trade is recorded. Open outcry is one type of auction.

Open-end mutual fund

Most mutual funds are open-end funds. This means they issue and redeem shares on a continuous basis, and grow or shrink in response to investor demand for their shares.

Open-end mutual funds trade at their net asset value (NAV), and if the fund has a front-end sales charge, that sales charge is added to the NAV to determine the selling price.

NAV is the value of the fund's investments, plus money awaiting investment, minus operating expenses, divided by the number of outstanding shares.

An open-end fund is the opposite of a closed-end fund, which issues shares only once. After selling its initial shares, a closed-end fund is listed on a securities market and trades like stock. The sponsor of the fund is not involved in those transactions.

However, an open-end fund may be closed to new investors at the discretion of the fund management, usually because the fund has grown very large.

Open-market operations

Open-market operations allow the Fed to implement its monetary policy and regulate the money supply.

The Federal Reserve's Open Market Committee (FOMC) regularly instructs the securities desk of the Federal Reserve Bank of New York to buy or sell government securities as part of the process of increasing or decreasing the cash available for lending.

Opening

The first transaction in each security or commodity when trading begins for the day occurs at what's known as its opening, or opening price.

Sometimes the opening price on one day is the same as the closing price the night before. But that's not always the case, especially with stocks or contracts that are traded in after-hours markets or when other factors affect the markets when the stock or commodity is not trading.

The opening also refers to the time that the market opens for trading or the time a particular instrument begins trading. For example, New York Stock Exchange (NYSE) opens at 9:30 ET. The first transaction in a single security may be at that time or at a later time.

Opportunity cost

When you make an investment decision, there is often a next best alternative that you decided not to take, such as buying one stock and passing up the opportunity to buy a different one.

The difference between the value of the decision you did make and the value of the alternative is the opportunity cost.

If you decide to invest in a risky stock hoping to realize a high return, you give up the return you might have earned on a bond or blue chip stock. So if the risky stock fails to perform, and you only make 3% on it when you might have made 6% on a blue chip, then the opportunity cost of the risky investment is 3%.

Of course, if your stock pick pays off, there will have been no opportunity cost, because you will make more than the 6% available from the safer investment.

Businesses must also consider opportunity costs in their decision-making. If a company is considering a capital investment, it must also consider the return it would earn if, instead of going ahead with the capital project, it invested the same amount of money in some other way.

In general, a business will only make a capital investment if the opportunity cost is lower than the projected earnings from the new project.

Option

Buying an option gives you the right to buy or sell a specific financial instrument at a specific price, called the strike price, during a preset period of time.

In the United States, you can buy or sell listed options on individual stocks, stock indexes, futures contracts, currencies, and debt securities.

If you buy an option to buy, which is known as a call, you pay a one-time premium that's a fraction of the cost of buying the underlying instrument.

For example, when a particular stock is trading at $75 a share, you might buy a call option giving you the right to buy 100 shares of that stock at a strike price of $80 a share. If the price goes higher than the strike price, you can exercise the option and buy the stock at the strike price, or sell the option, potentially at a net profit.

If the stock price doesn't go higher than the strike price before the option expires, you don't exercise. Your only cost is the money that you paid for the premium.

Similarly, you may buy a put option, which gives you the right to sell the underlying instrument at the strike price. In this case, you may exercise the option or sell it at a potential profit if the market price drops below the strike price.

In contrast, if you sell a put or call option, you collect a premium and must be prepared to deliver (in the case of a call) or purchase (in the case of a put) the underlying instrument. That will happen if the investor who holds the option decides to exercise it and you're assigned to fulfill the obligation. To neutralize your obligation to fulfill the terms of the contract before an option you sold is exercised, you may choose to buy an offsetting option.

Option premium

When you buy an option, you pay the seller a nonrefundable amount, known as the option premium, for the right to exercise that option before it expires.

If you sell an option, you receive a premium from the buyer. In fact, collecting the premium is often one motive for selling options, including those you anticipate will expire without being exercised.

An option premium is not a fixed amount, and typically increases as the option moves in-the-money and decreases if it doesn't move in-the-money.

However, factors such as the price and volatility of the underlying instrument, current interest rates, and the amount of time left before the option expires also affect the premium price.

You can look at the current range of premium prices in the Options Quotations tables in newspapers or on options websites, such as the Options Clearing Corporation (OCC) website.

Options chain

Options chains are charts showing all the options currently available on a particular underlying instrument.

A chain, also called an options string, provides the latest price quotes for all those contracts as well as the most recent price for the underlying instrument and whether that price is up or down.

Because all this information is available in one place, options chains allow you to assess the market for a particular option quickly and easily. They're a popular feature of online trading and financial information sites.

Options class

An options class includes all the calls or all the puts on a single underlying instrument that share some of the same terms, such as contract size and exercise style.

For example, in the case of listed equity options, where all contracts are American-style and cover 100 shares, all the puts on Stock A are members of the same class.

Options Clearing Corporation (OCC)

The Options Clearing Corporation issues all exchange-listed securities options in the United States and guarantees all transactions in those options.

The OCC also assigns exercised options for fulfillment, and handles the processing, delivery, and settlement of all options transactions.

The OCC is responsible for maintaining a fair and orderly market in options and is overseen by the Securities and Exchange Commission (SEC). It's jointly owned by the exchanges that trade options.

For an overview of what you should know about options trading, you can check the OCC publication, "Characteristics and Risks of Standardized Options."

Options series

An options series includes all the contracts within an options class that have identical terms, including expiration date and strike price. For example, all the calls on Stock A that expire in March and have a strike price of 45 are members of the same options series.

Order imbalance

An order imbalance occurs when there are substantially more buy orders in a particular security than there are sell orders, or the reverse. The result is a wide spread between bid and ask prices.

A specialist on an exchange floor might ease a minor imbalance by purchasing shares if there was not enough demand or selling shares if there was more demand than supply.

Major imbalances typically result in a suspension of trading until the situation that caused the imbalance is resolved. Either very good or very bad news about a company may trigger an imbalance.

Order protection rule

The order protection rule, part of Regulation NMS—for National Market System—adopted by the Securities and Exchange Commission (SEC) in 2005, requires that every stock trading center establish and enforce a policy that ensures no transaction will be traded-through, or executed at a price that's lower than a protected quotation in that security displayed by another trading center.

A protected quotation is one that's immediately and automatically accessible. The order protection rule, also called Rule 611, does allow certain exceptions, which apply to limit orders, immediate-or-cancel (IOC) orders, and intermarket sweep orders (ISOs).

Original issue discount

A bond or other debt security that is issued at less than par but can be redeemed for full par value at maturity is an original issue discount security.

The appeal, from an investor's perspective, is being able to invest less up front while anticipating full repayment later on.

Issuers like these securities as well because they don't have to pay periodic interest. Instead, the interest accrues during the term of the bond so that the total interest when combined with the principal equals the full par value at maturity.

Zero-coupon bonds are a popular type of original issue discount security. The drawback, from the investor's perspective is that the imputed interest that accumulates is taxable each year even though that interest has not been paid.

The exceptions are interest on municipal zero-coupons, which are tax exempt, or on zeros held in a tax-deferred or tax-exempt accounts.

Origination fee

An origination fee is an amount, usually calculated as a percentage of a mortgage loan or home equity loan, which a lender charges for processing your application. The origination fee may be subtracted from the amount of the loan or you may pay the fee separately.

OTC Bulletin Board (OTCBB)

During the trading day, the electronic OTC bulletin board (OTCBB) provides continuously updated real-time bid and ask prices, volume information, and last-sale prices.

The OTCBB lists this information for unlisted US and overseas stocks, warrants, unit investment trusts (UITs), and American Depositary Receipts (ADRs).

It also lists Direct Participation Programs (DPPs) that are not listed on an organized market but are being traded over-the-counter (OTC).

Approximately 3,600 companies are tracked on the OTCBB. To qualify for inclusion, they must report their financial information to the Securities and Exchange Commission (SEC) or appropriate regulatory agency.

Out-of-the-money

An option is out-of-the-money when the market price of an instrument on which you hold an option is not close to the strike price.

Call options—which you buy when you think the price is going up—are out-of-the-money when the market price is below the strike price.

Put options—which you buy when you think the price of the underlying instrument is going down—are out-of-the-money when the market price is higher than the strike price.

For example, a call option on a stock with a strike price of 50 would be out-of-the-money if the current market price of the stock were $40.

And a put option at 50 on the same stock would be out-of-the-money if its market price were $60. When an option expires out-of-the-money, it has no value.

Outstanding shares

The shares of stock that a corporation has issued and not reacquired are described as its outstanding shares. Some of but not all these shares are available for trading in the marketplace.

A corporation's market capitalization is figured by multiplying its outstanding shares by the market price of one share. The number of outstanding shares is often used to derive much of the financial information that's provided on a per-share basis, such as earnings per share or sales per share.

However, some analysts prefer to use floating shares rather than outstanding shares in calculating market cap and various ratios.

Floating shares are the outstanding shares that are available for trading as opposed to those held by founding partners, in pension funds, employee stock ownership plans (ESOP), and similar programs.

Over-the-counter (OTC)

Securities that trade over-the-counter (OTC) are not listed on an organized stock exchange, such as the New York Stock Exchange (NYSE) or the Nasdaq Stock Market.

Common stocks, corporate, government, and municipal bonds (munis), money market instruments, and other products, such as forward contracts and certain options, may trade OTC.

Generally speaking, the OTC market is a negotiated market conducted between brokers and dealers using telephone and computer networks.

Overbought

When a stock or entire securities market rises so steeply in price that technical analysts think that buyers are unlikely to push the price up further, analysts consider it overbought. For these analysts, an overbought market is a warning sign that a correction—or rapid price drop—is likely to occur.

Overdraft

An overdraft is a withdrawal from a bank account that exceeds the funds you have available.

If you overdraw your account and you have overdraft protection, the bank will transfer money up to the limit on your line of credit to your account to cover the withdrawal. Although you will pay interest on the amount the bank transfers to your account from your line of credit, it is likely to be less than the substantial fees you pay for each overdraft.

Overdraft protection

Overdraft protection is a bank line of credit. It's activated if you have insufficient funds to cover a check written against your account, up to a predetermined limit.

As with other forms of credit, you are charged interest once the line of credit is activated. If you qualify for it, overdraft protection can help you avoid the fees, inconvenience, and embarrassment of accidentally bouncing a check.

However, because banks often charge relatively high interest rates for the service, it's best to repay the transferred amounts quickly. And some banks charge a monthly fee for having overdraft protection linked to your account, even if you don't use it. Others may not offer the protection on low-cost accounts.

Oversold

A stock, a market sector, or an entire market may be described as oversold if it suddenly drops sharply in price, despite the fact that the country's economic outlook remains positive.

For technical analysts, an oversold market is poised for a price rise, since there would be few sellers left to push the price down further.

Oversubscribed

An initial public offering (IPO) is over-subscribed when investor demand for the shares is greater than the number of shares being issued.

What typically happens is that the share price climbs, sometimes dramatic-ally, as trading begins in the secondary market, though the price may drop back closer to the offering price after a period of active trading.

The group of investment banks, known as a syndicate, that underwrites a hot IPO may have an agreement, known as a green shoe clause, with the issuing company to sell additional shares at the same offering price.

Overvaluation

A stock whose price seems unjustifiably high based on standard mea-sures, such as its earn-ings history, is considered overvalued.

One indication of overvaluation is a price-to-earnings ratio (P/E) significantly higher than average for the market as a whole or for the industry of which the corporation is a part. The consequence of overvaluation is usually a drop in the stock's price—sometimes a rather dramatic one.

Overweighted

When you own more of a security, an asset class, or a subclass than your target asset allocation calls for, you are said to be overweighted in that security, asset class, or subclass.

For example, if you have decided to invest 60% of your portfolio in stock and other equity investments, but your equity holdings account for 80% of your portfolio, you are overweighted in equity.

In another use of the term, a securities analyst might recommend overweighting a particular security, which you might reasonably interpret as advice to buy.

Own-occupation policy

If you purchase an own-occupation disability insurance policy, you are entitled to receive benefits if a disability prevents you from performing the skilled work for which you have been trained.

Some other disability policies pay a benefit only if you are unable to do any type of work for which you're qualified.

Paid-up policy

A paid-up policy is a whole life insurance policy for which no additional premium payments are required to keep it in force.

Generally, a standard paid-up policy lasts the rest of your lifetime or until you reach a specific age, such as 100. Some policies are designed to be fully paid up at an age specified in the contract, such as whole life policies for which you pay no more premiums after age 65.

Paper

Short-term, unsecured debt securities that a corporation issues are often referred to as paper—for short-term commercial paper. The term is sometimes used to refer to any corporate bonds, whether secured or unsecured, short or long term.

Paper profit (or loss)

If you own an asset that increases in value, any increase in value is a paper profit, or unrealized gain. If you sell the asset for more than you paid to buy it, your paper profit becomes an actual profit, or realized gain.

The same relationship applies if the asset has lost value. You have a paper loss until you sell, when it becomes a realized loss.

You owe no capital gains tax on a paper profit, though you use the paper value when calculating gains or losses in your investment portfolio, for example. The risk with a paper profit is that it may disappear before you realize it. On the other hand, you may postpone selling because you expect the value to increase further.

Par value

Par value is the face value, or named value, of a stock or bond.

With stocks, the par value, which is frequently set at $1, is used as an accounting device but has no relationship to the actual market value of the stock.

But with bonds, par value, usually $1,000, is the amount you pay to purchase at issue and the amount you receive when the bond is redeemed at maturity.

Par is also the basis on which the interest you earn on a bond is figured. For example, if you are earning 6% annual interest on a bond with a par value of $1,000, that means you receive 6% of $1,000, or $60.

While the par value of a bond typically remains constant for its term, its market value does not. That is, a bond may trade at a premium, or more than par, or at a discount, which is less than par, in the secondary market.

BUY BOND AT PAR   **RECEIVE INTEREST**   **REDEEM BOND AT PAR**

The market price is based on changes in the interest rate, the bond's rating, or other factors.

Participating policy

When policyholders have what is called a participating policy from a mutual insurance company, they are eligible to receive dividends based on the company's financial performance.

When claims are low and the company's investments perform well, dividends tend to rise. On the other hand, when claims are high and investment returns slump, dividends are likely to fall.

The dividends on a participating policy aren't guaranteed, so they may not be paid every year. Unlike the dividends paid to a company's shareholders, participating policy dividends are considered a return of premium. As a result, the dividends are not taxed as income.

Dividends may typically be paid out as cash, as additional insurance coverage, or may be used to reduce policyholders' premiums or repay policy loans. Rules vary from company to company.

Pass-through security

When a corporation or government agency buys loans from lenders to pool and package as securities for resale to investors, the products may be pass-through securities.

That means regular payments of interest and return of principal that borrowers make on the original loans are funneled, or passed through, to the investors.

Unlike standard bonds, whose principal is repaid at maturity, the principal of a pass-through security is repaid over the life of the debt.

The best known pass-throughs are the mortgage-backed bonds offered by Fannie Mae, Freddie Mac, and Ginnie Mae. However, you can also buy pass-through securities backed by car loans, credit card debt, and other types of borrowing. Those are known as asset-backed securities.

Passive income

You collect passive income from certain businesses in which you aren't an active participant.

They may include limited partnerships where you're a limited partner, rental real estate that you own but don't manage, and other operations in which you're an investor but have a hands-off relationship.

For example, if you invest as a limited partner, you realize passive income or passive losses because you don't participate in operating the partnership and have no voice in the decisions the general partner makes.

In some cases, income from renting real estate is also considered passive income. On the other hand, any money you earn or realize on your investment portfolio of stocks, bonds, and mutual funds is considered active income. That includes dividends, interest, annuity payments, capital gains, and royalties.

Any losses you realize from selling investments in your portfolio are similarly active losses.

Internal Revenue Service (IRS) regulations differentiate between passive and active income (and losses) and allow you to offset passive income only with passive losses and active income with active losses.

Passive losses

You have passive losses from businesses in which you aren't an active participant. These include limited partnerships, such as real estate limited partnerships, and

other types of activities that you don't help manage.

You can deduct losses from passive investments against income you earn on similar ventures. For example, you can use your losses from rental real estate to reduce gains from other limited partnerships.

Or you can deduct those losses from any profits you realize from selling a passive investment. However, you can't use passive losses to offset earned income, income from your actively managed businesses, or investment income.

Passively managed

An index mutual fund or exchange traded fund is described as passively managed because the securities in its portfolio change only when the make-up of the index it tracks is changed.

For example, a mutual fund that tracks the Standard & Poor's 500 Index buys and sells only when the S&P index committee announces which companies have been added to and dropped from the index.

In contrast, when mutual funds are actively managed, their managers select investments with an eye to enabling the fund to achieve its investment objective and outperform its benchmark index. Their portfolios tend to change more frequently as a result. They also tend to have higher fees.

The performance of passively managed indexed investments and their risk profiles tend to correspond closely to the asset class or subclass that the index tracks. They tend to be more popular in bull markets when their returns reflect the market strength and less popular in bear markets when active managers may provide stronger returns.

Payable-on-death

A bank account titled payable-on-death (POD) lets you name one or more beneficiaries to whom the assets are paid when you die.

POD accounts can be useful estate planning tools in the states where they are available, since the assets in the account can pass to your beneficiaries directly, outside the probate process.

A similar type of registration is available in some states for securities and brokerage accounts, known as transferable-on-death, or TOD, accounts.

Payout ratio

A payout ratio, expressed as a percentage, is the rate at which a company distributes earnings to its shareholders in the form of dividends.

For example, a company that earns $5 a share and pays out $2 a share has a payout ratio of 2 to 5, or 40%.

A normal range for companies that do pay dividends is 25% to 50% of earnings. But the percentage may vary if a company keeps the amount of its dividend consistent with past dividends regardless of a drop in its earnings.

Penny stock

Stocks that trade for less than $1 a share are often described as penny stocks.

Penny stocks change hands over-the-counter (OTC) and tend to be extremely volatile. Their prices may spike up one day and drop dramatically the next.

The fluctuations reflect the unsettled nature of the companies that issue them and the relatively small number of shares in the marketplace. While some penny stocks may produce big returns over the long term, many turn out to be worthless.

Institutional investors tend to avoid penny stocks, and brokerage firms typically warn individual investors of the risks involved before handling transactions in these stocks.

However, penny stocks are sometimes marketed aggressively to unsuspecting investors.

Pension

A pension is an employer plan that's designed to provide retirement income to employees who have vested—or worked enough years to qualify for the income.

These defined benefit plans promise a fixed income, usually paid for the employee's lifetime or the combined lifetimes of the employee and his or her spouse.

The employer contributes to the plan, invests the assets, and pays out the benefit, which is typically based on a formula that includes final salary and years on the job.

You pay federal income tax on your pension at your regular rate, so a percentage is withheld from each check. If the state where you live taxes income, those taxes are withheld too. However, you're not subject to Social Security or Medicare withholding on pension income.

In contrast, the retirement income you receive from a defined contribution plan depends on the amounts that were added to the plan, the way the assets were invested, and their investment performance.

The way a particular plan is structured determines if you, your employer, or both you and your employer contribute and what the ceiling on that contribution is.

Pension Benefit Guaranty Corporation (PBGC)

The PBGC was created to ensure that participants in defined benefit pension plans under its jurisdiction will receive at least a basic pension if the plans are terminated because they're underfunded and so unable to meet their obligations.

The maximum benefit is adjusted each year for plans terminated in that year to reflect increases in Social Security.

Covered plans, which include those with 25 or more participants, must pay annual premiums to the PBGC to help fund this federal corporation.

The PBGC also tries to find people who participated in, and are due benefits from, plans that are no longer operating.

Pension maximization

Pension maximization is a strategy that begins with selecting a single life annuity for income to be paid from your retirement plan, rather than a joint and survivor annuity.

The next step involves using some of your annuity income to buy a life insurance policy. At your death, the annuity income ends and the life insurance death benefit is paid to your beneficiary, often your surviving spouse.

You do receive more income from a single life annuity than from a joint and survivor annuity, which translates to a larger pension while you're alive.

However, pension max, as this approach is sometimes called, has some potentially serious drawbacks. These include the cost of the insurance premiums, including sales charges, and an increased burden on your beneficiary for turning the death benefit into a source of lifetime income.

Per capita

Per capita is the legal term for one of the ways that assets being transferred by your will can be distributed to the beneficiaries of your estate.

Under a per capita distribution, each person named as beneficiary receives an equal share. However, the way your will is drawn up and the laws of the state where the will is probated may produce different results if one of those beneficiaries has died.

For example, if you specify that your children inherit your estate per capita, in some states only those children who survive you would inherit. In other states your surviving children and the surviving descendants of your deceased children would receive equal shares. That could result in your estate being split among more heirs than if all your children outlive you.

Per stirpes

Per stirpes is the legal term for transferring the assets of your estate to your children and their descendants.

With a per stirpes distribution, each of your children who is named as a beneficiary is entitled to an equal share. If one of your children is no longer alive, that person's children or children's children divide his or her share.

For example, if you had two children each of whom had two children and one of your children died before you did, under a per stirpes bequest, your surviving child would receive 50% of your estate and the children of your deceased child would each receive 25%.

Periodic interest rate

The periodic interest rate, sometimes called the nominal rate, is the interest rate a lender charges on the amount you borrow.

Lenders are also required to tell you what a loan will actually cost per year, expressed as an annual percentage rate (APR).

The APR combines any fees the lender may charge with a year of interest charges to give you the true annual interest rate. That allows you to compare loans on equal terms.

For example, suppose you take a $10,000 loan at 10% interest. You pay an origination fee of $350, so you actually borrow $9,650. Since you are getting a smaller loan, but repaying the full $10,000 with interest, the APR is closer to 10.35%.

The periodic rate is also the interest rate a bank or other financial institution pays on amounts you deposit. If you're earning compound interest, the periodic rate will be lower than the annual percentage yield (APY).

Permanent insurance

Permanent insurance is a life insurance policy that provides a death benefit as long as you live, or in some cases until you turn 100, provided you continue to pay the required premiums.

With this type of policy, a portion of your premium pays for the insurance and the rest goes into a tax-deferred account in your name.

With many permanent life policies, you can borrow against the cash value that has accumulated in the tax-deferred account. Any amount that you've borrowed and have not repaid at the time of your death reduces the death benefit.

If you terminate the policy, you get the cash surrender value back. Cash surrender value is the cash value minus fees and expenses.

Permanent life insurance, also known as cash value insurance, is available in several varieties, including conventional policies known as straight life or whole life, as well as universal life and variable universal life.

Personal identification number (PIN)

A personal identification number is a combination of numbers, letters, or both that you use to access your checking and savings accounts, credit card accounts, or investment accounts electronically.

You also need a PIN to authorize certain debit card purchases as well as for identification in other situations, such as accessing cell phone messages.

A PIN is one way to help protect your accounts against unauthorized use since presumably no other person would know the four- to six-letter code you have chosen. PINs are not foolproof, however, if you don't take steps to ensure that your code remains private.

Phantom gains

Phantom gains are capital gains on which you owe tax even if your actual return on the investment is negative.

For instance, if a mutual fund sells stock that has increased in price, you, as a fund shareholder, are liable for taxes on the portion of the gain the fund distributes to you.

The rule applies even if you bought shares of the fund after the stock price increased, and didn't benefit from the stock's rising value. You also owe the tax if you purchase shares in the fund after the stock has been sold but before the fund has made its distribution.

Phantom gains can also occur in a falling market, when a mutual fund may sell investments to raise cash to repurchase shares from shareholders who are leaving the fund.

If you're still an owner of the fund at the time any gains from those sales are distributed, you'll owe tax even though the value of your investment has decreased.

Phishing

Phishing is one way that identity thieves use the Internet to retrieve your personal information, such as passwords and account numbers.

The thieves' techniques include sending hoax emails claiming to originate from legitimate businesses and establishing phony websites designed to capture your personal information.

For example, you may receive an urgent email claiming to come from your bank and directing you to a website where you're asked to update or verify your account number or password. By responding you give identity thieves an opportunity to steal your confidential information.

Phishing is difficult to detect because the fraudulent emails and websites are often indistinguishable from legitimate ones and the perpetrators change identities regularly.

Piggyback

A broker who piggybacks acts illegally by buying or selling a security for his or her own account after—and presumably because—a client has authorized that same transaction.

One speculation is that a broker in this situation thinks the client is acting on information that the broker doesn't have.

Pink Sheets

Pink Sheets LLC is a centralized financial information network.

It provides current prices and other information in both print and electronic formats to the over-the-counter (OTC) securities markets.

Its Electronic Quotation Service reports real-time OTC equity and bond quotations to market makers and brokers, and its website provides a broad range of historical and current data.

The name pink sheet derives from the pink paper on which the National Quotation Bureau originally printed information on OTC stocks. Comparable information on OTC bonds was printed on yellow paper.

PITI

PITI is an acronym for principal, interest, taxes, and insurance—the four elements of a monthly mortgage payment.

Principal is the loan amount. Interest is the rate at which the finance charge you pay for borrowing is calculated. Taxes are the real estate taxes for which you are responsible, and insurance is the homeowners insurance that your lender requires you to have.

If your lender also requires private mortgage insurance (PMI), this amount may be included in the monthly payment or paid separately. Lenders use PITI to calculate your monthly mortgage obligation and how much you can afford to borrow. Most lenders prefer that you spend no more than 28% of your gross monthly income on PITI.

Plan administrator

A plan administrator is the person or company your employer selects to manage its retirement savings plan. The administrator works with the plan provider to ensure that the plan meets government regulations.

PLAN MANAGER

The administrator is also responsible for ensuring employees have the information needed to enroll, select, and change investments in the plan, apply for a loan if the plan allows loans, and request distributions.

Plan participant

If you're enrolled in an employee retirement plan, such as a 401(k) or pension plan, you're a plan participant with certain rights and protections guaranteed by federal rules.

The plan in which you participate may be subject to administration and investment rules set by the Employee Retirement Income Security Act (ERISA).

As a participant, you have the right to certain information about your plan, such as a summary plan description, which outlines how it works. You also have the right to see copies of the tax reporting form that your plan must file with the IRS each year (Form 5500), as well as statements showing your estimated retirement benefits. If you have problems with your plan, you also have the right to bring claims against it.

Plan provider

The plan provider of a retirement savings plan, such as a 401(k), 403(b),

or 457 plan, is the mutual fund company, insurance company, brokerage firm, or other financial services company that creates, sells, and manages the plan your employer selects.

Plan sponsor

The plan sponsor of a retirement savings plan is an employer who offers a retirement savings plan to employees.

The sponsor is responsible for choosing the plan, the plan provider, and the plan administrator, and for deciding which investments will be offered through the plan.

Points

The term points can mean different things in different contexts.

With regard to stock, a point represents a $1 change in market price, so if a share of stock rises two points, its price has risen $2. With bonds, a point is a 1% change above or below its par, or face, value, so if a bond has a par value of $1,000, a point equals $10.

But in the case of futures and options, a point usually represents a price change of one-hundredth of one cent. And you may also hear about points if you're applying for a mortgage.

In this case, points—also called discount points—are prepaid interest some lenders require at closing as a condition of approving the loan. One point is 1% of the mortgage principal, or 100 basis points. So if you are borrowing $200,000 and your lender charges 2 points, you owe $4,000, in addition to other closing costs.

Prepaid interest is tax deductible in most cases, and your long-term interest rate will be lowered slightly—often 0.25% or 25 basis points—for each point you pay. But because points increase your closing costs, you may decide to choose a lender that doesn't require points if you plan to move or refinance within a few years.

Policyholder or policy owner

If you own an insurance contract or policy, you are a policyholder, also known as the policy owner.

As a policyholder, you may also be the person covered by the policy—referred to as the insured—although you may own a policy that names someone else as the insured.

Policyholders have certain rights. For instance, if you're the policyholder for a life insurance policy, you can change the beneficiary or transfer ownership of the policy to someone else.

In contrast, if you're covered by a group policy, such as a group health policy or group life insurance policy offered by an employer, the policyholder is the organization that offers you a chance to participate in the coverage. You may be given certain options, but in this case you're not the policyholder.

Portable benefits

Benefits or accumulated assets that you can take with you when you leave your employer or switch jobs are described as portable.

For instance, if you contribute to a 401(k), 403(b), 457, or other defined contribution plan at your current job, you can roll over your assets to an individual retirement account (IRA) or to a new employer's plan if the plan accepts rollovers.

In contrast, credits accumulated toward benefits from a pension—otherwise known as a defined benefit plan—usually aren't portable.

Insurance benefits under an employer sponsored group health plan may also be portable as the result of The Health Insurance Portability and Accountability Act (HIPAA). If you have had group coverage and move to a new employer who offers health insurance, your new group health plan can't impose exclusions for preexisting conditions.

HIPAA may also give you a right to purchase individual coverage if you are not eligible for group health plan coverage and have exhausted the 18-month extension of your previous coverage under the Consolidated Omnibus Budget

Reconciliation Act (COBRA) or similar coverage.

Other job benefits, such as health savings accounts (HSAs), are also be portable, but flexible spending plans (FSAs) are not.

Portfolio

If you own more than one security, you have an investment portfolio.

You build your portfolio by buying additional stock, bonds, annuities, mutual funds, or other investments. Your goal is to increase the portfolio's value by selecting investments that you believe will go up in price.

According to modern portfolio theory, you can reduce your investment risk by creating a diversified portfolio that includes different asset classes and individual securities chosen from different segments, or subclasses, of those asset classes. That diversification is designed to take advantage of the potential for strong returns from at least some of the portfolio's investments in any economic climate.

Portfolio manager

A portfolio manager is responsible for overseeing a collection of investments, either for an institution—such as a mutual fund, brokerage firm, insurance company, or pension fund—or for an individual.

It's the portfolio manager's job to invest the client's assets in a way that's appropriate to meet the client's goals. A portfolio manager develops investment strategies, selects individual investments, evaluates performance, and rebalances the portfolio as necessary.

Portfolio managers may also be referred to as fund managers or money managers and may be paid fees based on the value of the assets under management, the performance of the portfolio, or both.

Portfolio turnover

Portfolio turnover is the rate at which a mutual fund manager buys or sells securities in a fund, or an individual investor buys and sells securities in a brokerage account.

A rapid turnover rate, which frequently signals a strategy of capitalizing on opportunities to sell at a profit, has the potential downside of generating short-term capital gains.

That means the gains are usually taxable as ordinary income rather than at the lower long-term capital gains rate. Rapid turnover may also generate higher trading costs, which can reduce the total return on a fund or brokerage account.

As a result, you may want to weigh the potential gains of rapid turnover against the costs, both in your own buy and sell decisions and in your selection of mutual funds.

You can find information on a fund's turnover rate in the fund's prospectus.

Positive yield curve

A positive yield curve results when the yield on long-term US Treasury bonds is higher than the yield on on short-term Treasury bills.

You create the curve by plotting a graph with yield on the vertical axis and maturity date on the horizontal axis and connecting the dots. When the curve is positive the highest point is to the right.

In most periods, the yield curve is positive because investors demand more for tying up their money for a longer period.

When the reverse is true, and yields on short-term investments are higher than the yields on long-term investments, the curve is negative, or inverted.

That typically occurs if inflation spikes after a period of relatively stable growth or if the economic outlook is uncertain. The yield curve can also be flat, if the rates are essentially the same.

Post-trade processing

Each securities transaction goes through post-trade processing during which the details of the trade are compared, cleared, and settled.

This involves matching the details of the buy order with those of the sell order, changing the records of ownership, and finalizing the payment.

Power of attorney

A power of attorney is a written document that gives someone the legal authority to act for you as your agent or on your behalf. To be legal, it must be signed and notarized.

You may choose to give someone a limited, or ordinary, power of attorney. That authority is revoked if you are no longer able to make your own decisions.

In contrast, if you give an attorney, family member, or friend a durable power of attorney, he or she will be able to continue to make decisions for you if you're unable to make them. Not all states allow a durable power of attorney, however.

A springing power of attorney takes effect only at the point that you are unable to act for yourself.

It's a good idea have an attorney draft or review a power of attorney to be sure the document you sign will give the person you're designating the necessary authority to act for you but not more authority than you wish to assign.

You always have the right to revoke the document as long as you are able to act on your own behalf.

Preexisting condition

A preexisting condition is a health problem that you already have when you apply for insurance.

If you have a preexisting condition, an insurer can refuse to cover treatment connected to that problem for a period of time. That period is often the first six months, but may be for the entire term of your policy.

Insurers can also deny you coverage entirely because of a preexisting condition. And they can end a policy if they discover a preexisting condition that you did not report, provided you knew it existed when you applied for your policy.

However, if you're insured through your employer's plan and switch to a job that also provides health insurance, the new plan must cover you regardless of a preexisting condition.

Preapproval

When you're preapproved for a mortgage, the lender guarantees in advance the maximum you can borrow, provided your financial situation doesn't change before you find a home.

You'll need to fill out a mortgage application with the lender to be pre-approved, as well as provide verification of a regular source of income and authorize a credit check. Then the lender provides a letter confirming how much you'll be able to borrow.

The preapproval process usually takes a week or two, but it may take only a few minutes if you apply for a mortgage online. Some, but not all, lenders charge a fee for preapproval.

Preapproval is not a binding commit-ment for either the buyer or lender, but it can give you a competitive advantage. You know in advance how much you can afford, and sellers are confident your mortgage application won't be turned down. Plus it can speed the process of closing the sale.

If you're a first-time homebuyer or you're self-employed, it may be a good idea to consider getting preapproved.

Preferred provider organization (PPO)

A preferred provider organization (PPO) is a network of doctors and other health-care providers that offers discounted care to members of a sponsoring organization, usually an employer or union.

You may also arrange private insurance coverage through a PPO.

If you're insured through a PPO, you make a copayment for each visit to a healthcare provider, though certain diag-nostic tests may not require copayment.

You typically have the option to go to a doctor or other provider outside the network, but you pay a larger percentage of the cost, called coinsurance, than if you used a network doctor.

Preferred stock

Some corporations issue preferred as well as common stock.

Preferred stock can be an attractive investment because it typically pays a fixed dividend on a regular schedule. The share prices also tend to be less volatile than the prices of common stock.

In fact, preferred stock prices tend to move with changing interest rates in the same way that bond prices do. That's one reason this type of stock is sometimes described as a hybrid investment because it shares some characteristics with common stock and some with fixed-income securities.

What preferred stock doesn't gener-ally offer is the right to vote on corporate matters or the opportunity to share in the corporation's potential for increased profits in the form of increased share prices and dividend payments.

Convertible preferred shares can be exchanged for a specific number of common shares of the issuing company at an agreed-upon price. The process is similar to the way that a convertible bond can be exchanged for common stock.

Premium

A premium is the purchase price of an insurance policy or an annuity contract. You may pay the premium as a single lump sum, in regular monthly or quarterly installments, or in some cases on a flexible schedule over the term of the policy or contract.

When you pay over time, the premium may be fixed for the life of the policy, assuming the coverage remains the same. That's the case with many permanent life insurance policies.

With other types of coverage, the premium changes as you grow older or as costs for the issuing company increase.

Used in another sense, the term premium refers to the amount above face value that you pay to buy, or you receive from selling, an investment. For example, a corporate bond with a par value of $1,000 with a market price of $1,050 is selling at a $50 premium.

Prepayment penalty

Most lenders allow you to prepay the outstanding balance of a loan at any time without a fee, but some lenders charge a prepayment penalty, often about 2% of the amount you borrowed.

If your loan agreement doesn't have a prepayment clause, which excludes a fee for early termination, the penalty may apply.

Many states prohibit prepayment fees, and they're not allowed on any mortgage loans purchased by Fannie Mae or Freddie Mac. But they are allowed in other states, and lenders may offer a lower rate on loans with prepayment penalties because they are locking in their long-term profit.

Similarly lenders who offer to waive closing costs and points when you

refinance may impose a penalty if you pay off the loan within the first few years. But if you're not planning to move, this refinancing deal could save you money.

Prequalification

When you prequalify for a mortgage, the lender calculates the approximate amount you'd be able to borrow, based on your current income and debt.

Many lenders offer free mortgage calculators—sometimes called prequalification calculators—on their websites to help you estimate how large a mortgage you'd be approved for.

Since you don't complete a mortgage application or provide financial details, prequalification is not a guarantee, and simply helps you determine how much you should plan to spend on a home. But before you're approved for a mortgage, you'll have to go through the mortgage application process, including a credit check, and provide financial documentation.

Prerefunding

Prerefunding may occur when a corporation plans to redeem a callable bond before its maturity date. If that's the case, the bond is identified as a pre-refunded bond.

To prerefund, the issuer sells a second bond with a longer maturity or a lower coupon rate, or both, and invests the amount it raises in US Treasury notes or other securities that are essentially free of default risk.

The specific securities are typically chosen because their maturity dates correspond to the date on which the company will use the money to redeem the first bond.

Present value

The present value of a future payment, or the time value of money, is what money is worth now in relation to what you think it'll be worth in the future based on expected earnings.

For example, if you have a 10% return, $1,000 is the present value of the $1,100 you expect to have a year from now.

The concept of present value is useful in calculating how much you need to invest now in order to meet a certain future goal, such as buying a home or paying college tuition.

Many financial websites and personal investment handbooks provide calculators and other tools to help you compute these amounts based on different rates of return.

Inflation has the opposite effect on the present value of money, accounting for loss of value rather than increase in value. For example, in an economy with 5% annual inflation, $100 is the present value of $95 next year.

Present value also refers to the current value of a securities portfolio. If you compare the present value to the acquisition cost of the portfolio, you can determine its profit or loss.

Further, you can add the present value of each projected interest payment of a fixed income security with one year or more duration to calculate the security's worth.

Pretax contribution

A pretax contribution is money that you agree to have subtracted from your salary and put into a retirement savings plan or other employer sponsored benefit plan.

Your taxable earnings are reduced by the amount of your contribution, which reduces the income tax you owe in the year you make the contribution.

Some pretax contributions, including those you put into your 401(k), 403(b), or 457, are taxed when you withdraw the amount from your plan. Other contributions, such as money you put into a flexible spending plan, are never taxed.

Pretax income

Pretax income, sometimes described as pretax dollars, is your gross income before income taxes are withheld.

Any contributions you make to a salary reduction retirement plan, such as a traditional 401(k) or 403(b) plan, or to a flexible spending account comes out of your pretax income.

The contribution reduces your current income and the amount you owe in current income taxes.

Price improvement

Price improvement occurs when you pay less or receive more on a securities transaction than the bid and ask prices being currently quoted.

In other words, the price you pay to buy is lower than the ask price or the price you collect for selling is higher than the bid price.

Price improvement may occur for a variety of reasons, from a change in market price to the diligence of your broker in seeking out the best price. For example, your broker may fill your order from the firm's inventory or net it against a sell order from another client of the firm. Or the order might be sent to a particular market for execution if a better price is available.

Price-to-book ratio

Some financial analysts use price-to-book ratios to identify stocks they consider to be overvalued or undervalued.

You figure this ratio by dividing a stock's market price per share by its book value per share.

Other analysts argue that book value reveals very little about a company's financial situation or its prospects for future performance.

Price-to-cash flow

You find a company's price-to-cash flow ratio by dividing the market price of its stock by its cash receipts minus its cash payments over a given period of time, such as a year.

Some institutional investors prefer price-to-cash flow over price-to-earnings as a gauge of a company's value.

They believe that by focusing on cash flow, they can better assess the risks that may result from the company's use of leverage, or borrowed money.

Price-to-earnings ratio (P/E)

The price-to-earnings ratio (P/E) is the relationship between a company's earnings and its share price, and is calculated by dividing the current price per share by the earnings per share.

A stock's P/E, also known as its multiple, gives you a sense of what you are paying for a stock in relation to its earning power.

PRICE TO EARNINGS RATIO

$$\frac{\text{Current share price}}{\text{Earnings per share}} = \begin{array}{l}\text{PRICE TO} \\ \text{EARNINGS RATIO}\end{array}$$

For example, a stock with a P/E of 30 is trading at a price 30 times higher than its earnings, while one with a P/E of 15 is trading at 15 times its earnings. If earnings falter, there is usually a sell-off, which drives the price down. But if the company is successful, the share price and the P/E can climb even higher.

Similarly, a low P/E can be the sign of an undervalued company whose price hasn't caught up with its earnings potential. Conversely, a low P/E can be a clue that the market considers the company a poor investment risk.

Stocks with higher P/Es are typical of companies that are expected to grow rapidly in value. They're often more volatile than stocks with lower P/Es because it can be more difficult for the company's earnings to satisfy investor expectations.

The P/E can be calculated two ways. A trailing P/E, the figure reported in newspaper stock tables, uses earnings for the last four quarters. A forward P/E generally uses earnings for the past two quarters and an analyst's projection for the coming two.

Price-to-sales ratio

A price-to-sales ratio, or a stock's market price per share divided by the revenue generated by sales of the company's products and services per share, may sometimes identify companies that are undervalued or overvalued within a particular industry or market sector.

For example, a corporation with sales per share of $28 and a share price of $92 would have a price-to-sales ratio of 3.29, while a different stock with the same sales per share but a share price of $45 would have a ratio of 1.61.

Some financial analysts and money managers suggest that, since sales figures are less easy to manipulate than either earnings or book value, the price-to-sales ratio is a more reliable indicator of how the company is doing and whether you are likely to profit from buying its shares.

Other analysts believe that steady growth in sales over the past several years is a more valuable indicator of a good investment than the current price-to-sales ratio.

Primary market

If you buy stocks or bonds when they are initially offered for sale, and the money you spend goes to the issuer, you are buying in the primary market.

In contrast, if you buy a security at some point after issue, and the amount you pay goes to an investor who is selling the security, you're buying in the secondary market.

The term primary market also applies the leading or main markets for trading various products. For example, the New York Stock Exchange (NYSE) is a primary market for stocks.

Prime rate

The prime rate is a benchmark for interest rates on business and consumer loans.

For example, a bank may charge you the prime rate plus two percentage points on a car loan or home equity loan.

The prime rate is determined by the federal funds rate, which is the rate banks charge each other to borrow money overnight. If banks must pay more to borrow, they raise the prime rate. If their cost drops, they drop the prime rate. The difference between the two rates is three percentage points, with the prime rate always the higher number.

The federal funds rate itself is determined by supply and demand, prompted by the actions of the Open Market Committee of the Federal Reserve to increase or decrease the money supply.

Principal

Principal can refer to an amount of money you invest, the face amount of a bond, or the balance you owe on a debt, distinct from the finance charges you pay to borrow.

A principal is also a person for whom a broker carries out a trade, or a person who executes a trade on his or her own behalf.

Private equity

Private equity is an umbrella term for large amounts of money raised directly from accredited individuals and institutions and pooled in a fund that invests in a range of business ventures.

The attraction is the potential for substantial long-term gains. The fund is generally set up as a limited partnership, with a private equity firm as the general partner and the investors as limited partners.

Private equity firms typically charge substantial fees for participating in the partnership and tend to specialize in a particular type of investment.

For example, venture capital firms may purchase private companies, fuel their growth, and either sell them to other private investors or take them public. Corporate buyout firms buy troubled public firms, take them private, restructure them, and either sell them privately or take them public again.

Private letter ruling

A private letter ruling explains a position the Internal Revenue Service (IRS) has taken on a specific issue or action that affects the amount of income tax a taxpayer owes.

While these rulings are not the law, and there's no guarantee that they won't be overturned by new IRS opinions, they can provide guidance on how to handle financial decisions that have potential tax consequences. There is a fee when you request such a ruling.

Private mortgage insurance (PMI)

When you buy a home with a down payment of less than 20% of the purchase price, your lender may require you to buy private mortgage insurance (PMI), which protects the lender against the risk that you may fail to repay your loan.

The premiums you can expect to pay will vary, but typically come to about 0.5% of the total amount you borrow.

For instance, on a $150,000 mortgage, a typical annual PMI premium would be $750, which is 0.5% of $150,000. Divided into monthly payments, this premium would come out to $62.50 a month.

You can usually cancel your PMI when you meet certain criteria. Generally, this is when the balance of the mortgage is paid down to 80% of either your home's original purchase price or its appraisal value at the time you took out the loan. You can check if it's possible to cancel your PMI by reviewing your annual mortgage statements or by calling your mortgage lender.

If you forget to cancel your PMI, your lender is required by federal law to end the insurance once your outstanding balance reaches 78% of the original purchase price or appraisal value at

the time you took the loan, or you have reached the mid-point of the loan term, provided you meet certain requirements.

The lender must give you information about the termination requirement at closing. There are some exceptions to the termination rule, including high risk mortgages, VA and FHA mortgages, and those negotiated before July 29, 1999.

Private placement

If securities are sold directly to an institutional investor, such as a corporation or bank, the transaction is called a private placement.

Unlike a public offering, a private placement does not have to be registered with the Securities and Exchange Commission (SEC), provided the securities are bought for investment and not for resale.

Privatization

Privatization is the conversion of a government-run enterprise to one that is privately owned and operated. The conversion is made by selling shares to individual or institutional investors.

The theory behind privatization is that privately run enterprises, such as utility companies, airlines, and telecommunications systems, are more efficient and provide better service than government-run companies.

But in many cases, privatization is a way for the government to raise cash and to reduce its role as service provider.

Probate

Probate is the process of authenticating, or verifying, your will so that your executor can carry out the wishes you expressed in the document for settling your estate and appointing a guardian for your minor children.

While the probate process can run smoothly if everything is in order, it can also take a long time and cost a great deal of money if your will isn't legally acceptable or it's contested by potential beneficiaries who object to its terms.

If you die without a will, the same court that handles probate resolves what happens to your assets based on the laws of the state where you live through a process known as administration. The larger or more complex your estate is, the greater the potential for delay and expense.

Probate estate

Your probate estate includes all the assets that will pass to your heirs through your will.

It doesn't include anything that you have sold, given away, put into trusts, or passed directly to recipients by naming them as beneficiaries of specific accounts.

Assets you can pass directly to beneficiaries include money in retirement plans, insurance policies, payable-on-death bank accounts, and transferable-on-death securities accounts.

In addition, any property you own jointly with rights of survivorship passes directly to your co-owner outside the probate process. However, all the assets you own at the time of your death, including half the value of property you own jointly, are considered part of your estate for purposes of calculating whether estate taxes are due.

Profit

Profit, which is also called net income or earnings, is the money a business has left after it pays its operating expenses, taxes, and other current bills.

When you invest, profit is the amount you make when you sell an asset for a higher price than you paid for it. For example, if you buy a stock at $20 a share and sell it at $30 a share, your profit is $10 a share minus sales commission and capital gains tax if any.

Profit margin

A company's profit margin is derived by dividing its net earnings, after taxes, by its gross earnings minus certain expenses. Profit margin is a way of measuring how well a company is doing, regardless of size.

For example, a $50 million company with net earnings of $10 million and a $5 billion company with net earnings of $1 billion both have profit margins of 20%.

Profit margins can vary greatly from one industry to another, so it can be difficult to make valid comparisons among companies unless they are in the same sector of the economy.

Profit sharing

A profit-sharing plan is a type of defined contribution retirement plan that employers may establish for their workers.

The employer may add up to the annual limit to each employee's profit-sharing account in any year the company has a profit to share, though there is no obligation to make a contribution in any year.

The annual limit is stated as a dollar amount and as a percentage of salary, and the one which applies to each employee is the lower of the two alternatives.

Employers get a tax deduction for their contribution. Employees owe no income tax on the contributions or on any of the earnings in their accounts until they withdraw money.

In some cases, employees in the plan may be able to borrow from their accounts to pay for expenses such as buying a home or paying for college.

Profit-sharing plans offer employers certain flexibility. For example, in a year without profits, they don't have to contribute at all. And they can vary the amount of each year's contribution to reflect the company's profitability for that year.

However, each employee in the plan must be treated equally. This means that if an employer contributes 10% of one employee's salary to the plan, the employer must also contribute 10% of the salaries of all other employees in the plan.

Profit taking

Profit taking is the sale of securities after a rapid price increase to cash in on gains.

Profit taking sometimes causes a temporary market downturn after a period of rising prices as investors sell off shares to lock in their gains.

Program trading

Program trading is the purchase or sale of a basket, or group, of 15 or more stocks with the combined value of $1 million or more.

In some cases, programmed trades are triggered automatically when prices hit predetermined levels.

In other cases, institutional investors, arbitrageurs, and other large investors use program trading to take advantage of the spread between a basket of stocks replicating an index and a futures contract on the same index.

Large-scale program trading can cause abrupt price changes in a stock or group of stocks and may even have a dramatic effect on the overall market. The New York Stock Exchange (NYSE) and other exchanges have instituted a series of circuit breakers, which halt trading for a period of time when prices fall by specific percentages in a single day, to help prevent such disruption.

Progressive tax

In a progressive, or graduated, income tax system, taxpayers with higher incomes are taxed at higher rates that those with lower incomes.

Those in favor of this approach say that the greatest tax burden falls on those who can afford to carry it. Opponents argue that it imposes an unfair burden on the people whose ingenuity and hard work make the economy strong.

Proprietary fund

Proprietary mutual funds are offered for sale by the financial institution—such as a bank, investment company, or brokerage firm—that sponsors the funds.

Characteristically, the funds' names include the name of the institution. For example, a hypothetical bank called Last Bank might offer a Last Bank Growth Fund or a Last Bank Capital Appreciation Fund.

Some institutions market only their proprietary funds, while others offer both their own funds and funds sponsored by others.

Prospectus

A prospectus is a formal written offer to sell stock to the public. It is created by an investment bank that agrees to underwrite the stock offering.

The prospectus sets forth the business strategies, financial background, products, services, and management of the issuing company, and information about how the proceeds from the sale of the securities will be used.

The prospectus must be filed with the Securities and Exchange Commission (SEC) and is designed to help investors make informed investment decisions.

Each mutual fund provides a prospectus to potential investors, explaining its objectives, management team and policies, investment strategy, and performance. The prospectus also summarizes the fees the fund charges and analyzes the risks you take in investing in the fund.

Proxy

If you own common stock in a US corporation, you have the right to vote on certain company policies and elect the board of directors by casting a proxy, or vote.

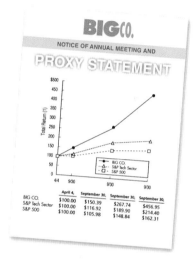

You may vote in person at the annual meeting, by phone, or online.

Proxy statement

The Securities and Exchange Commission (SEC) requires that all publicly traded companies provide a proxy statement to their shareholders prior to the annual meeting.

The proxy statement presents the candidates who have been nominated to the board of directors and any proposed changes in corporate management that require shareholder approval.

The statement also states the position the board of directors takes on the nominations and proposals. By law, the proxy statement must also present shareholder proposals even if they are at odds with the board's position.

SEC rules also require that the proxy statement shows, in chart form, the total compensation of the company's five highest paid executives and compares the stock's performance to the performance of similar companies and the appropriate benchmark.

Prudent man rule

The prudent man rule is the basic standard a fiduciary, who is responsible for other people's money, must meet.

It mandates acting as a thoughtful and careful person would, given a particular set of circumstances. A trustee, for example, observes the prudent man rule by preserving a trust's assets for its beneficiaries.

The prudent man rule has sometimes been described as a defensive approach to money management, putting greater emphasis on preservation than on growth. The newer prudent investor rule differs by putting greater emphasis on achieving a reasonable rate of return and by delegating decision-making to investment professionals.

Public company

The stock of a public company is owned and traded by individual and institutional investors.

In contrast, in a privately held company, the stock is held by company founders, management, employees, and sometimes venture capitalists.

Many privately held companies eventually go public to help raise capital to finance growth. Conversely, public companies can be taken private for a variety of reasons.

Pump and dump

In a pump and dump scheme, a scam artist manipulates the stock market by buying shares of a low-cost stock and then artificially inflating the price by spreading rumors, typically using the Internet and phone, that the stock is about to hit new highs.

Investors who fall victim to the get-rich-quick scheme begin buying up shares, and the increased demand drives up the price. At the peak of the market, the scammer sells out at a profit, shuts down the rumor mill, and disappears. The price of the stock invariably drops dramatically and the investors who got caught in the scam lose their money.

Put option

Buying a put option gives you the right to sell the specific financial instrument underlying the option at a specific price, called the exercise or strike price, to the writer, or seller, of the option before the option expires.

You pay the seller a premium for the option, and if you exercise your right to sell, the seller must buy.

Selling a put option means you collect a premium at the time of sale. But you must buy the option's underlying instrument if the option buyer exercises the option and you are assigned to meet the contract's terms.

Not surprisingly, buyers and sellers have different goals. Buyers hope that the price of the underlying instrument drops so they can sell at the exercise price, which is higher than the market price. This way, they could offset the price of the premium, and hopefully make a profit as well.

Sellers, on the other hand, hope that the price stays the same or increases, so they can keep the premium they've collected and not have to lay out money to buy.

Put-call ratio

Since investors buy put options when they expect the market to fall, and call options when they expect the market to rise, the relationship of puts to calls, called the put-call ratio, gives analysts a way to measure the relative optimism or pessimism of the marketplace.

The customary interpretation is that when puts predominate, and the mood is bearish, stock prices are headed for a tumble.

The reverse is assumed to be true when calls are more numerous. The contrarian investor, however, holds just the opposite view. For example, a contrarian believes that by the time investors are concentrating on puts, the worst is already over, and the market is poised to rebound.

Quadruple witching day

Once every quarter—on the third Friday of March, June, September, and December—stock options, stock index options, stock index futures contracts, and single stock futures expire on the same day in the United States.

In the past, when all contracts expired at the same hour of the day, trading could be extremely volatile as professional investors attempted to capitalize on pricing differences.

But in recent years, various adjustments in the trading schedule have helped to reduce the pace.

Qualified domestic trust (QDOT)

If your spouse isn't a US citizen and your estate is large enough to risk being vulnerable to estate taxes, you can use a qualified domestic trust (QDOT) to allow your spouse to enjoy the benefit of the marital deduction until his or her own death.

In short, the marital deduction means that one spouse can leave the other all his or her assets free of estate tax. The inherited assets become part of the estate of the surviving spouse, and unless the combined value is less than the exempt amount, estate tax could be due at the death of that spouse.

The difference, with a QDOT, is that at the death of the surviving, noncitizen spouse, the assets in the trust don't become part of his or her estate, but are taxed as if they were still part of the estate of the first spouse to die. Income distributions from the trust are subject to income tax alone, but distributions of principal may be subject to estate tax.

Qualified retirement plan

A qualified retirement plan is an employer sponsored plan that meets the requirements established by the Internal Revenue Service (IRS) and the US Congress.

Pensions, profit-sharing plans, money purchase plans, cash balance plans, SEP-IRAs, SIMPLEs, and 401(k)s are all examples of qualified plans, though each type works a little differently.

Employers may take a tax deduction for contributions to qualified plans, and in some plans employees may make tax-deferred contributions.

Among the other requirements, a qualified plan must provide for all eligible employees equivalently. That means the plan can't treat highly paid employees more generously than it does less-well paid employees, though one group of employees, such as those within five years of the official retirement age, may receive different treatment than another group.

In contrast, a nonqualified plan may be available to some employees and not others. In some plans, nonqualified contributions are made with after-tax dollars, either by the employer or the employee, although any earnings in the plan are tax deferred.

In other plans, future benefits are promised but contributions are not actually deposited in an account established for the employee.

Mandatory federal withdrawal rules that apply to qualified plans do not apply in the same way to nonqualified plans, though nonqualified plans are subject to stringent regulation as well.

Qualitative analysis

When a securities analyst evaluates intangible factors, such as the integrity and experience of a company's management, the positioning of its products and services, or the appeal of its marketing campaign, that seem likely to influence future performance, the approach is described as qualitative analysis.

While this type of evaluation is more subjective than quantitative analysis—which looks at statistical data—advocates of this approach believe that success or failure in the corporate world is often driven as much by qualitative factors as by financial data.

Quantitative analysis

When a securities analyst focuses on a corporation's financial data in order to project potential future performance, the process is called quantitative analysis.

This methodology involves looking at profit-and-loss statements, sales and earnings histories, and the state of the economy rather than at more subjective factors such as management experience, employee attitudes, and brand recognition.

While some people feel that quantitative analysis by itself gives an incomplete picture of a company's prospects, advocates assert that numbers tell the whole story.

Quarter

The financial world splits up its calendar into four quarters, each three months long.

If January to March is the first quarter, April to June is the second quarter, and so on, though a company's first quarter does not have to begin in January.

The Securities and Exchange Commission (SEC) requires all publicly held US companies to publish a quarterly report, officially known as Form 10-Q, describing their financial results for the quarter. These reports and the predictions that market analysts make about them often have an impact on a company's stock price.

For example, if analysts predict that a certain company will have earnings of 55 cents a share in a quarter, and the results beat those expectations, the price of the company's stock may increase. But if the earnings are less than expected, even by a penny or two, the stock price may drop, at least for a time.

However, this pattern doesn't always hold true, and other forces may influence investor sentiment about the stock.

Quasi-public corporation

In the United States, quasi-public corporations have links to the federal government although they are technically in the private sector.

This means that their managers and executives work for the corporation, not the government. And, in many cases, you can buy stock in a quasi-public corporation, expecting to share in its profits.

Many quasi-public corporations were originally federal agencies that have been privatized. Among the best known are Fannie Mae, Freddie Mac, and Sallie Mae. They securitize consumer loans and sell them in the secondary market.

The US Postal Service is also a quasi-public corporation, as is the Tennessee Valley Authority (TVA).

Qubes

The Nasdaq Stock Market sells shares in a unit investment trust (UIT) that tracks the Nasdaq 100 Stock Index.

This market capitalization weighted index includes the largest 100 companies trading on the Nasdaq and is adjusted quarterly to keep it focused on the strongest performers.

The name Qubes comes from the UIT's trading symbol: QQQQ.

Qubes resemble Standard & Poor's Depositary Receipts (SPDR), which reflect the performance of the Standard & Poor's 500 Index (S&P 500) and the DIAMOND (DIA), which tracks the Dow Jones Industrial Average (DJIA).

These investments are also described as exchange traded funds.

Quotation (Quote)

On a stock market, a quotation combines the highest bid to buy and the lowest ask to sell a stock.

For example, if the quotation on DaveCo stock is "20 to 20.07," it means that the highest price that any buyer wants to pay is $20, and the lowest price that any seller wants to take is $20.07.

How that spread is resolved depends on whether the stock is traded on an auction market, such as the New York Stock Exchange (NYSE), or on a dealer market, such as the Nasdaq Stock Market, where the price is negotiated by market makers.

R-squared

R-squared is a statistical measurement that determines the proportion of a security's return, or the return on a specific portfolio of securities, that can be explained by variations in the stock market, as measured by a benchmark index.

For example, an r-squared of 0.08 shows that 80% of a security's return is the result of changes in the market—specifically that 80% of its gains are due to market gains and 80% of its losses are due to market losses. The other 20% are the result of factors particular to the security itself.

Rally

A rally is a significant short-term recovery in the price of a stock or commodity, or of a market in general, after a period of decline or sluggishness.

Stocks that make a particularly strong recovery in a particular sector or in the market as a whole are often said to be leading the rally, a reference to the term's origins in combat, where an officer would lead his rallying troops back into battle. While a rally may signal the beginning of a bull market, it doesn't necessarily do so.

Random walk theory

The random walk theory holds that it is futile to try to predict changes in stock prices.

Advocates of the theory base their assertion on the belief that stock prices react to information as it becomes known, and that, because of the randomness of this information, prices themselves change as randomly as the path of a wandering person's walk.

This theory stands in opposition to technical analysis, whose practitioners believe you can predict future stock behavior based on statistical patterns of prior performance.

Ranking

Ranking is a method of assigning a value to an investment in relation to comparable investments by using a scale.

The scale might be a straightforward numerical (1 to 5) or alphabetical (A to E) system, or one that also uses stars, checks, or some other icon to convey the evaluation.

Research firms and individual analysts typically establish and publish their criteria—though not their methodology—for establishing their rankings.

These criteria, which also differ by investment type, may include quantitative information such as past earnings, price trends, and the issuing company's financial fundamentals, or more qualitative assessments, such as the state of the marketplace.

Ranking can be a useful tool in evaluating potential investments or in reviewing your current portfolio. Before depending on a ranking, though, you'll want to understand how it has been derived and how accurate the system for assigning the values has been over time.

Rate of return

Rate of return is income you collect on an investment expressed as a percentage of the investment's purchase price. With a common stock, the rate of return is dividend yield, or your annual dividend divided by the price you paid for the stock.

However, the term is also used to mean percentage return, which is a stock's total return—dividend plus change in value—divided by the investment amount.

With a bond, rate of return is the current yield, or your annual interest income divided by the price you paid for the bond. For example, if you paid $900 for a bond with a par value of $1,000 that pays 6% interest, your rate of return is $60 divided by $900, or 6.67%.

Rating

Rating means evaluating a company, security, or investment product to determine how well it meets a specific set of objective criteria.

For example, a bond issue may be rated along a spectrum from highest quality investment grade to speculative, or from AAA to D.

Rating typically affects the interest rate a fixed-income security must pay to attract investors, forcing lower-rated bond issuers to pay higher rates. Other investors may shun low-rated investments entirely, unwilling to take the risk that the issuer might default. However, ratings are not infallible, even in industries, such as insurance, that are regularly scrutinized.

Rating differs from ranking, which assigns the relative standing of two or more similar items in relation to each other.

Rating service

A rating service, such as A.M. Best, Moody's Investors Service, or Standard & Poor's, evaluates bond issuers to determine the level of risk they pose to would-be investors.

Though each rating service focuses on somewhat different criteria in making its evaluation, the assessments tend to agree on which investments pose the least default risk and which pose the most.

These rating services also evaluate insurance companies, including those offering fixed annuities and life insurance, in terms of how likely a provider is to meet its financial obligations to policyholders.

Real estate investment trust (REIT)

REITs are publicly traded companies that pool investors' capital to invest in a variety of real estate ventures, such as apartment and office buildings, shopping centers, medical facilities, industrial buildings, and hotels.

After an REIT has raised its investment capital, it trades on a stock market just as a closed-end mutual fund does.

There are three types of REITs: Equity REITs buy properties that produce income. Mortgage REITs invest in real estate loans. Hybrid REITs usually make both types of investments.

All three are income-producing investments, and by law 90% of a REIT's taxable income must be distributed to investors. That means the yields on REITs may be higher than on other equity investments.

Real interest rate

Your real interest rate is the interest rate you earn on an investment minus the rate of inflation.

For example, if you're earning 6.25% on a bond, and the inflation rate is 2%, your real rate is 4.25%. That's enough higher than inflation to maintain your buying power and have some in reserve, which you could use to build your investment base.

But if the inflation rate were 5%, your real rate would be only 1.25%.

Real property

Real property is what's more commonly known as real estate, or realty.

A piece of real property includes the actual land as well as any buildings or other structures built on the land, the plant life, and anything that's permanently in the ground below it or the air above it. In that sense, real property is different from personal property, which you can move from place to place with you.

Real property tax

A real property tax is a local tax on the value of real estate. The property may be assessed at full value, which is presumably the price that the owner could sell it for in the current market, or using some other valuation method.

The taxing agency, such as a county, city, town, or village, sets a tax rate, which is multiplied by the assessed value of each property to determine the tax due on that property.

You may be able to deduct real property taxes on your federal income tax return, but large deductions for real estate taxes are one of the factors that may result in your owing the alternative minimum tax (AMT).

Real rate of return

You find the real rate of return on an investment by subtracting the rate of inflation from the nominal, or named, rate of return.

For example, if you have a return of 6% on a bond in a period when inflation is averaging 2%, your real rate of return is 4%. But if inflation were 4%, your real rate of return would be only 2%.

REAL RATE OF RETURN	
Earned interest rate	10%
− Inflation rate	− 3%
REAL RATE OF RETURN	= 7%

Finding real rate of return is generally a calculation you have to do on your own. It isn't provided in annual reports, prospectuses, or other publications that report investment performance.

Real time

When an event is reported as it happens—such as a quick jump in a stock's price or the constantly changing numbers on a market index—you are getting real-time information.

Traditionally, this type of information was available to the public with a 15- or 20-minute time delay or was reported only periodically by news services.

Because of the Internet and cable TV, however, more and more individual investors have access to real-time financial news. Knowing what's happening enables you and others to make buy and sell decisions based on the same information that institutional investors and financial services organizations are using.

Real time, when used in computer technology, means that there is an interactive program that collects data and reports results immediately. The alternative, called batch processing, occurs when data is collected, stored, and then reported later in the evening or the next day.

Realized gain

When you sell an investment for more than you paid, you have a realized gain.

For example, if you buy a stock for $20 a share and sell it for $35 a share, you have a realized gain of $15 a share. In contrast, if the price of the stock increases, and you don't sell, your gain is unrealized, or a paper profit.

Realizing your gains means you lock in any increase in value, which could potentially disappear if you continued to hold the investment.

But it also means you may owe tax on that profit when you sell unless the investment is tax exempt or you hold it in a tax-deferred or tax-free account. In a tax-deferred account, you can postpone paying the tax until you begin withdrawing from the account.

However, if taxes are due and you have owned the investment for more than a year when you sell, you pay tax at the long-term capital gains rate, which, for most types of investments, is lower than the rate at which you pay federal income tax on ordinary income.

Recapture

When you recapture assets, you regain them, usually because of the provisions of a contract or legal precedent.

When a contract is involved, you may be entitled to recapture a percentage of the revenues from something you produce in addition to being paid the cost of producing it.

For example, a hotel developer might be entitled to recapture a portion of the hotel's profits. Most of the time, recapture works in your favor, but depending on the situation, it can also mean a financial loss.

A negative form of recapture occurs when the government makes you repay tax benefits that you've profited from in the past. For example, say that your divorce settlement calls for you to pay $150,000 to your ex-spouse over three years. If you pay all the money in the first two years in order to qualify for a tax deduction, and pay nothing in the third year, the IRS may force you to recapture part of your deduction in the third year and pay taxes on it.

Recession

Broadly defined, a recession is a downturn in a nation's economic activity. The consequences typically include increased unemployment, decreased consumer and business spending, and declining stock prices.

Recessions are typically shorter than the periods of economic expansion that they follow, but they can be quite severe even if brief. Recovery is slower from some recessions than from others.

The National Bureau of Economic Research (NBER), which tracks recessions, describes the low point of a recession as a trough between two peaks, the points at which a recession began and ended—all three of which can be identified only in retrospect.

The Conference Board, a business research group, considers three consecutive monthly drops in its Index of Leading Economic Indicators a sign of decline and potential recession up to 18 months in the future. The Board's record in predicting recessions is uneven, having correctly anticipated some but expected others that never materialized.

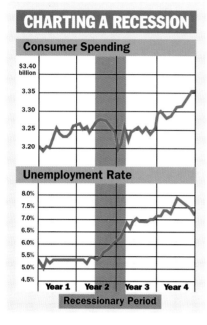

CHARTING A RECESSION

Consumer Spending

Unemployment Rate

Year 1 | Year 2 | Year 3 | Year 4
Recessionary Period

Recharacterization

When you have converted one type of individual retirement account (IRA) to another type—such as a traditional IRA to a Roth IRA—and then convert it back to the original type, you are recharacterizing the IRA.

Similarly, you can recharacterize a contribution you've made to one type of IRA as a contribution to another type of IRA. In either case, when the recharacterization is handled correctly, the original conversion or contribution is erased, as if it never happened. To be valid, a recharacterization must be handled as a transfer between IRA providers or internally by a single provider.

Further, it must be completed before the date your tax return is due, including extensions. You must also report the action to the IRS, and in some cases, you must file an additional form.

Record date

To be paid a stock dividend, you must own the stock on the day that the corporation's board of directors names as the record date, also known as the date of record.

For example, if a company declares a dividend of 50 cents a share payable on September 1 to shareholders of record as of August 10, you must own the shares on August 10 to be entitled to the dividend.

To be the legal owner on the record date you must buy the stock at least three

business days before the record date. That is the last day on which trades will settle on the record date.

If you buy the stock after that day, you are buying the stock ex-dividend, which means you are not entitled to the dividend. The first day the buyer is not entitled to receive the dividend is called the ex-dividend date and is currently two days before the record date in most cases.

Red herring

When a security is offered to the public for the first time, the underwriter prepares a preliminary prospectus, called a red herring.

While the name may refer to the parts of the document printed in red ink, the implication is that the document has been written to present the company in the best possible light. The reference is to the rather distinctive odor of the fish in question, which, the story goes, fleeing fugitives sometimes used to throw bloodhounds off their scent.

Although the preliminary prospectus contains important information about the company, its offerings, financial projections, and investment risk, it is customarily revised before the final version is issued.

Redemption

When a fixed-income investment matures, and you get your investment amount back, the repayment is known as redemption.

Bonds are usually redeemed at par, or face value, traditionally $1,000 per bond. However, if a bond issuer calls the bond, or pays it off before maturity, you may be paid a premium, or a certain dollar amount over par, to compensate you for lost interest.

You can redeem, or liquidate, open-end mutual fund shares at any time. The fund buys them back at their net asset value (NAV), which is the dollar value of one share in the fund.

Redemption fee

Some open-end mutual funds impose a redemption fee when you sell shares in the fund, often during a specific, and sometimes brief, period of time after you purchase those shares.

The fee is usually a percentage of the value of the shares you sell, but it may also be a flat fee, or fixed amount.

The purpose of the fee is to prevent large-scale withdrawals from the fund in response to changes in the financial markets, which might require the fund manager to sell holdings at a loss in order to meet the fund's obligation to buy back your shares.

Refinancing

Refinancing is the process of paying off an existing loan by taking a new loan and using the same property as security.

Homeowners may refinance to reduce their mortgage expense if interest rates have dropped, to switch from an adjustable to a fixed rate loan if rates are rising, or to draw on the equity that has built up during a period of rising home prices.

Closing costs for a refinance are generally comparable to those for any mortgage. If you're refinancing to reduce your payments, you'll want to calculate how long it will take before you recover the closing costs and begin to save money.

If you're planning to move within a few years, refinancing may not actually save you enough to justify the closing expenses. And if you refinance to use some of your home equity, you run the added risk that prices could drop and you could end up owing more on your mortgage than you could realize from selling your home.

Regional exchange

Stock exchanges in cities other than New York are called regional exchanges. They list both regional stocks, which may or may not be listed on the New York exchanges, as well as stocks that are listed in New York.

Because of the National Market System, securities listed on one exchange can be traded on any other exchange if the price there is better than the price on the exchange where the stock is listed.

The number of regional exchanges is shrinking, however, as the result of mergers and acquisitions by larger exchanges.

Registered bond

When a bond is registered, the name of the owner and the particulars of the bond are recorded by the issuer or the issuer's agent.

When registered bonds are issued in certificate form, a bond can be sold only if the owner endorses the certificate, or signs it over to someone else. In contrast, bearer bonds are considered the property of whoever holds them, since there is no record of ownership.

Currently, however, most bonds are registered electronically, so there are no certificates to endorse. Instead, you authorize the transaction over the phone or by computer.

Registered investment adviser (RIA)

Investment advisory firms that register with the Securities and Exchange Commission (SEC) and agree to be regulated by SEC rules are known as registered investment advisers.

Only a small percentage of all investment firms, and an even smaller number of individuals, register, though being registered is often interpreted as a sign that the adviser meets a higher standard.

Registered representative

Registered representatives are licensed to act on investors' orders to buy and sell and to provide advice relevant to portfolio transactions.

They may be paid a salary, a commission, usually a percentage of the market price of the investments their clients buy and sell, or by annual fee figured as a percentage of the value of a client's account.

Registered reps work for a broker-dealer that belongs to the exchange or operates in the market where the trades are handled. The reps must pass a series of exams administered by NASD to qualify for their licenses and are subject to NASD oversight.

Regressive tax

A regressive or flat income tax system taxes everyone at the same rate, as sales tax does.

Advocates say it's simpler and does away with the kinds of tax breaks that tend to favor the wealthy. Opponents say that middle-income taxpayers carry too large a proportion of the total tax bill.

Regulation D

Both the Securities and Exchange Commission (SEC) and the Federal Reserve have regulations known as Regulation D.

The SEC's Regulation D specifies which securities can be sold within the United States without having to be registered with the Commission.

Among the other restrictions, these securities can be made available only to accredited investors—individuals with a net worth of at least $1 million or an annual income of $200,000 or more, and institutions with assets of $5 million or more.

The Federal Reserve's Regulation D sets the requirements for depositary institutions, including the amount of cash the bank must hold in reserve and the number of transfers or withdrawals permitted for a savings account—which is six transfers every four week cycle with no more than three by check or electronic payment.

Regulation T

Regulation T is the Federal Reserve Board rule that governs how much you can borrow through your margin account to cover the purchase price of a security. This initial margin is 50% of the total cost.

The New York Stock Exchange (NYSE) and NASD additionally require your account to have a minimum margin of $2,000 or the full cost of the purchase, whichever is less, at the time you trade, plus a maintenance margin of at least 25% of the total market value of the securities in your account at all times.

Individual broker-dealers may and often do require higher minimum and maintenance margins.

Regulation Z

Under Regulation Z, a Federal Reserve Board rule covering provisions of the Consumer Credit Protection Act of 1968, lenders have to tell you certain terms of the credit they're offering, in writing, before you borrow.

Also known as the Truth in Lending Act, the regulation stipulates that lenders must disclose the true cost of loans. For example, they must make the interest rate, annual percentage rate (APR), and other terms of the loan simple to understand.

Regulation Z establishes uniform methods for calculating the cost of credit, disclosing credit terms, and resolving errors on certain types of credit accounts.

Rehypothecation

Rehypothecation occurs when your broker, to whom you have hypothecated—or pledged—securities as collateral for a margin loan, pledges those same securities to a bank or other lender to secure a loan to cover the firm's exposure to potential margin account losses.

When you open a margin account, you typically sign a general account agreement with your broker, in which you authorize your broker to rehypothecate.

Reinvestment

When you own certain stocks and most mutual funds, you can reinvest the dividends or distributions to buy more shares instead of receiving a cash payout.

In a corporate Dividend Reinvestment Plan (DRIP), for example, a company offers you the right to reinvest any cash dividends automatically to buy more stock. When you open a mutual fund account, you're generally offered an automatic reinvestment option as well.

One benefit of reinvestment programs is that in most cases you can make the new investments without incurring the usual sales charges, so it can be a lower cost way to build your investment portfolio.

One potential drawback, if you're reinvesting in a taxable account, is that you acquire shares at different prices, so figuring the cost basis for capital gains or losses when you sell can be more complicated than if you made fewer, larger purchases. It's also true that you owe income or capital gains tax in the year the money is reinvested, which isn't the case in a tax-deferred or tax-free account.

You will also want to consider the impact of reinvestment on the diversification of your portfolio, since buying additional shares increases the percentage of your portfolio that is allocated to a particular stock or mutual fund.

Reinvestment risk

Reinvestment risk occurs when you have money from a maturing fixed-income investment, such as a certificate of deposit (CD) or a bond, and want to make a new investment of the same type.

The risk is that you will not be able to find the same rate of return on your new investment as you were realizing on the old one. In fact, the return could be significantly lower, based on what's happening in the economy at large, though it could also be higher.

For example, if a bond paying 6% interest matures when the current rate is 4%, you must settle for a lower return if you buy a new bond unless you're willing to buy one of lower quality.

One way to limit reinvestment risk is by using an investment technique known as laddering, which means splitting your investment among a number of bonds or CDs that mature gradually over a series of years.

That way only part of your total investment will mature and have to be reinvested at any one time.

Renewable term

A renewable term life insurance policy allows you to extend your coverage for an additional period without having to requalify for coverage, provided that you have paid your premiums in full and on time.

Being able to renew your policy can be an important advantage if your health has declined since your original purchase. That's because another insurer might refuse to sell you a policy or might charge more for comparable coverage.

Renewable term policies do not guarantee the same rate for the new coverage period. In fact, at each renewal, the cost is likely to increase to reflect the fact that you're older and therefore pose a greater risk to the insurer.

Required beginning date (RBD)

Your required beginning date is the date by which you must take your first minimum required distribution from retirement savings plans that require distributions.

For an individual retirement account (IRA), it's April 1 of the year following the year you turn 70½. For a 401(k), it's either the April 1 of the year following the year you turn 70½ or the April 1 following the year you retire, unless you own 5% or more of the company sponsoring the plan. If that's the case, your deadline is April 1 of the year after the year you turn 70½.

Reserve requirement

The Federal Reserve requires its member banks to keep a certain percentage of their customer deposits in cash and other liquid assets in reserve at all times.

The required percentage may be revised at the Fed's discretion, but it has not been changed in recent years.

When a bank finds itself with excess reserves, it can lend them to other banks that may need them. These very short-term loans are known as federal funds and the interest rate the lenders charge is called the federal funds rate. That's also the benchmark rate for many corporate and international government loans.

Restricted security

Restricted securities are stocks or warrants that you acquire privately, through stock options or a corporate merger, rather than by buying them in the open market.

For example, you may receive restricted stock if you put money into a startup company.

If the company has not yet registered with the Securities and Exchange Commission (SEC) for an initial public offering (IPO), its securities cannot be transferred or resold until the issuing company meets the SEC registration requirements for publicly traded securities.

If you exercise stock options and buy stock at a reduced price, you may be required to hold those stocks for a period of time before liquidating them.

Retained earnings

Retained earnings, also known as retained surplus, are the portion of a company's profits that it keeps to reinvest in the business or pay off debt, rather than paying them out as dividends to its investors.

Retained earnings are one component of the corporation's net worth and increase the supply of cash that's available for acquisitions, repurchase of outstanding shares, or other expenditures the board of directors authorizes.

Smaller and faster-growing companies tend to have a high ratio of retained earnings to fuel research and development plus new product expansion. Mature firms, on the other hand, tend to pay out a higher percentage of their profits as dividends.

Return

Your return is the profit or loss you have on your investments, including income and change in value.

Return can be expressed as a percentage and is calculated by adding the income and the change in value and then dividing by the initial principal or investment amount. You can find the annualized return by dividing the percentage return by the number of years you have held the investment.

For example, if you bought a stock that paid no dividends at $25 a share and sold it for $30 a share, your return would be $5. If you bought on January 3, and sold it the following January 4, that would be a 20% annual percentage return, or the $5 return divided by your $25 investment.

But if you held the stock for five years before selling for $30 a share, your annualized return would be 4%, because the 20% gain is divided by five years rather than one year.

Percentage return and annual percentage return allow you to compare the return provided by different investments or investments you have held for different periods of time.

Return on equity

Return on equity (ROE) measures how much a company earns within a specific period in relation to the amount that's invested in its common stock.

It is calculated by dividing the company's net income before common stock dividends are paid by the company's net worth, which is the stockholders' equity.

If the ROE is higher than the company's return on assets, it may be a sign that management is using leverage to increase profits and profit margins.

In general, it's considered a sign of good management when a company's performance over time is at least as good as the average return on equity for other companies in the same industry.

Return on investment

Your return on investment (ROI) is the profit you make on the sale of a security or other asset divided by the amount of your investment, expressed as an annual percentage rate.

For example, if you invested $5,000 and the investment was worth $7,500 after two years, your annual return on investment would be 25%. To get that result, you divide the $2,500 gain by your $5,000 investment, and then divide the 50% gain by 2.

RETURN ON INVESTMENT	
$7,500	Current value
− 5,000	Investment amount
$2,500	Profit
÷ 5,000	Investment amount
50%	Percentage return
÷ 2	Years investment held
25%	Annual percentage return (return on investment)

Return on investment includes all the income you earn on the investment as well as any profit that results from selling the investment. It can be negative as well as positive if the sale price plus any income is lower than the purchase price.

Revenue

Revenue is the money you collect for providing a product or service.

Revenue is different from earnings, which is what's left of your revenue after subtracting the costs of producing or delivering the product or service and any taxes you paid on the amount you took in.

When corporations release their financial statements, those that provide services, such as power or telecommunications companies, describe their income as revenues, while those that manufacture products, such as lightbulbs or books, describe their income as sales.

The money a government collects in taxes is also called revenue. The US body that collects those taxes is called the Internal Revenue Service (IRS). In the United Kingdom, it's Inland Revenue.

Revenue bond
Revenue bonds are municipal bonds issued to finance public projects, such as airports and roadways. The bonds are backed by revenue to be generated by the project.

For example, if the construction of a tunnel is financed with municipal revenue bonds, the tolls paid by motorists are used to pay back the bondholders. However, bondholders usually have no claims on the bond issuer's other assets or resources.

Reverse merger
In a reverse merger, a privately held company purchases a publicly held company and, as part of the new entity, becomes public without an initial public offering (IPO).

It's described as reverse because in the more typical merger pattern a public company purchases a private company to expand its business.

Reverse mortgage
A reverse mortgage is a loan available to a homeowner 62 or older who may be eligible to borrow against the equity in his or her home.

Generally with a reverse mortgage, you receive money from a lender while you stay in your home. You don't have to pay the money back for as long as you live there and keep the property in good repair, but the loan must be repaid when you die, sell your home, or move to a different primary residence.

The amount you can borrow depends on your age, your home's value, your equity in it, and current interest rates. You can access the money as a lump sum, a line of credit, or a combination of these methods.

All reverse mortgages require closing costs, much like a regular mortgage, and they can charge fixed or variable interest rates. The fees can make a reverse mortgage an expensive way to borrow.

More than 90% of reverse mortgages, officially known as home equity conversion mortgages (HECMs), are insured by the US government's Federal Housing Administration (FHA). The FHA caps the size of reverse mortgages depending on the county in which your home is located and guarantees that you will receive the full amount of your loan.

Private alternatives to HECMs, called proprietary reverse mortgages, often offer higher limits. These loans may have higher costs, however.

Reverse stock split
If a company's stock is trading at a low price, the company may decide to reduce the number of existing shares and increase their price by consolidating the shares.

For example, a 1-for-2 reverse stock split halves the number of existing shares and doubles the price. In that case, if you hold 100 shares of a stock selling at $5 a share, for a combined value of $500, in a 1-for-2 reverse stock split, you would own 50 shares valued at $10 a share, which would still give you a combined value of $500. Stocks may be reverse split 1-for-5, or 5-for-10, or in any ratio the company chooses.

Reverse splits are generally used to ensure that a stock will continue to meet listing requirements on the market where it is traded or to encourage purchases by institutional investors, who may not buy stocks priced below a specific point.

Revocable trust
A revocable trust is a living trust that can be modified or revoked by the grantor, or person who establishes the trust and transfers property to it.

The trust can be a useful estate-planning tool because, when you die, the assets in the trust pass directly to the beneficiaries you've named in the trust rather than through your will.

But because you haven't relinquished control over the assets, as you do when you transfer them to an irrevocable trust, they are still included in your estate. If its total value, including the trust assets, is greater than the exempt amount, federal or state estate taxes may be due.

For the same reason, during your lifetime, you continue to collect the income that the assets in the revocable trust produce, and you owe income or capital gains taxes on those earnings at your regular rates. That's not the case with an irrevocable trust, which has its own tax identity.

Revolving credit

A revolving credit arrangement allows you to borrow up to your credit limit without having to reapply each time you need cash. As you repay the money you have borrowed, it is available to be borrowed again.

For example, if you have a credit card with a credit limit of $1,500 and you make a purchase of $400, the amount of credit you have available is $1,100. But when you repay the $400, your credit limit goes back to $1,500—assuming you haven't charged anything else on the card.

At any given time, your balance due may fluctuate from zero to the maximum credit limit. If you don't use the credit line in any billing cycle, no fees apply in most cases. But if you have a balance due and don't repay the full amount, finance charges are added to your next bill.

Some revolving credit arrangements, such as a home equity line of credit, may have a predetermined end date, but the majority are open-ended as long as you make at least the minimum required payment on time.

Rider

A rider is a modification to an insurance policy that typically adds a new coverage or higher coverage in return for higher premiums.

For example, you might add a rider to your life insurance policy to provide coverage for your spouse, or a rider to your homeowners policy to provide additional liability insurance for a specific event. Dental care and prescription insurance are typical riders on health insurance policies.

Rights of survivorship

If two or more people own property jointly with rights of survivorship and one of the owners should die, the deceased owner's share of the property automatically passes to the surviving owners.

This arrangement for joint ownership is in contrast to the arrangement known as tenants-in-common, in which a deceased owner's share becomes part of his or her estate and can be sold or distributed to heirs according to the terms of his or her will.

Couples who own their own home jointly often opt for right of survivorship to allow the surviving partner to enjoy full ownership rights to their home.

Rights offering

In a rights offering, also known as a subscription right, a company offers existing shareholders the opportunity to buy additional shares of company stock in proportion to the number they already own before any new shares are offered to the public.

Such an offering is usually mandated by the corporate charter.

To act on the offering, you turn over the rights you receive, typically one for each share of stock you own, and the money needed to make the purchase within the required period, often two to four weeks. The amount of money that's required is known as the subscription price.

You don't have to buy the additional shares, and you can transfer your rights to someone else if you prefer. But buying helps you maintain the same percentage of ownership you had in the company before the new shares were issued rather than having that percentage diluted.

Risk

Risk is the possibility you'll lose money if an investment you make provides a disappointing return. All investments carry a certain level of risk, since investment return is not guaranteed.

According to modern investment theory, the greater the risk you take in making an investment, the greater your return has the potential to be if the investment succeeds.

For example, investing in a startup company carries substantial risk, since there is no guarantee that it will be profitable. But if it is, you're in a position to realize a greater gain than if you had invested a similar amount in an already established company.

As a rule of thumb, if you are unwilling to take at least some investment risk, you are likely to limit your investment return.

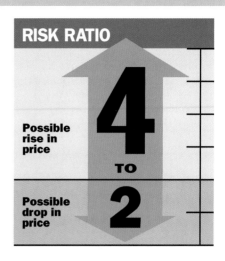

Critics point out that it is impossible to provide an accurate estimate of future prices, rendering risk ratios meaningless.

Risk premium

A risk premium is one way to measure the risk you'd take in buying a specific investment. Some analysts define risk premium as the difference between the current risk-free return—defined as the yield on a 13-week US Treasury bill—and the potential total return on the investment you're considering.

Other measures of risk premium, which are applied specifically to stocks, are a stock's beta, or the volatility of that stock in relation to the stock market as a whole, and a stock's alpha, which is based on an evaluation of the stock's intrinsic value.

Similarly, the higher interest rates that bond issuers typically offer on bonds below investment grade may be considered a risk premium, since the higher rate, and potentially greater return, is a way to compensate for the greater risk.

Risk ratio

Some investors and financial analysts try to estimate the risk an investment poses by speculating on how much the investment is likely to increase in value as opposed to how much it could decline.

For example, a stock priced at $50 that analysts think could increase to $90 or decrease to $30 has a 4:2 risk ratio, because they estimate the stock could go up $40 but down $20.

Risk tolerance

Risk tolerance is the extent to which you as an investor are comfortable with the risk of losing money on an investment. If you're unwilling to take the chance that an investment that might drop in price, you have little or no risk tolerance.

On the other hand, if you're willing to take some risk by making investments that fluctuate in value, you have greater risk tolerance. The probable consequence of limiting investment risk is that you are vulnerable to inflation risk, or loss of buying power.

Risk-adjusted performance

When you evaluate an investment's risk-adjusted performance, you aren't looking simply at its straight performance figures but at those figures in relation to the amount of risk you took (or would have taken) to get the return the investment produced.

One method is to investigate the investment's price volatility over various periods of time, including different market environments.

For example, you might consider how far the price fell in the most recent bear market against its price in a bull market, or how it performed in a recent market correction. In general, the greater the volatility, the greater the risk.

However, many analysts believe that looking exclusively at past performance can be deceptive in evaluating the risk you are taking in making a certain investment, since it can't predict what will happen in the future.

Risk-free return

When you buy a US Treasury bill that matures in 13 weeks, you're making a risk-free investment in the sense that there's virtually no chance of losing your principal (since the bill is backed by the US government) and no threat from inflation (since the term is so short).

Your yield, or the amount you earn on that investment, is described as risk-free return. By subtracting the risk-free return from the return on an investment that has the potential to lose value, you can figure out the risk premium, which is one measure of the risk of choosing an investment other than the 13-week bill.

Rollover

If you move your assets from one investment to another, it's called a rollover.

For example, if you move money from one IRA to another IRA, that transaction is a rollover. In the same vein, if you move money from a qualified retirement plan, such as a 401(k), into an IRA, you create a rollover IRA.

Similarly, when a bond or certificate of deposit (CD) matures, you can roll over the assets into another bond or time deposit.

Rollover IRA

A rollover IRA is an individual retirement account or annuity you create with tax-deferred assets you move from an employer sponsored retirement plan to a self-directed investment account.

If you arrange for a direct rollover, the trustee of your employer's plan transfers the assets to the trustee you select for your IRA. In that case the total value of the account moves from one to the other.

If you handle the rollover yourself, by getting a check from your employer's plan and depositing it in your IRA, your employer must withhold 20% of the total to prepay taxes that will be due if you fail to redeposit the full amount of the money you're moving into a tax-deferred account within 60 days.

The required withholding forces you to supply the missing 20% from another source to meet the deposit deadline if you want to maintain the tax-deferred status of the full amount and avoid taxes and a potential early withdrawal tax penalty on the amount you don't deposit in the IRA.

Roth 401(k)

The Roth 401(k), which was introduced in 2006, allows you to make after-tax contributions to your account in an employer sponsored plan.

Earnings may be withdrawn tax free, provided that you have left your job, are at least 59½, and your account has been open five years or more.

Both the Roth 401(k) and the traditional 401(k) have the same contribution limits and distribution requirements. You can add no more than the annual federal limit each year, and you must begin taking minimum required distributions (MRD) by April 1 of the year following the year you reach age 70½. You can postpone MRDs if you are still working.

You may not move assets between traditional and Roth 401(k) accounts, though you may be able to split your annual contribution between the two. If you leave your job or retire, you can roll Roth 401(k) assets into a Roth IRA, just as you can roll traditional 401(k) assets into a traditional IRA.

Most 401(k) plans, including the Roth, are self-directed, which means you must choose specific investments from among those offered through the plan.

Roth IRA

A Roth IRA is a variation on a traditional individual retirement arrangement (IRA).

Because contributions are made with after-tax dollars, the Roth IRA allows you to withdraw your earnings completely tax free any time after you reach age 59½, provided your account has been open at least five years.

You may also be able to withdraw money earlier without penalty if you qualify for certain exceptions, such as using up to $10,000 toward the purchase of a first home. And since a Roth IRA has no required withdrawals, you can continue to accumulate tax-free earnings as long as you like.

You can make a nondeductible annual contribution, up to the annual federal limit, any year you have earned income, even after age 70½, though you can never contribute more than you earn. If you are 50 or older, you may also make annual catch-up contributions.

To make a full contribution to a Roth IRA, your modified adjusted gross income (MAGI) must be less than the annual limit set by Congress.

You may make partial contributions on a sliding scale if your MAGI is between the amounts that Congress sets for your filing status. These annual limits are lower if you file as a single than if you're married and file a joint return.

You may also qualify to convert a traditional IRA to a Roth IRA if your MAGI in the year you convert is less than the cap, currently $100,000, which applies whether you are single or married. The amount you're converting is not included in that total.

Round lot

A round lot is the normal trading unit for stocks and bonds on an organized securities exchange or market, also called a trading platform.

For example, shares of stock traded in multiples of 100 are typically considered round lots, as are bonds with par values of $1,000 and $5,000.

Rule of 78

A practice, called the Rule of 78, means that lenders front-load the interest they charge on a short-term loan to guarantee their profit if you pay off your loan before the end of its term.

In other words, you pay most of the interest before you begin to make substantial repayment of principal.

For example, on a one-year loan, you'd pay 15% of the interest in the first month, 14% in the second month, and only 1% in the last month. The practice is called the Rule of 78 because that's the sum of the twelve payments in a one-year loan $(1+2+3+...+12 = 78)$.

It's illegal to calculate loans with terms longer than 61 months using the Rule of 78, and a number of states outlaw the practice for all loans. But where the Rule of 78 is used, the loans may be described as precomputed or precalculated loans, or as loans that offer a rebate of finance charges if you prepay.

Russell 1000 Index

This capitalization-weighted index, published by the Frank Russell Company tracks the 1000 largest stocks that are included in the Russell 3000 Index and represents approximately 92% of the market value of US stock.

The Index is rebalanced annually, at the end of June, and is widely used as a benchmark of large-cap US stock performance.

Russell 2000 Index

The Russell 2000 Index, published by the Frank Russell Company tracks the stocks of the 2,000 smallest companies in the Russell 3000 index.

The index includes many of the initial public offerings (IPOs) of recent years and is considered the benchmark index for small-cap investments.

Russell 3000 Index

The Russell 3000 Index, a market capitalization weighted index published by the Frank Russell Company, tracks the 3,000 largest companies in the United States. Its subsets, the Russell 1000 and the Russell 2000, are widely used benchmarks of the US large-cap and small-cap markets.

Safekeeping

Safekeeping occurs when a broker-dealer holds securities that are registered in a client's name for the client.

The advantage from the client's perspective is that the securities are safe and the broker-dealer has them available to sell at the client's instruction.

The disadvantage from the broker-dealer's perspective is that securities held in a client's name are not fully negotiable or fungible, so they can't be used to settle trades, for example. Thus, it's a service for which many firms charge a fee.

Instead of being registered in their own names, clients' securities may be registered in the broker-dealer's name or in the name of a depository. That's known as being registered in street name or nominee name.

With this type of registration, the client's ownership rights are fully protected but the stock is fungible. The broker-dealer may use a limited portion of the holding to settle trades or for other purposes.

Salary reduction plan

A salary reduction plan is a type of employer-sponsored retirement savings plan. Typical examples are traditional 401(k)s, 403(b)s, 457s, and SIMPLE IRAs.

TAKE HOME PAY — SALARY REDUCTION PLAN

A salary reduction plan allows you, as an employee, to contribute some of your current income to a retirement account in your name and to accumulate tax-deferred earnings on those contributions. In most plans, you contribute pretax income, which reduces your current income tax, and you pay tax at withdrawal at your regular rate.

Your employer may match some of or all your contribution according to a formula that applies on an equal basis to all participating employees. All salary reduction plans have an annual contribution cap that's set by Congress and allow annual catch-up contributions for participants 50 and older.

With Roth 401(k) and similar plans, you contribute after-tax income but qualify for tax-free withdrawals if you are older than 59½ and your account has been open at least five years.

Sale-leaseback

In a sale-leaseback arrangement—also known as a leaseback—an owner sells his or her property, and then immediately leases it back from the buyer as part of the same transaction.

This way, the seller gets the profits from the sale while keeping possession and use of the property, while the buyer is assured immediate long-term income on the property.

Sale-leaseback transactions are most commonly used in commercial real estate, but can also apply to commercial vehicles and other types of property.

Sales charge

A sales charge is the fee you pay to buy shares of a load mutual fund or other investment purchased through a financial professional.

The charge is typically figured as a percentage of the amount you invest. As the size of your investment increases, the rate at which you pay the sales charge may decrease.

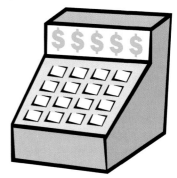

Each dollar amount at which there is a corresponding reduction in the charge is known as a breakpoint. For example, the rate may drop from 4.5% to 4.25% with an investment of $25,000.

The sales charge on a mutual fund may be imposed as a front-end load when you buy (also known as Class A shares), as a back-end load when you sell (also known as Class B shares), or as a level load each year you own the fund (also known as Class C shares).

Sales tax

A sales tax is a tax imposed by state and local governments on transactions that occur within their jurisdictions.

The taxing authority determines which transactions are subject to tax and the flat rate at which the tax is calculated. Some countries, though not the United States, impose a national sales tax often called a value added tax (VAT).

Sallie Mae

This corporation purchases student loans from various lenders, such as banks, and packages the loans as bonds or short-term or medium-term notes. After issue, these debt securities trade on the secondary market.

Sallie Mae guarantees repayment of the bonds and notes, and uses the money it raises through the sale of these securities to provide additional loan money for post-secondary school students. Sallie Mae also arranges financing for state student loan agencies. Its shares trade on the New York Stock Exchange (NYSE).

Sarbanes-Oxley Act of 2002

Named after its main Congressional sponsors, Senator Paul Sarbanes and Representative Michael Oxley, the Sarbanes-Oxley Act of 2002 introduced new financial practices and reporting requirements, including executive certification of financial reports, plus more stringent corporate governance procedures for publicly traded US companies . It also added protections for whistleblowers.

Officially the Corporate and Auditing Accountability, Responsibility, and Transparency Act, the law is known more colloquially as SarbOx or SOX. It was passed in response to several high-profile corporate scandals involving accounting fraud and corruption in major US corporations.

The law also created the Public Company Accounting Oversight Board (PCAOB), a private-sector, nonprofit corporation that regulates and oversees public accounting firms.

The law has seen its share of controversy, with opponents arguing that the expense and effort involved in complying with the law reduce shareholder value, and proponents arguing that increased corporate responsibility and transparency far outweigh the costs of compliance.

Savings account

A savings account is a deposit account in a bank or credit union that pays interest on your balance—though some institutions require that you have at least a minimum amount in the account to qualify for earnings.

You can deposit and withdraw from savings accounts as you wish, but you can't transfer money from the account directly to other people or organizations.

While savings accounts typically pay interest at a lower rate than other bank accounts, that may not always be the case. Savings accounts are insured by the Federal Deposit Insurance Corporation (FDIC) or the National Credit Union Share Insurance Fund.

You're covered up to $100,000 in each of three different categories of account in a single bank, or up to $250,000 if an account is a self-directed retirement account (IRA). Different branches of the same bank count as one bank.

Savings bonds

The US government issues two types of savings bonds: Series EE and Series I.

You buy electronic Series EE bonds through a Treasury Direct account for face value and paper Series EE for half their face value. You earn a fixed rate of interest for the 30-year term of these bonds, and they are guaranteed to double in value in 20 years. Series EE bonds issued before May 2005 earn interest at variable rates set twice a year.

Series I bonds are sold at face value and earn a real rate of return that's guaranteed to exceed the rate of inflation during the term of the bond. Existing Series HH bonds earn interest to maturity, but no new Series HH bonds are being issued.

The biggest difference between savings bonds and US Treasury issues is that there's no secondary market for savings bonds since they cannot be traded among investors. You buy them in your own name or as a gift for someone else and redeem them by turning them back to the government, usually through a bank or other financial intermediary.

The interest on US savings bonds is exempt from state and local taxes and is federally tax deferred until the bonds are cashed in. At that point, the interest may be tax exempt if you use the bond proceeds to pay qualified higher education expenses, provided that your adjusted gross income (AGI) falls in the range set by federal guidelines and you meet the other conditions to qualify.

Screen

A screen is a set of criteria against which you measure stocks or other investments to find those that meet your criteria.

For example, you might screen for stocks that meet a certain environmentally or socially responsible standard, or for those with current price-to-earnings ratios (P/E) less than the current market average.

A socially responsible mutual fund describes the screens it uses to select investments in its prospectus.

Scrip

Scrip is a certificate or receipt that represents something of value but has no intrinsic value. What's essential is that the issuer and the recipient must agree on the value that the scrip represents.

For example, in the past, after a corporate stock split or spin-off, a company might issue scrip representing a fractional share of stock for each share you owned. On or before a specific date, you could combine the certificates and convert the value they represented into full shares.

But most companies today make a cash payment for fractional shares based on the closing price of the stock on a specific date.

Scripophily

Scripophily is the practice of collecting antique stocks, bonds, and other securities.

The most valuable documents are usually the most beautiful, or those that have some historical significance because of the role the issuing company played in the economy. Sometimes those with distinctive errors are also especially valuable.

Secondary market

When investors buy and sell securities through a brokerage account, the transactions occur on what's known as the secondary market.

While the secondary market isn't a place, it includes all of the exchanges, trading rooms, and electronic networks where these transactions take place.

The issuer—company or government—that sold the security initially receives no proceeds from these trades, as it does when the securities are sold for the first time.

Secondary offering

The most common form of secondary offering occurs when an investor, usually a corporation, but sometimes an individual, sells a large block of stock or other securities it has been holding in its portfolio to the public.

In a sale of this kind, all the profits go to the seller rather than the company that issued the securities in the first place. The seller usually pays all the commissions.

Secondary offerings can also originate with the issuing companies themselves. In these cases, a company issues additional shares of its stock, over and above those sold in its initial public offering (IPO), or it reissues shares that were issued and have been bought up by the company over time. Reissued shares are known as Treasury stock.

Sector

A sector is a segment of the economy that shares distinctive characteristics, such as telecommunications or energy.

Sectors tend to do better during certain parts of the economic cycle and worse in others. Sectors also respond to a variety of factors, including consumer sentiment.

The performance of any single stock in a sector can be measured against the performance of the sector as a whole, showing where that stock ranks in relation to its peers.

Sector indexes, some broad and some very narrow, track many of the major sectors of the economy.

Sector fund

Sector mutual funds, also called specialty or specialized funds, concentrate their investments in a single segment of an industry, such as biotechnology, natural resources, utilities, or regional banks, for example.

Sector funds tend to be more volatile and erratic than more broadly diversified funds, and often dominate both the top and bottom of annual mutual fund performance charts. A sector that thrives in one economic climate may wither in another one.

Secular market

A secular market is one that moves in the same direction—up or down—for an extended period.

Benchmark indexes continue to rise to new, higher levels during a secular bull market despite some short-term corrections. Similarly, during a secular bear market, index levels decline or remain flat despite short-term rallies.

In addition, the average price-to-earnings ratio increases substantially during a secular bull market before reaching a top and falls during secular bear markets before hitting a bottom.

Secular markets tend to move in cycles, or predictable though not regular patterns, so that a secular bull market is followed by a secular bear market, which is followed by a secular bull market, and so on.

For example, the bull market of 1982 through 1999 followed the bear market of 1966-1981. The length of secular markets varies, from as few as 4 or 5 years to more than 20 years, though when one begins and ends becomes clear only in retrospect.

Secured bond

The issuer of a bond or other debt security may guarantee, or secure, the bond by pledging, or assigning, collateral to investors. If the issuer defaults, the investors may take possession of the collateral.

A mortgage-backed bond is an example of a secured issue, since the underlying mortgages can be foreclosed and the properties sold to recover some of or all the amount of the bond.

Holders of secured bonds are at the top of the pecking order if an issuer misses an interest payment or defaults on repayment of principal.

Secured credit card

A secured credit card is linked to a savings account you open with the bank or other financial institution offering the card.

You deposit a sum of money in the account, and you can borrow up to that amount using your card. If you don't repay what you borrowed, the creditor can access your account to cover your debt. The creditor may also change substantial fees for a secured card.

Secured credit cards look the same as other credit cards, so no merchant can identify a card as secured. But if you have trouble qualifying for credit, perhaps because you've just started working, you can use a secured card as a first step toward establishing a record of using credit responsibly.

Secured loan

A secured loan is a loan that's guaranteed with collateral, such as a home or car. If you default and fail to make payments on time, the lender can take possession of your collateral and sell it to recover the loan amount.

In most cases, lenders charge a lower interest rate on a secured loan than on an unsecured loan of comparable size. An unsecured loan is guaranteed only by your promise to pay, not by collateral.

Securities and Exchange Commission (SEC)

The Securities and Exchange Commission (SEC) is an independent federal agency that oversees and regulates the securities industry in the United States and enforces securities laws.

The SEC requires registration of all securities that meet the criteria it sets, and of all individuals and firms who sell those securities. It's also a rule making body, with a mandate to turn the law into rules that the investment industry can follow.

Established by Congress in 1934, the SEC sets standards for disclosure by publicly traded corporations, and works to protect investors from misleading or fraudulent practices, including insider trading.

It has four divisions: Corporate Finance, Market Regulation, Investment Management, and Enforcement.

Securities Investor Protection Corporation (SIPC)

The Securities Investor Protection Corporation (SIPC) is a nonprofit corporation created by Congress to insure investors against losses caused by the failure of a brokerage firm.

Through SIPC, assets in your brokerage account are insured up to $500,000, including up to $100,000 in cash, but only against losses that result from the brokerage firm going bankrupt, not against market losses caused by trading decisions or other causes.

All brokers and dealers must register with the Securities and Exchange Commission (SEC) and are required to be SIPC members though they can lose their affiliation under certain circumstances. Clients of nonmember firms are not insured.

Securitization

Securitization is the process of pooling various types of debt—mortgages, car loans, or credit card debt, for example—and packaging that debt as bonds, pass-through securities, or collateralized mortgage obligations (CMOs), which are sold to investors.

The principal and interest on the debt underlying the security is paid to the investors on a regular basis, though the method varies based on the type of security. Debts backed by mortgages are known as mortgage-backed securities, while those backed by other types of loans are known as asset-backed securities.

Security

Traditionally, a security was a physical document, such as stock or bond certificate, that represented your investment in that stock or bond.

But with the advent of electronic recordkeeping, paper certificates have increasingly been replaced by electronic documentation.

In current general usage, the term security refers to the stock, bond, or other investment product itself rather than to evidence of ownership.

Self-amortizing loan

A self-amortizing loan is one that's paid off over a specific period of time as the borrower makes regular installment payments.

Part of each payment covers some interest on the loan, and the rest is applied to the principal. When the last payment is made, both principal and interest have been paid in full.

Self-amortizing loans can be bundled together and offered for sale as debt securities, such as those available through Ginnie Mae (GNMA). If you buy GNMA or similar bonds, you get back part of your principal as well as the interest you've earned each time you receive an interest payment. There is no lump-sum repayment of principal when the bond matures.

Self-directed retirement plan

If you participate in an employer's retirement savings plan, such as a 401(k) or a 403(b), you usually must select the investments into which your contribution goes from a menu of choices your plan offers.

When that's the case, your plan is self-directed, and the income you receive when you retire is determined in part by the investment choices you make.

Individual retirement accounts are also self-directed, as you choose the way that the assets in the account are invested. Individual retirement annuities may or may not be self-directed, depending on the contract you chose.

In contrast, if you're part of a defined benefit pension plan, your employer is responsible for making the investment decisions. If you own a fixed annuity, the insurance company makes the investment decisions.

Self-regulatory organization (SRO)

All securities and commodities exchanges in the United States are self-regulatory organizations (SROs), as is NASD.

These bodies establish the standards under which their members conduct business, monitor the way that business is conducted, and enforce their own rules.

For example, the New York Stock Exchange (NYSE) requires that client orders delivered to the floor of the exchange be filled before orders that originate with traders on the floor, who buy and sell for their own accounts.

Sell short

Selling short is a trading strategy that's designed to take advantage of an anticipated drop in a stock's market price.

To sell short, you borrow shares through your broker, sell them, and use the money you receive from the sale as collateral on the loan until the stock price drops.

If it does, you then buy back the shares at a lower price using the collateral, and return the borrowed shares to your broker plus interest and commission. If you realize a profit, it's yours to keep.

Suppose, for example, you sell short 100 shares of stock priced at $10 a share. When the price drops to $7.50, you buy 100 shares, return them to your broker, and keep the $2.50-per-share profit minus commission. The risk is that if the share price rises instead of falls, you may have to buy back the shares at a higher price and suffer the loss.

During the period of the short sale, the lender of the stock is no longer the registered owner because the stock was sold. If any dividends are paid during that period, or any other corporate actions occur, the short seller must make the lender whole by paying the amount that's due. However, that income is taxed at the lender's regular rate, not the lower rate that applies to qualifying dividend income.

Sell side

Brokerage firms and other financial services companies that buy and sell investments as agents for retail investors as well as for their own accounts are described as the sell side of Wall Street.

Sell-side institutions employ analysts to research potential investments and make buy, hold, or sell recommendations that the firm's brokers may make available to their clients to help guide their investment decisions.

Sell-off

A sell-off is a period of intense selling of securities and commodities triggered by declining prices. Sell-offs—sometimes called dumping—usually cause prices to plummet even more sharply.

Senior bond

Senior bonds offer slightly lower interest rates than subordinated or junior bonds because they are considered less risky.

A senior bond has priority in interest payments, and if a bond issuer defaults, or runs into difficulty paying off debt, holders of senior bonds have a prior claim in receiving whatever monies are available.

Separate account

An insurance company's separate account is established to hold the premiums you use to purchase funds included in variable annuity contracts the company offers.

The separate account is distinct from the company's general account, which holds the company's assets as well as premiums for fixed annuities and fixed-income separate account funds.

Assets in a company's separate account are not vulnerable to the claims of creditors, as assets in the general account are. But they can be affected by the ups and downs of the marketplace. Any gain or loss in the annuity's value results from the investment performance of the investments in the separate account funds you select.

Separate account fund

Each variable annuity contract offers a number of separate account funds.

Each of those funds owns a collection of individual investments chosen by a professional manager who is striving to achieve a particular objective, such as long-term growth or regular income.

You allocate your variable annuity premiums among different separate account funds offered in your contract to create a diversified portfolio of funds, sometimes called investment portfolios or subaccounts.

If you're comparing different contracts to decide which to purchase, among the factors to consider are the variety of funds each contract offers, the past performance of those funds, the experience of the professional manager, and the fees.

In evaluating the past performance and other details of the funds a contract offers, or the funds you are using in the contract you selected, you can use the prospectus the annuity company provides for each separate account fund. You may be able to find independent research on the funds from firms such as Morningstar, Inc., Standard & Poor's, and Lipper.

Series 6

The Series 6 is a licensing examination that you must pass to be entitled to sell mutual funds and variable annuities to investors.

The examination, which is administered by NASD, is a 100-question multiple choice test that puts primary emphasis on knowledge of the products plus the securities and tax regulations that apply.

Anyone taking the exam must be sponsored by either an NASD member firm or an industry self-regulatory organization (SRO).

Series 63

The Series 63 is a licensing examination that most states require for anyone who wants to sell securities within the state.

Developed by the North American Securities Administrators Association (NASAA), the test covers state securities laws, known informally as blue sky laws, as reflected in the Uniform Securities Act as amended by NASAA.

To sell securities anywhere in the United States, applicants must also pass the Series 6 (for a license to sell mutual funds and annuities) or Series 7 (for a license to sell all securities) administered by NASD.

Series 7

To be licensed to sell securities to individual investors, brokers must pass the Series 7 exam, also called the General Securities Registered Representative Examination.

The six-hour test requires knowledge of specific securities, the concept of suitability, the securities markets, and various aspects of maintaining customer accounts, stocks, bonds, options, mutual funds, direct participation programs, and variable annuities, but not commodities or futures contracts.

Anyone taking the exam must be sponsored by an NASD member firm or an industry self-regulatory organization (SRO).

Settlement agent

In some states, a settlement agent, or closing agent, handles the real estate transaction when you buy or sell a home.

He or she oversees title searches, legal documents, fee payments, and other details of transferring property, acting on your behalf to ensure that the conditions of the contract have been met and appropriate real estate taxes have been paid.

A settlement agent also represents you at the closing, so you don't need to be present.

Settlement date

The settlement date is the date by which a securities transaction must be finalized.

By that date, the buyer must pay for the securities purchased in the transaction, and the seller must deliver those securities.

For stocks, the settlement date is three business days after the trade date, or what's referred to as T+3. For options and government securities, the settlement date is one day, or T+1, after the trade date.

In figuring long- and short-term capital gains on your tax return, you use the trade date—the date you buy or sell a security—rather than the settlement date as the date of record.

Share

A share is a unit of ownership in a corporation or mutual fund, or an interest in a general or limited partnership. Though the word is sometimes used interchangeably with the word stock, you actually own shares of stock.

Share class

Some stocks and certain mutual funds subdivide their shares into classes or groups to designate their special characteristics.

For example, the differences between Class A shares and Class B shares of stock may focus on voting rights, resale rights, or other provisions that enhance the power of certain shareholders.

In fact, in the United States, most dual class shares involve one class that is publicly traded and another class that is privately held.

In some overseas countries, Class A shares can be purchased by citizens only, while Class B shares can be purchased by noncitizens only.

In the case of mutual funds, class designations indicate the way that sales charges, or loads, are levied. Class A shares have front-end loads, Class B shares have back-end loads, also called contingent deferred sales charges, and Class C shares have level loads.

Shareholder

If you own stock in a corporation, you are a shareholder of that corporation.

You're considered a majority share-holder if you alone or in combination with other shareholders own more than half the company's outstanding shares, which allows you to control the outcome of a corporate vote. Otherwise, you are considered a minority shareholder.

In practice, however, it is possible to gain control by owning less than 51% of the shares, especially if there are a large number of shareholders or you own shares that carry extra voting power.

Sharpe ratio

Using the Sharpe ratio is one way to compare the relationship of risk and reward in following different investment strategies, such as emphasizing growth or value investments, or in holding different combinations of investments.

To figure the ratio, the risk-free return is subtracted from the average return of an investment portfolio over a period of time, and the result is divided by the standard deviation of the return.

A strategy with a higher ratio is less risky than one with a lower ratio.

This type of analysis, which is done using sophisticated computer programs, is named for William P. Sharpe, who won the Nobel Prize in economics in 1990.

Short interest

Short interest is the total number of shares of a particular stock that investors have sold short in anticipation of a decline in the share price and have not yet repurchased.

Short interest is often considered an indicator of pessimism in the market and a sign that prices will decline.

However, some analysts see short interest as a positive sign, pointing out that short sales have to be covered, and that the need to repurchase can trigger increased demand and therefore higher prices.

Short position

If you sell stock short and have not yet repurchased shares to replace the ones you borrowed, you are said to have a short position in that stock.

Similarly, if you sell an options contract that commits you to meet the terms of the contract at some date in the future if the option is exercised, you have a short position in that contract.

SIMPLE

A SIMPLE, also known as a SIMPLE IRA, is short for Savings Incentive Match Plans for Employees, an employer sponsored retirement savings plan that may be offered by companies with fewer than 100 employees.

Employers must contribute to eligible employees' accounts each year in one of two ways. They can make a contribution equal to 2% of salary for every employee, or match dollar-for-dollar each employee's contribution to the plan, up to 3% of that employee's annual salary.

A SIMPLE may be set up by establishing an IRA in each employee's name or as a 401(k). Congress sets an annual dollar limit on the tax-deferred amount an employee may contribute, based on the type of SIMPLE it is. Contribution ceilings for SIMPLE-IRAs are lower than for other employer sponsored plans.

You may withdraw assets from a SIMPLE without penalty if you are 59½ or older and retired. And you must begin taking minimum required distributions by April 1 of the year following the year you turn 70½ unless you're still working. Taxes are due on distributions at your regular tax rate.

You may roll your assets over into another employer plan or an IRA if you leave your job for any reason or retire.

Two key differences between SIMPLEs and other employer plans are that your account must be open at least two years before you can withdraw or move the money, and the federal tax penalty for early withdrawal is 25% of the amount you take, rather than 10%.

Simple interest

If you earn simple interest on money you deposit in a bank or use to purchase a certificate of deposit (CD), the interest is figured on the amount of your principal alone.

For example, if you had $1,000 in an account that paid 5% simple interest for five years, you'd earn $50 a year ($1,000 x .05 = $50) and have $1,250 at the end of five years.

In contrast, if you had been earning compound interest, you'd have $1,276.29 at the end of five years, since the interest you earned each year, as well as your principal, would have earned interest.

Simplified employee pension plan (SEP)

An SEP is a qualified retirement plan set up as an individual retirement arrangement (IRA) in an employee's name.

You can establish an SEP for yourself if you own a small business, or you may participate as an employee if you work for a company that sponsors such a plan.

The federal government sets the requirements for participation, the maximum annual contribution limits, and the rules governing withdrawals.

Sinking fund

To ensure there's money on hand to redeem a bond or preferred stock issue, a corporation may establish a separate custodial account, called a sinking fund, to which it adds money on a regular basis.

Or the corporation may be required to establish such a fund to fulfill the terms of its issue. The existence of the fund allows the corporation to present its investments as safer than those issued by a corporation without comparable assets.

However, sinking fund assets may be used to call bonds before they mature, reducing the interest the bondholders expected to receive.

Slow market

A slow market is one with sluggish trading and static prices. In this environment, it may be difficult to find buyers willing to pay the price at which you'd like to sell your securities or other assets.

So to reduce the risk of losing principal or limiting gains, you may decide not to sell in a slow market unless you have a pressing need for the money that your asset might produce.

On the other hand, you might choose to buy in a slow market because lackluster trading volume might depress the prices of attractive investments.

The term slow market is also used to describe an exchange or market where transactions take relatively longer to execute than they do in other trading environments.

Slump

In an investment slump, prices fall. The slump may affect an individual investment as the result of company-specific problems or it may affect an entire investment market. Often a slump is short-term, but it may also signal a long-term decline.

Small-capitalization stock

Shares of relatively small publicly traded corporations with a total market capitalization of less than $2.3 billion are typically considered small-capitalization, or small-cap, stocks.

That number is not used uniformly, however, and you may find small-cap defined as below $1.5 billion. Market capitalization is calculated by multiplying the market price per share by the number of outstanding shares.

Small-cap stocks, which are tracked by the Russell 2000 Index, tend to be issued by young, potentially fast-growing companies. Over the long term—though not in every period—small-cap stocks as a group have produced stronger returns than any other investment category. Mutual funds that invest in this type of stock are known as small-cap funds.

Social Security

Social Security is a federal government program designed to provide income for qualifying retired people, their dependents, and disabled people who meet the Social Security test for disability.

You qualify for retirement benefits if you have had at least the minimum required payroll tax withheld from your wages for 40 quarters, the equivalent of 10 years.

The minimum for each quarter is set by Congress and increases slightly each year. You earn credits toward disability coverage in the same way.

The amount you receive in Social Security retirement benefits, up to the annual cap, is determined by the payroll taxes you paid during your working life, which were matched by an equal tax paid by your employers. Some of your benefit may be subject to income tax if your income plus half your benefit is higher than the ceiling Congress sets.

Socially responsible fund

When socially responsible mutual funds, also known as green funds or conscience funds, select securities to meet their investment goals, the securities must also satisfy the fund's commitment to certain principles spelled out in the fund's prospectus.

For example, a socially responsible fund might not buy shares of a manufacturing company that operates factories that fund managers consider sweatshops. Or the fund might not buy shares of a food company that sells out-of-date products in emerging markets.

Since the priorities of these funds vary, you may need to do some investigating to find one that matches your values.

Soft dollars

Soft dollars are amounts that money managers, including mutual fund managers, pay out of their clients' accounts to a brokerage firm to cover the cost of research the firm provides. Soft dollars also cover transaction fees for executing trades.

The alternative would be for the managers to purchase the research with their own money, or hard dollars, and pay for the transaction fees with their clients' money.

Using soft dollars isn't a violation of the manager's fiduciary duty, provided that the money pays for research that is consistent with SEC requirements and for actual transaction costs. In fact, it may make valuable research information available to both the managers and their clients.

The practice is controversial, however, for a number of reasons, including whether soft dollar relationships conflict with the managers' obligation to seek best execution of the trades they place.

Soft market

A soft market, also known as a buyer's market, is one in which there is inactive trading in an individual stock or the market as a whole at current prices.

As a result, a large sell order can easily push the price of the stock or the market down. If investors move in to buy at this lower level, the market is sometimes said to be firming up. Another way to describe a soft market is as one with more supply than demand.

Sole proprietor

A sole proprietor is the owner and operator of a business that isn't registered as either a corporation or a limited liability company.

As a sole proprietor, you are personally liable for all your business's debts and report any business profits or losses on your individual tax return.

Special situation

An undervalued stock that one or more analysts expects to increase in price in the very near future because of an anticipated—and welcome—change within the company is known as a special situation.

That change could be the introduction of a major new product, a corporate restructuring, or anything else that has the potential to increase earnings.

In some cases, the fact that a stock is identified as a special situation creates a flurry of investor interest and actually helps drive the price up even before the change has had time to take effect.

A stock that is extremely volatile over the short term because of important recent news about the company, such as a takeover or spin-off, is also described as a special situation.

Specialist

A specialist or specialist unit is a member of a securities exchange responsible for maintaining a fair and orderly market in a specific security or securities on the exchange floor.

Specialists execute market orders given to them by other members of the exchange known as floor brokers or sent to their post through an electronic routing system.

Typically, a specialist acts both as agent and principal. As agent, the specialist handles limit orders for floor brokers in exchange for a portion of their commission.

Those orders are maintained in an electronic record known as the limit order book, or specialist's book, until the stock is trading at the acceptable price. As principal, the specialist buys for his or her own account to help maintain a stable market in a security.

For example, if the spread, or difference, between the bid and ask, or the highest price offered by a buyer and the lowest price asked by a seller, gets too wide, and trading in the security hits a lull, the specialist might buy, sell, or sell short shares to narrow the spread and stimulate trading.

But because of restrictions the exchange puts on trading, a specialist is not permitted to buy a security when there is an unexecuted order for the same security at the same price in the limit order book.

Specialist's display book

A display book was traditionally a written chronological record of all limit, stop, and short sale orders that had been placed with a specialist for an individual security on behalf of specific clients plus an inventory of the specialist's own holdings in the security.

The New York Stock Exchange (NYSE) Display Book is an electronic extension of that recordkeeping. It's part of an integrated telecommunications system that not only displays orders but executes and reports transactions, handles trade comparison, and links to a number of other functions.

Speculator

When you make a financial commitment because you believe something will happen in the market where you're trading that will provide a profit, you are acting as a speculator.

THE SPECULATORS

Seek to profit on price changes	Buy when they think prices are lowest	Sell when they think prices are highest

For example, you might invest in a bankrupt company because you expect that it will emerge from bankruptcy and its stock price will rise at some point in the future. Or you might purchase futures contracts or buy or sell options because you think the contracts might increase in value.

In contrast, hedgers buy futures and options to protect their financial interests. For example, a baker who buys a wheat futures contract in order to protect the cost of producing bread is hedging the risk that wheat prices will rise. She's willing to spend a certain amount to protect against a potentially larger loss.

Spending plan

A spending plan can help you manage your money more effectively, live within your income limits, reduce your reliance on consumer credit, and save for the things you want.

You create a spending plan, or budget, by dividing up your income so that it covers your regular expenses—both essential and nonessential.

It's a good idea to include some income for your emergency fund—typically about three months of income—and ideally some for your investment account. As a starting point, some people use what they spent the previous year to figure out their spending plan for the next year.

You may want to check the Bureau of Labor Statistics website (www.bls.gov) for the average nationwide expenditures for housing, food, and other costs. But you may have to modify that information to reflect local costs and your own situation.

Spin-off

In a spin-off, a company sets up one of its existing subsidiaries or divisions as a separate company.

Shareholders of the parent company receive stock in the new company based on an evaluation established for the new entity. In addition, they continue to hold stock in the parent company.

The motives for spin-offs vary. A company may want to refocus its core businesses, shedding those that it sees as unrelated. Or it may want to set up a company to capitalize on investor interest.

In other cases, a corporation may face regulatory hurdles in expanding its business and spin off a unit to be in compliance. Sometimes, a group of employees will assume control of the new entity through a buyout, an employee stock ownership plan (ESOP), or as the result of negotiation.

Split-funded annuity

A split-funded annuity lets you begin receiving income from a portion of your principal immediately, while the rest of the money goes into a deferred annuity.

The advantage of split-funding is that you have the benefit of some income right away for immediate needs or wants, while the balance compounds tax deferred, allowing you to build your retirement assets.

One goal of a split-funded annuity is providing a larger future income when you begin to draw on the deferred portion than you would receive if you annuitized the entire principal now.

Spoofing

Some market analysts maintain that the increased volatility in stock markets may be the result of an illegal practice known as spoofing, or phantom bids.

To spoof, traders who own shares of a certain stock place an anonymous buy order for a large number of shares of the stock through an electronic communications network (ECN). Then they cancel, or withdraw, the order seconds later.

As soon as the order is placed, however, the price jumps. That's because investors following the market closely enter their own orders to buy what seems to be a hot stock and drive up the price.

When the price rises, the spoofer sells shares at the higher price, and gets out of the market in that stock. Investors who bought what they thought was a hot stock may be left with a substantial loss if the price quickly drops back to its prespoof price.

Spoofing is a variant of the scam known as pump and dump.

Spot market

Commodities and foreign currencies are traded for immediate delivery and payment on the spot market, also known as a cash market.

The term refers to the fact that the current market price is paid in cash on the spot, or within a short period of time.

A cash sale, whether arranged in person, over the telephone, or electronically, is the opposite of a forward contract, where delivery and settlement are set for a date in the future.

The same is true for a futures contract, which is an agreement to trade a commodity today for a set price at delivery on a specific date in the future.

Spot price

The spot, or cash, price is the price of commodities and foreign currencies that are being sold for immediate delivery with payment in cash.

Spread

In the most general sense, a spread is the difference between two similar measures. In the stock market, for example, the spread is the difference between the highest price bid and the lowest price asked.

With fixed-income securities, such as bonds, the spread is the difference between the yields on securities having the same investment grade but different maturity dates. For example, if the yield on a long-term Treasury bond is 6%, and the yield on a Treasury bill is 4%, the spread is 2%.

The spread may also be the difference in yields on securities that have the same maturity date but are of different investment quality. For example, there is a 3% spread between a high-yield bond paying 9% and a Treasury bond paying 6% that both come due on the same date.

The term also refers to the price difference between two different derivatives of the same class.

For instance, there is typically a spread between the price of the October wheat futures contract and the January wheat futures contract. Part of that spread is known as the cost of carry. However, the spread widens and narrows, caused by changes in the market—in this case the wheat market.

Standard & Poor's (S&P)

Standard & Poor's is a private, independent source of financial market intelligence for investors and other market participants.

Its products include indexes, risk evaluation, investment research and data, and credit ratings on public companies, financial institutions, insurance firms, sovereign nations, municipal and state governments, and many non-profit organizations such as hospitals and universities.

Standard & Poor's Depositary Receipt (SPDR)

When you buy SPDRs—pronounced spiders—you're buying shares in a unit investment trust (UIT) that owns a portfolio of stocks included in Standard & Poor's 500 Index (S&P 500). A share is priced at about 1/10 the value of the S&P 500.

SPDR

Like an index mutual fund that tracks the S&P 500, SPDRs provide a way to diversify your investment portfolio without having to own shares in all the S&P 500 companies yourself.

However, while the net asset value (NAV) of an index fund is set only once a day, at the end of trading, the price of SPDRs, which are listed on the American Stock Exchange (AMEX), changes throughout the day, reflecting the constant changes in the index.

SPDRs, which are part of a category of investments known as exchange traded funds (ETFs), can be sold short or bought on margin as stocks can.

Each quarter you receive a distribution based on the dividends paid on the stocks in the underlying portfolio, after trust expenses are deducted. If you choose, you can reinvest those distributions to buy additional shares.

Standard & Poor's/Citigroup Growth and Value Indexes

To provide benchmarks for specific investment styles, Standard & Poor's offers complementary sets of style indexes for the US market that subdivide the S&P 500, the S&P MidCap 400, the S&P SmallCap 600, the Composite 1500, the S&P 1000, and the S&P 900 into to growth and value segments.

One set, called the style index series, divides each of the indexes into approximately equal halves, with one half comprising growth stocks and the other value stocks. Stocks that don't fit clearly into either category are distributed between growth and value.

The other set, called the pure style index series, tracks only those stocks that fit clearly into the growth category or the value category. Stocks in these indexes are weighted by their style scores rather than their market cap to eliminate the impact of size on the index return.

Standard & Poor's 500 Index (S&P 500)

The benchmark Standard & Poor's 500 Index, widely referred to as the S&P 500, tracks the performance of 500 widely held large-cap US stocks in the industrial, transportation, utility, and financial sectors.

In calculating the changing value of this capitalization-weighted index, also called a market value index, stocks with the greatest number of floating shares trading at the highest share prices are weighted more heavily than stocks with lower market value.

This can mean that a relatively few stocks have a major impact on the movement of the index at any point in time. The stocks included in the index, their relative weightings, and the number of stocks from each of the sectors vary from time to time, at S&P's discretion.

Standard deviation

Standard deviation is a statistical measurement of how far a variable quantity, such as the price of a stock, moves above or below its average value. The wider the range, which means the greater the standard deviation, the riskier an investment is considered to be.

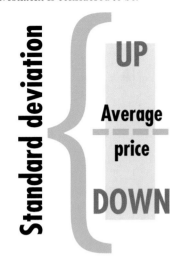

Some analysts use standard deviation to predict how a particular investment or portfolio will perform. They calculate the range of the investment's possible future performances based on a history of past performance, and then estimate the probability of meeting each performance level within that range.

Start-up
While any new company could be considered a start-up, the description is usually applied to aggressive young companies that are actively courting private financing from venture capitalists, including wealthy individuals and private equity partnerships. In many cases, the start-ups plan to use the cash infusion to prepare for an initial public offering (IPO).

State guaranty funds
State guaranty funds, which are offered in every state, protect contract owners against the insolvency of an insurance company that has issued insurance contracts, including annuity contracts.

However, each state's laws set different limits on benefits and coverage. The guaranty funds are backed by an association of insurance companies, not the state or federal government.

But all insurance companies in the state must belong to and contribute to the fund in order to be licensed to sell their products. However, if you buy your contract from a highly rated company, its financial strength and reputation stand behind your contract.

Rating services such as Standard & Poor's, Moody's, A.M. Best, and Fitch rank insurance companies on their overall financial condition, which underlies their ability to meet their obligations. You can request these reports from the insurance company. They are also available in public libraries, on the Internet, and from your financial adviser.

Statutory voting
When shareholders vote for candidates nominated to serve on a company's board of directors, they usually cast their ballots using statutory voting.

Under this system, each shareholder gets one vote for each share of stock he or she owns, and may cast that number of votes for or against each candidate.

For example, if you owned 100 shares, and there were three candidates, you could cast 100 votes for each of them. That means the shareholders owning greater numbers of shares have greater influence on the outcome of the election.

In cumulative voting, on the other hand, a shareholder may cast the total number of his or her votes—one vote for every share of stock multiplied by the number of candidates for the board—for or against a single nominee, divide them between two nominees, cast an equal number of shares for each candidate, or any other combination.

For example, if you owned 100 shares, and there were three candidates, you could cast 300 votes for one of them and ignore the others. With this system, people owning a smaller number of shares can concentrate on one or two candidates. That means they may have a better chance of influencing the makeup of the board.

Step-up in basis
When you inherit assets, such as securities or property, they are stepped-up in basis.

That means the assets are valued at the amount they are worth when your benefactor dies, or as of the date on which his or her estate is valued, and not on the date the assets were purchased. That new valuation becomes your cost basis.

For example, if your father bought 200 shares of stock for $40 a share in 1965, and you inherited them in 2000 when they were selling for $95 a share, they would have been valued at $95 a share.

If you had sold them for $95 a share, your cost basis would have been $95, not the $40 your father paid for them originally. You would not have had a capital gain and would have owed no tax on the amount you received in the sale.

In contrast, if your father had given you the same stocks as a gift where there is no step-up, your basis would have been $40 a share. So if you sold at $95 a share, you would have had a taxable capital gain of $55 a share (minus commissions).

Stochastic modeling

Stochastic modeling is a statistical process that uses probability and random variables to predict a range of probable investment performances.

The mathematical principles behind stochastic modeling are complex, so it's not something you can do on your own.

But based on information you provide about your age, investments, and risk tolerance, financial analysts may use stochastic modeling to help you evaluate the probability that your current investment portfolio will allow you to meet your financial goals.

Appropriately enough, the term stochastic comes from the Greek word meaning "skillful in aiming."

Stock

Stock is an equity investment that represents part ownership in a corporation and entitles you to part of that corporation's earnings and assets.

Common stock gives shareholders voting rights but no guarantee of dividend payments. Preferred stock provides no voting rights but usually guarantees a dividend payment.

In the past, shareholders received a paper stock certificate—called a

security—verifying the number of shares they owned. Today, share ownership is usually recorded electronically, and the shares are held in street name by your brokerage firm.

Stock certificate

A stock certificate is a paper document that represents ownership shares in a corporation.

In the past, when you bought stock, you got a certificate that listed your name as owner, and showed the number of shares and other relevant information. When you sold the stock, you endorsed the certificate and sent it to your broker.

Stock certificates have been phased out, however, and replaced by electronic records. That means you don't have to safeguard the certificates, and can sell shares by giving an order over the phone or online.

The chief objection that's been raised to the new system is largely nostalgic and aesthetic, since the certificates, with their finely engraved borders and images, are distinctive and often beautiful.

Stock market

A stock market may be a physical place, sometimes known as a stock exchange, where brokers gather to buy and sell stocks and other securities.

The term is also used more broadly to include electronic trading that takes place over computer and telephone lines. In fact, in many markets around the world, all stock trading is handled electronically.

Stock option

A stock option, or equity option, is a contract that gives its buyer the right to buy or sell a specific stock at a preset price during a certain time period.

The exact terms are spelled out in the contract. The same contract obligates the seller, also known as the writer, to meet its terms to buy or sell the stock if the option is exercised. If an option isn't exercised within the set period, it expires.

The buyer pays the seller a premium for the privilege of having the right to exercise, and the seller keeps that premium whether or not the option is exercised. The buyer has the right to sell the contract at any point before expiration, and might choose to sell if the sale provides a profit. The seller has the right to buy an offsetting contract at any time before expiration, ending the obligation to meet the contract's terms.

Stock options are also a form of employee compensation that gives employees—often corporate executives—the right to buy shares in the company at a specific price known as the strike price. If the stock price rises, and an employee has a substantial number of options, the rewards can be extremely handsome.

However, if the stock price falls, the options can be worthless. Often, there are time limits governing when employees can exercise their options and when they can sell the stock. These options, unlike equity options, can't be traded among investors.

Stock split

When a company wants to make its shares more attractive and affordable to a greater number of investors, it may authorize a stock split to create more shares selling at a lower price.

A 2-for-1 stock split, for example, doubles the number of outstanding shares and halves the price. If you own 100 shares of a stock selling at $50 a share, for a total value of $5,000, and the company's directors authorize a 2-for-1 split, you would own 200 shares priced at $25, with the same total value of $5,000.

Announcements of stock splits, or anticipated stock splits, often generate a great deal of interest. Buyers may simply want to take advantage of the lower share price, or they may believe that the split stock will increase in value, moving back toward its presplit price.

While 2-for-1 splits are the most common, stocks can be also be split 3-for-1, 10-for-1, or any other combination. In addition, a company can reverse the process and consolidate shares to reduce their number by authorizing a reverse stock split.

Stop order

You can issue a stop order, which instructs your broker to buy or sell a security once it trades at a certain price, called the stop price.

Stop orders are entered below the current price if you are selling and above the current price if you are buying. Once the stop price is reached, your order becomes a market order and is executed.

For example, if you owned a stock currently trading at $35 a share that you feared might drop in price, you could issue a stop order to sell if the price dropped to $30 a share to protect yourself against a larger loss.

The risk is that if the price drops very quickly, and other orders have been placed before yours, the stock could actually end up selling for less than $30. You can give a stop order as a day order or as a good 'til canceled (GTC) order.

You might use a buy stop order if you have sold stock short anticipating a downward movement of the market price of the security. If, instead, the price rises to the stop price, the order will be executed, limiting your loss.

However, there is a risk with this type of order if the market price of the stock rises very rapidly. Other orders entered ahead of yours will be executed first, and you might buy at a price considerably higher than the stop limit, increasing your loss.

Stop price

When you give an order to buy or sell a stock or other security once it has reached a certain price, the price you name is known as the stop price.

When you ask your broker to buy, your stop price is higher than the current market price. When you're selling, the stop price is lower than the current price.

In either case, once the stop price has been reached, your broker will execute the order even if a flurry of trading drives the stock's price up or down quickly. That might mean you end up paying more than the stop price if you're buying or get less than the stop price if you're selling.

Stop-limit order

A stop-limit is a combination order that instructs your broker to buy or sell a stock once its price hits a certain target, known as the stop price, but not to pay more for the stock, or sell it for less, than a specific amount, known as the limit price.

For example, if you give an order to buy at "40 stop 43 limit," you might end up spending anywhere from $40 to $43 a share to buy a stock, but not more than $43.

A stop-limit order can protect you from a rapid run-up in price—such as those that may occur with an initial public offering (IPO)—but you also run the risk that your order won't be executed because the stock's price leapfrogs your limit.

Straddle

A straddle is hedging strategy that involves buying or selling a put and a call option on the same underlying instrument at the same strike price and with the same expiration date.

If you buy a straddle, you expect the price of the underlying to move significantly, but you're not sure whether it will go up or down. If you sell a straddle, you hope that the underlying price remains stable at the strike price.

Your risk in buying a straddle is limited to the premium you pay. As a seller, your risk is much higher because, if the price of the underlying security moves significantly, you may be assigned at exercise to purchase or sell the underlying security at a potential loss.

Similarly, if you choose to buy offsetting contracts when the prices move, it may cost you more than the premium you collected.

Straight life

A straight life insurance policy is a type of permanent insurance that provides a guaranteed death benefit and has fixed premiums. This traditional life insurance is sometimes also known as whole life insurance or cash value insurance.

With a straight life policy, a portion of your premium pays for the insurance and the rest accumulates tax deferred in a cash value account.

You may be able to borrow against the cash value, but any amount that you haven't repaid when you die reduces the death benefit.

If you end the policy, you get the cash surrender value back, which is the cash value minus fees and expenses. However, ending the policy means you no longer have life insurance and no death benefit will be paid at your death.

Strangle

A strangle is a hedging strategy in which you buy or sell a put and a call option on the same underlying instrument with the same expiration date but at different strike prices that are equally out-of-the-money.

That is, the strike price for a put is above the current market price of the stock, stock index, or other product, and the strike price for a call is below the market price.

If you buy a strangle, you hope for a large price move in one direction or another that would allow you to sell one of the contracts at a significant profit. If you sell a strangle, you hope there's no significant price move in either direction so that the contracts expire out-of-the-money and you keep the premium you received.

Street name

Street name is a way to identify stock that is registered in a broker-dealer's name rather than in the name of the actual, or beneficial, owner.

Stock registered in street name is also said to be held in nominee name. The advantage of having your stocks registered in street name is that the shares are secure and at the same time can be traded more easily. That's because you don't have to sign and deliver the stock certificates before a sale can be completed.

There's an advantage from the broker-dealer's perspective as well, since stocks held in street name can be used to complete a trade or in other transactions, subject to regulatory limits.

Strike price

The strike price, also called the exercise price, is the price at which you as an options holder can buy or sell the stock or other financial instrument underlying the options contract if you choose to exercise before expiration.

While the strike price is set by the exchange on which the option trades, and changes only if there's a stock split, merger, or some other corporate action that affects the underlying instrument, the market price of the underlying instrument rises and falls during the life of the contract.

As a result, the underlying instrument might reach a price that would put the strike price in-the-money and make exercising the option at the strike price, or selling the option in the marketplace financially advantageous, or it might not. If not, you let the option expire.

STRIPS

STRIPS, an acronym for separate trading of registered interest and principal of securities, are special issues of US Treasury zero-coupon bonds. They're created and sold by brokerage firms, not by the government.

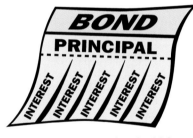

The bonds are prestripped, which means that the issue is separated into the principal and a series of individual interest payments, and each of those parts is offered separately as a zero-coupon security.

Structured product

Financial institutions create investment products, known generically as structured products, that trade on a stock exchange and link the return on an investor's principal to the performance of an underlying security, such as a stock or basket of stocks, or to a derivative, such as a stock index.

For example, the return on debt securities known as structured notes is determined by the performance of a stock index such as the Standard & Poor's 500 (S&P 500) rather than the market interest rate. The objective is to provide the potential for higher returns than are available through a conventional investment.

Each product has a distinctive name, often expressed as an acronym, and its terms and conditions vary somewhat from those offered by its competitors.

For example, in some cases the principal is protected and in others it isn't. But some features are characteristic of these complex investments—their value always involves an underlying financial instrument and they require investors to commit a minimum investment amount for a specific term, such as three years.

Stub stock

When a company has a negative net worth as a result of being bought out or going bankrupt, it may convert some of the bonds it has issued into shares of common stock.

Perhaps because each share is worth only a portion of the original bond's value, this new stock is known as stub stock.

The issuing company's financial instability makes stub stock a volatile investment. But if the company regains its strength, stub stock can increase dramatically in value.

Subaccount

The separate account funds to which you allocate your variable annuity premiums are sometimes called subaccounts.

Each subaccount is managed by an investment specialist, or team of specialists, who make buy and sell decisions based on the subaccount's objective and their analysts' research.

If you're comparing different contracts to decide which to purchase, among the factors to consider are the variety of sub-accounts each contract offers, the past performance of those subaccounts, the experience of the professional manager, and the fees.

In evaluating the past performance and other details of the subaccounts a contract offers, or those you select in the contract you choose, you can use the prospectus the annuity company provides for each subaccount. You may also be able to find independent research from firms such as Morningstar, Inc., Standard & Poor's, and Lipper. However, past performance is not indicative of future results.

Subclass

Each asset class—stock, bonds, and cash equivalents, for example—is made up of a number of different groups of investments called subclasses.

Each member of a subclass shares distinctive qualities with other members of the subclass.

For example, some of the subclasses of the asset class bonds are US Treasury bonds, mortgage-backed agency bonds, corporate bonds, and high-yield bonds.

Similarly, some of the subclasses of stock are large-, medium-, and small-company stock, blue chip stock, growth stock, value stock, and income stock.

Because different subclasses of an asset class perform differently, carry different risks, and may go up and down in value at different times, you may be able to increase your return and offset certain risks by diversifying your portfolio, which means holding individual securities within a variety of subclasses within each asset class.

Subordinated debt

Subordinated debt generally refers to debt securities that have a secondary or lesser claim to the issuer's assets than more senior debt, should the issuer default on its obligations.

In fact, there are also levels of subordinated debt, with senior subordinated debt having a higher claim to repayment than junior subordinated debt.

Subscription price

The subscription price is the discounted price at which a current shareholder can buy additional shares of company stock before these newly available shares are offered for sale to the general public.

In some cases the shareholder can buy the new shares without incurring a brokerage fee.

Subscription right

If a corporation's charter has a pre-emptive rights clause, before the company offers a new issue of securities to the public, it must offer existing shareholders the opportunity to buy new shares of stock in proportion to the number they already own.

That obligation is known as a subscription right, or a rights offering, and allows you to maintain the same percentage of ownership you had before the new issue.

Usually you receive one right for every share you already own, although the number of rights you need to buy a share depends on the number of outstanding shares in relation to the number in the proposed new issue.

Rights are transferable, and may be traded on the secondary market. For example, if you don't wish to purchase additional shares, you may choose to sell your rights.

If you need additional rights to make a purchase, you may buy them. Rights have expiration dates, so you typically must act promptly to take advantage of the offer.

Substitute check

Substitute checks are digital copies of the fronts and backs of paper checks that provide the same legal protections and obligations as the originals, including serving as proof of payment.

Each check is formatted on a separate piece of paper a little larger than the original with the words "This is a legal copy of your check" appearing next to the image.

Using digital copies, which can be transmitted electronically, allows banks to process payments faster and more efficiently than they could when paper checks had to be routed through the check clearing system. Most banks destroy original checks once they've archived the substitutes, which means that you probably no longer receive cancelled checks with your bank statement.

Your bank may send you substitute checks but is more likely to provide either a line item statement or an image statement that has photocopies of the fronts and backs of cancelled checks grouped on a page. These are not substitute checks, although they can often be used as proof of payment.

If you need an actual copy of a substitute check, you can request it from your bank. However, there may be a fee.

Suitability rules

Self-regulatory organizations (SROs), such as NASD, securities exchanges, and individual brokerage firms require that stockbrokers ensure that the investments they buy for you are suitable for you.

This means, for example, that the investments are appropriate for your age, financial situation, investment objectives, and tolerance for risk.

Brokerage firms require investors opening accounts to provide enough information about their financial picture to enable the broker to know what investments would be suitable.

Surrender fee

A surrender fee is the penalty you owe if you withdraw money from an annuity or mutual fund within a certain time period after purchase. The period is set by the seller.

In the case of a mutual fund, it's designed to prevent in-and-out trading in a fund, which might require the fund manager to liquidate holdings in order to redeem your shares.

In the case of an annuities contract, there's the additional motive of covering the sales charge paid to the investment professional who sold you the product.

Survivorship life

Survivorship life insurance, also known as a second-to-die policy, is permanent insurance that covers the lives of two people and pays the death benefit only after the death of the second person.

Survivorship life may be appropriate for married couples with substantial wealth if estate taxes might be due after the death of the second person.

The death benefit would be available to cover the amount due at the federal or state level, protecting some of or all the assets from having to be sold to cover these tax bills.

However, the premiums on survivorship life policies are often higher than the cost of other types of permanent insurance.

Suspended trading

Suspended trading means that an exchange has temporarily stopped trading in a particular stock or other security.

Trading is typically halted either because an important piece of information

about the issuing company is about to be released or because there's a serious imbalance between buy and sell orders, often triggered by speculation.

In the case of an expected announcement, the affected company generally notifies the exchange that the news is imminent. The suspension, or trading halt, provides time for the marketplace to absorb the announcement, good or bad, and helps reduce volatility in the stock price.

Examples of news that could cause a suspension are a poorer than expected earnings report, a major innovation or discovery, a merger, or significant legal problems. The Securities and Exchange Commission (SEC) can also suspend trading in the stock of a company it suspects of misleading or illegal activity.

Swap

When you swap or exchange securities, you sell one security and buy a comparable one almost simultaneously.

Swapping enables you to change the maturity or the quality of the holdings in your portfolio. You can also use swaps to realize a capital loss for tax purposes by selling securities that have gone down in value since you purchased them.

More complex swaps, including interest rate swaps and currency swaps, are used by corporations doing business in more than one country to protect themselves against sudden, dramatic shifts in currency exchange rates or interest rates.

Sweep account

A brokerage firm or bank may automatically transfer—or sweep—a client's uninvested or surplus funds into a designated account.

For instance, at the end of each business day, a bank might sweep a business client's surplus cash from a checking account into a high-yield money market or savings account, where the money earns interest overnight. The next morning, the bank would make these funds again available to the customer.

Individuals are more likely to have sweep arrangements with their brokerage firm to handle investment earnings.

Syndicate

When a group of investment banks works together to underwrite and distribute a new security issue, they are acting as a syndicate.

Syndicates are temporary, forming to purchase the securities from the issuer and dissolving once the issue is distributed.

However, new syndicates, involving some of or all the same banks, form on a regular basis to underwrite each new issue. You may also hear these underwriting syndicates called purchase groups, underwriting groups, or distributing syndicates.

In other financial contexts, syndicate may refer to any group of financial institutions that works together on a particular project. Syndicate also describes a group of investors who make a joint investment in a company.

Synthetic investment

A synthetic investment simulates the return of an actual investment, but the return is actually created by using a combination of financial instruments, such as options contracts or an equity index and debt securities, rather than a single conventional investment.

For example, an investment firm might create a synthetic index that seeks to outperform a particular index by purchasing options contracts rather than the equities the actual index owns, and using the money it saves to buy cash equivalents or other debt securities to enhance its return on the derivatives.

Options spreads, structured products, and certain investments in real estate and guaranteed investment contracts can be described as synthetic products.

While they are artificial, they can play a legitimate role in an individual or institutional investor's portfolio as a way to reduce risk, increase diversification, enjoy a stronger return, or meet needs that conventional investments don't satisfy.

However, synthetic investments may carry added fees and add more complexity than you are comfortable dealing with.

Systematic risk

Systematic risk, also called market risk, is risk that's characteristic of an entire market, a specific asset class, or a portfolio invested in that asset class.

It's the opposite of the risk posed by individual securities in a class or portfolio, also known as nonsystematic risk. The predictable impact that rising interest rates have on the prices of previously issued bonds is one example of systematic risk.

Systematic withdrawal

Systematic withdrawal is a method of receiving income in regular installments from your mutual fund accounts, retirement plans, or annuity contracts.

Generally, you decide how much you want to receive in each payment, and the schedule on which you want to receive the income. Those payments continue until you stop them or you run out of money.

Unlike the alternatives, such as a pension annuity, systematic withdrawal gives you the flexibility to stop payments at any time, adjust the amount you receive, or choose a different way to access your money.

By withdrawing the same amount on a regular schedule, you limit the risk of taking a large lump sum at a time when your account value has dropped because of a market decline.

The chief drawback of this withdrawal method is that there's no guarantee of lifetime income, so it's possible to deplete your account more quickly than the rate at which it's growing. That could mean running out of money.

After you reach 70½, you can use systematic withdrawals as a way to ensure you take out the minimum required distribution (MRD) from qualified retirement accounts and IRAs to avoid the risk of incurring IRS penalties.

Tailgating

When a broker places your order for a security, and then immediately places an order for his or her own account for the same security, the broker is tailgating.

Although this practice, which is also known as piggybacking, isn't illegal, it is considered unethical, because the assumption is that the broker is trying to profit from information the broker believes you have about the stock.

A broker will typically tailgate only when you buy stock in a sufficient quantity to potentially affect the price of the security.

Target date fund

A target date fund is a fund of funds that allows you to link your investment portfolio to a particular time horizon, typically your expected retirement date.

In fact, a target date fund characteristically has a date in its name, such as a 2015 Fund or a 2030 Fund.

A target fund aiming at a date in the somewhat distant future tends to have a fairly aggressive asset allocation, with a focus on growth. As the target date approaches, the fund is designed to become more conservative to preserve the assets that have accumulated and eventually to provide income.

Each fund company formulates its own approach to risk, so that the allocation of one 2025 Fund may be noticeably different from the allocation of a 2025 Fund from a different company.

You can find model portfolios and statements of investment strategy in the fund's prospectus. Each mutual fund company that offers target date funds tends to offer a series, with dates five or ten years apart.

Most companies populate their funds of funds with individual funds from their fund family, though some companies add mutual funds or exchange traded funds from other investment companies.

Like other funds of funds, the fees you pay for a target date fund may be higher than you would pay to own each of the individual funds separately. However, these fees pay for an additional level of professional oversight.

Target risk fund

A target risk fund is a fund of funds that maintains a specific asset allocation in order to provide an essentially level exposure to investment risk.

You may find a target risk fund attractive if you want a professional manager to keep your portfolio aligned with your risk tolerance as you pursue specific investment goals.

Target risk funds are generally available with conservative, moderate, and aggressive portfolios, and some mutual fund companies offer even more finely tuned approaches.

Like other funds of funds, the fees you pay for a target risk fund may be higher than you would pay to own each of the individual funds separately. However, these fees pay for an additional level of professional oversight.

Tax bracket

A tax bracket is a range of income that is taxed at a specific rate.

In the United States there are six brackets, taxed at 10%, 15%, 25%, 28%, 33%, and 35% of the amount that falls into each bracket.

For example, if your taxable income was high enough to cross three brackets, you'd pay tax at the 10% rate on income in the lowest bracket, at the 15% rate on income in the next bracket, and at the 25% rate on the rest.

The rates remain fixed until they are changed by Congress, but the dollar amounts in each bracket change slightly each year to adjust for inflation.

In addition, the income that falls into each bracket varies by filing status, so that if you file as a single taxpayer you may owe more tax on the same taxable income as a married couple filing a joint return.

Tax credit

A tax credit is an amount you can subtract from the tax you would otherwise owe. Unlike a deduction or exemption, a credit is a dollar-for-dollar reduction of your tax bill.

For example, if you pay someone to care for your young children or for elderly or disabled relatives, you may be able to subtract that money, up to a set limit.

Among the other tax credits for which you may qualify are the Hope scholarship and lifetime learning education credits, a credit for purchasing a hybrid car, or a credit for adopting a child. The list changes from time to time.

Some but not all credits are available to people whose income is less than the ceilings Congress sets. Other credits are available to anyone who has spent the money.

Tax deferred

A tax-deferred account allows you to post-pone income tax that would otherwise be due on employment or investment earnings you hold in the account until some point the future, often when you retire.

For example, you can contribute pretax income to employer retirement plans, such as a traditional 401(k) or 403(b).

You owe no tax on any earnings in these plans, or in traditional individual retirement accounts (IRAs), fixed and variable annuities, and some insurance policies until you withdraw the money. Then tax is due on the amounts you take out, at the same rate you pay on your regular income.

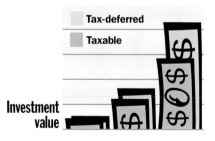

A big advantage of tax deferral is that earnings may compound more quickly, since no money is being taken out of the account to pay taxes. But in return for postponing taxes, you agree to limited access to your money before you reach 59½.

Tax exempt

Some investments are tax exempt, which means you don't have to pay income tax on the earnings they produce.

For example, the interest you receive on a municipal bond is generally exempt from federal income tax, and also exempt from state and local income tax if you live in the state where the bond was issued.

However, if you sell the bond before maturity, any capital gain is taxable.

Similarly, dividends on bond mutual funds that invest in municipal bonds are exempt from federal income tax. And for residents of the issuing state for single-state funds, the dividends are also exempt from state and local taxes.

Capital gains on these funds are never tax exempt.

Earnings in a Roth IRA are tax exempt when you withdraw them, provided your account has been open for five years or more and you're at least 59½ years old. And earnings in 529 college savings plans and Coverdell education savings accounts (ESAs) are also tax exempt if the money is used to pay qualified education expenses.

When an organization such as a religious, educational, or charitable institution, or other not-for-profit group, is tax exempt, it does not owe tax of any kind to federal, state, and local governments. In addition, you can take an income tax deduction for gifts you make to such organizations.

Tax-efficient funds

When a mutual fund minimizes the income earnings and capital gains it distributes to its shareholders, it may be described as a tax-efficient fund.

In general, the smaller a fund's turnover, or the less buying and selling it does, the more tax-efficient it has the potential to be. That's one reason why index funds, which buy and sell investments only when the composition of the index they track changes, are generally tax-efficient.

In addition to reducing turnover, actively managed funds may increase tax efficiency by emphasizing investments expected to grow in value over those that produce current taxable income, or yield. And they may postpone the sale of certain investments until they qualify as long-term capital gains, making them subject to a lower tax rate.

Funds that emphasize tax efficiency generally include that goal in their statement of investment objectives.

Teaser rate

A teaser rate is a low introductory interest rate on a credit card or an adjustable rate mortgage (ARM). The lender must tell you how long the teaser rate lasts and what the real cost of borrowing will be at the end of the introductory period.

Technical analysis

Technical analysts track price movements and trading volumes in various securities to identify patterns in the price behavior of particular stocks, mutual funds, commodities, or options in specific market sectors or in the overall financial markets.

The goal is to predict probable, often short-term, price changes in the investments that they study, which allows them to choose an appropriate trading strategy.

The speed and accuracy with which the analysts create their tracking charts has been enhanced by the development of increasingly sophisticated software.

Tenancy-in-common

When two or more people own property as tenants-in-common (TIC), they share in the property's tax benefits, any income it generates, and its growth in value, as well as expenses of ownership.

If one owner dies, that owner's share of the property becomes part of his or her estate, to be sold or distributed among heirs as the owner instructs.

TIC arrangements are a popular way to structure the ownership of real estate investments, in which two or more parties buy commercial property to generate income. However, siblings might also own family property in this way, as might business partners.

Tender offer

When a corporation or other investor offers to buy a large portion of outstanding shares of another company, called the target company, at a price higher than the market price, it is called a tender offer.

The tender is usually part of a bid to take over the target company. Current stockholders, individually or as a group, can accept or reject the offer.

If the tender offer is successful and the corporation accumulates 5% or more of another company, it has to report its holdings to the Securities and Exchange Commission (SEC), the target company, and the exchange or market on which the target company's shares are traded.

Term

A term is the length of time between when a fixed-income security, such as a bond or note, is offered for sale and its maturity date.

When the term ends, the issuer repays the par value of the security, often along with the final interest payment. In general, the longer the term, the higher the rate of interest the investment pays, to offset the increased risk of tying up your money for a longer period of time.

Term is also the lifespan of a certificate of deposit (CD), called a time deposit. If you hold a CD for the entire term, which may run from six months to five years, you collect the full amount of interest the CD has paid during the term and are free to roll the principal into a new CD or use the money for something else.

Term insurance

A term life insurance policy provides a guaranteed death benefit for a set period of time, such as five, ten, or 20 years, provided you continue to pay the premiums as they are due.

At the end of the term, the coverage ends unless you renew the policy or switch to another one.

Term life insurance policies have either a level term, which means that the annual premium remains the same for the life of the policy, or a graduated term, which means that the premium is smaller in the early years and grows larger each year. In most cases, level term policies cost less if you keep the policy in force for the entire term.

Term policies don't accumulate a cash value, so you get nothing back if you end your coverage before the end of the term. However, term insurance may be less expensive than a permanent policy providing the same coverage, although the cost of new coverage increases as you get older.

Thin market

A thin market is one where securities trade infrequently. The term can refer to an entire securities market, such as one in an emerging nation, a specific class of securities, such as micro-cap stocks, or an individual security.

Thinly traded

A particular stock, sector, or market is said to be thinly traded if transactions occur only infrequently, and there are a limited number of interested buyers and sellers.

Prices of thinly traded securities tend to be more volatile than those traded more actively because just a few trades can affect the market price substantially.

It can also be difficult to sell shares of thinly traded securities, especially in a downturn, if there is no ready buyer. Shares of small- and micro-cap companies are more likely to be thinly traded than those of mid- or large-cap stocks.

Third market

Exchange-listed securities, such as those that are traded on the New York Stock Exchange (NYSE) or the American Stock Exchange (AMEX), may also be bought and sold off the exchange, or over-the-counter (OTC), in what is known as the third market.

Typically, third-market transactions are large block trades involving securities firms and institutional investors, such as investment companies and pension funds.

With the growth of electronic communications networks (ECNs), more institutional investors are buying and selling in this way. Among the appeals of the third market are speed, reduced trading costs, and anonymity.

Tick

A tick is the minimum movement by which the price of a security, option, or index changes.

With stocks, a tick may be little as one cent. With US Treasury securities, the smallest increment is 1/32 of a point, or 31.25 cents.

An uptick represents an increase over the last different price, and a downtick a drop from the last different price.

Ticker (tape)

While the stock markets are in session, there is a running record of trading activity in each individual stock. Today's computerized system, still referred to as the ticker, actually replaces the scrolling paper tape of the past.

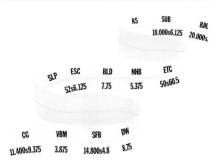

Ticker symbol

A ticker symbol, also known as a stock symbol, is a unique string of letters that identifies a particular stock on one of two electronic tapes that report market transactions.

The consolidated tape includes companies that trade on the New York Stock Exchange (NYSE), the American Stock Exchange (AMEX), regional exchanges and other markets. A second tape includes companies that trade on the Nasdaq Stock Market.

Most corporations have a say in what their symbol will be, and many choose one that's clearly linked to their name, such as IBM or AMZN for Amazon.com.

Various letters may be added to a ticker symbol to indicate where the trade took place or that there was something atypical about the transaction. For example, IBM.Pr would indicate that the trade involved preferred stock.

Time deposit

When you put money into a bank or savings and loan account with a fixed term, such as a certificate of deposit (CD), you are making a time deposit.

Time deposits may pay interest at a higher rate than demand deposit accounts, such as checking or money market accounts, from which you can withdraw at any time.

But if you withdraw from a time deposit account before the term ends, you may have to pay a penalty—sometimes as much as all the interest that has been credited to your account. Some other time deposits require you to give advance notice if you plan to withdraw money.

Time value of money

The time value of money is money's potential to grow in value over time.

Because of this potential, money that's available in the present is considered more valuable than the same amount in the future.

For example, if you were given $100 today and invested it at an annual rate of only 1%, it could be worth $101 at the end of one year, which is more than you'd have if you received $100 at that point.

In addition, because of money's potential to increase in value over time, you can use the time value of money to calculate how much you need to invest now to meet a certain future goal. Many financial websites and personal investment handbooks help you calculate these amounts based on different interest rates.

Inflation has the reverse effect on the time value of money. Because of the constant decline in the purchasing power of money, an uninvested dollar is worth more in the present than the same uninvested dollar will be in the future.

Title

A title is a legal document proving ownership of a piece of property.

If you are buying real estate you authorize a title search, or examination of property records, to insure that the seller holds the title and has the right to transfer it.

In most cases, if you're taking a mortgage to buy the property, the lender will require you to arrange title insurance to protect its interest until the full amount of the loan has been repaid. You may also arrange for your own title insurance to protect you from losing your property if your ownership is successfully contested.

Title insurance

Title insurance protects your lender's interest in your home and real property in case its ownership is contested in court.

Before you close on any property purchase, your lender will require a title search—an examination of all the property records by an attorney or title company, to ensure that the seller owns the property and has the right to sell it.

But just in case something is not revealed in the title search, your lender will usually require you to obtain title insurance as added protection until you have paid off your mortgage. You may also choose to purchase additional insurance to protect your own title and claim to the property.

Usually, you pay for title insurance as a one-time cost at closing. While some states regulate title insurance costs, others don't.

Title search

A title search is an examination of property records by a title company or attorney to ensure that the person from whom you are buying a piece of property is its legal owner, and that there are no outstanding legal claims against the property.

Your lender will require you to pay for a title search before the closing, or settlement, on your new home.

The title search consists of a close examination of public records, such as deeds, wills, court judgments, and trusts, to make sure that the seller has the right to sell the property to you and that all prior mortgages, liens, and judgments have been settled.

Sometimes the title search uncovers pending legal actions, undisclosed easements, or even claims on the property by heirs to prior owners. Since title examiners might miss problems and public records can contain errors, most lenders will require you to purchase title insurance at closing to protect their interest in the property.

Toehold purchase

A toehold purchase is one in which an individual investor or investment firm caps holdings in a potential target company at less than 5% of the company's outstanding stock.

Presumably that's because once an investor has acquired 5% or more of the stock, the investor must notify the company, the market where the company is listed, and the Securities and Exchange Commission (SEC). That notification must explain the next steps the investor intends to take, such as a possible takeover bid.

Total return

Total return is your annual gain or loss on an equity or debt investment.

It includes dividends or interest, plus any change in the market value of the investment. When total return is expressed as a percentage, it's figured by dividing the increase or decrease in value, plus dividends or interest, by the original purchase price.

On bonds you hold to maturity, however, your total return is the same as your yield to maturity (YTM).

TOTAL RETURN

$$\frac{\text{Change in value + earnings}}{\text{Cost of initial investment}} = \text{TOTAL RETURN (\%)}$$

Calculating total return is more complex if your earnings have been reinvested, as they often are in a mutual fund, to buy more shares. But fund companies do that calculation on a regular basis.

Total return index

A total return index is an equity market index that's calculated using the assumption that all the dividends that the stocks in the index pay are reinvested in the index as a whole.

Since an index is not an investment, but a statistical computation, the reinvestment occurs only on paper, or, more precisely, in a software program.

Tracking stock

Some corporations issue tracking stock, a type of common stock whose value is linked to the performance of a particular division or business within a larger corporation rather than to the corporation as a whole.

Tracking stock separates the finances of the division from those of the parent company, so that if the division falters or takes time to become profitable, the value of the traditional common stock won't be affected.

If you own tracking stock, you actually are invested in the parent company, since it continues to own the division that's being tracked, though typically you have no shareholder's voting rights in the corporation.

Trade date

The trade date is the day on which you buy or sell a security, option, or futures contract.

The settlement date, on which cash and securities are delivered, occurs one or more days after the trade date, depending on the type of security that you're trading.

Options and futures contracts settle on T+1, or one business day after the trade date, and stocks settle on T+3, or three business days after the trade.

Trader

Traders who are dealers or market makers select the securities in which they will specialize and provide quotes on those securities in the marketplace.

They commit their firm's capital by taking positions in those securities and are ready to buy and sell at the prices they quote.

Traders known as competitive or floor traders buy and sell securities for their own accounts. They don't pay commissions, so they can profit on small differences in price, but they must abide by the rules established by the exchange or market on which they trade.

The term trader also describes people who execute transactions at brokerage firms, asset management firms, and mutual fund companies.

Trading floor

The trading floor is the active trading area of a stock exchange, such as the New York Stock Exchange (NYSE).

Securities are traded double auction style on an exchange trading floor. That means the prices are set by competitive bidding between brokers representing buyers and brokers representing sellers, following a series of clearly established exchange rules.

Many market maker firms refer to the space in their offices that they have allocated for trading as their trading floor. The same term is used to describe the trading areas in banks and brokerage firms.

Trading range

A trading range means different things on different types of markets.

On a stock exchange or over-the-counter market, it's the spread between the highest and lowest prices at which a particular stock or market as a whole has been trading over a period of time.

Some of the commodities exchanges set a trading range for each commodity because of the minimum margin required to maintain a position. If the market price moves above or below the trading range, trading is halted to give the member firms the opportunity to issue margin calls and collect the required money from customers whose account values are below the margin requirements.

Trading symbol

All companies listed on the New York Stock Exchange (NYSE), the American Stock Exchange (AMEX), or the NASDAQ Stock Market are represented by a unique combination of one to five letters of the alphabet.

TICKER SYMBOLS

Single letter

F	Ford Motor Co. (NYSE)
T	AT&T (NYSE)
S	Sprint Nextel (NYSE)

Symbols for Smiles

DNA	Genentech (NYSE)
BOOT	La Crosse Footwear (Nasdaq)
TAP	Molson Coors (NYSE)

Simple Symbols

MSFT	Microsoft Corp. (Nasdaq)
IBM	International Business Machines (NYSE)
EBAY	eBay Inc. (Nasdaq)

Some, but not all, trading symbols are easily associated with their companies, such as GE for General Electric or YHOO for Yahoo!.

Sometimes, the exchange trading symbol varies slightly from the way the company is designated on the ticker.

Trading volume

Trading volume is the quantity of stocks, bonds, futures contracts, options, or other investments that are bought sold in a specific period of time, normally a day. It's an indication of the interest that investors have in that particular security or product at its current price.

Tranche

Certain securities, such as collateralized mortgage obligations (CMOs), are made up of a number of classes, called tranches, that differ from each other because they pay different interest rates, mature on different dates, carry different levels of risk, or differ in some other way.

When the security is offered for sale, each of these tranches is sold separately.

Similarly, a large certificate of deposit (CD) may be subdivided into smaller certificates for sale to individual investors. Each smaller certificate, or tranche, matures on the same date and pays the same rate of interest, but is worth a fraction of the total amount.

Transfer

In a transfer, a 401(k) or IRA custodian or trustee moves the assets in your existing account directly to the custodian or trustee of your new account.

With a transfer, you don't risk failing to deposit the full amount of your withdrawal within the 60-day deadline for rollovers. And, in the case of a transfer from a 401(k) or similar retirement savings plan, nothing is withheld for income taxes.

In contrast, if you handle the rollover yourself, your employer must withhold 20% of the account value.

When securities are sent to a transfer agent for reregistration of the ownership name, this process is also known as a transfer.

Securities may be registered in the actual, or beneficial, owner's name, or in the name of a nominee, known as street name. Most stocks that are held by brokerage firms for their clients are registered in nominee name on the transfer agent's books.

Transfer agent

A transfer agent is responsible to a corporation for keeping track of who owns the corporation's stock and bonds and whether those securities are registered in the name of an individual investor or a brokerage firm, which is known as street name registration.

In some cases, stocks can be registered directly on the books of an issuer or its transfer agent using the direct registration system (DRS).

Increasingly, ownership records are electronic, though a transfer agent may issue stock and bond certificates to new owners if they request them. The transfer agent also receives certificates that represent securities that have been sold or returned to be reregistered.

Transferable-on-death

A securities or brokerage account titled transferable-on-death (TOD) lets you name one or more beneficiaries, to whom the account assets are transferred when you die. TOD accounts are available only in some states, and laws may vary.

Nonetheless, TOD accounts can be useful estate planning tools where they are available, since the assets in the account can pass to your beneficiaries directly, outside the probate process.

A similar type of registration is available in some states for bank accounts. They're known as payable-on-death, or POD, accounts.

Transparency

Transparency is a measure of how much information you have about the markets where you invest, the corporations whose stocks or bonds you buy, or the mutual funds or other investments you select.

For example, in order to achieve maximum transparency in US markets, the Securities and Exchange Commission (SEC) requires corporations to disclose all information that might have an impact on their financial status so that investors can make fully informed decisions.

Real-time trading information, increasingly available to individuals as well as institutional investors, and linked pricing systems are other steps toward complete transparency.

Treasury bill (T-bill)

Treasury bills are the shortest-term government debt securities.

They are issued with a maturity date of 4, 13, or 26 weeks. The 13- and 26-week bills are sold weekly by competitive auction to institutional investors, and to noncompetitive bidders through Treasury Direct for the same price paid by the competitive bidders.

Treasury bond

Treasury bonds are long-term government debt securities with a maturity date of 30 years that are issued in denominations of $1,000.

You can buy any number of these bonds at issue in $1,000 increments, but not more than $5 million. Those purchases as well as sales can be made through a Treasury Direct account. Existing bonds trade in the secondary market.

While interest on Treasury bonds is federally taxable, it is exempt from state and local taxes. Treasury bonds are considered among the most secure investments in the world, since they are backed by the federal government.

However, like all debt securities, they are subject to market risk. This means their prices change to reflect supply and demand.

Treasury Direct

Treasury Direct is a direct investment system, offered through the US Department of the Treasury, that lets you make competitive or noncompetitive bids for new US Treasury issues.

Once you open a Treasury Direct account, you can buy, sell, or roll over your investments by mail, telephone, or online. Interest paid on your investments, and the value of any securities you redeem at maturity or by sale, are deposited directly into the bank account you designate.

Treasury inflation-protected securities (TIPS)

TIPS, or Treasury inflation-protected securities, are inflation-indexed Treasury bonds and notes.

TIPS pay a fixed rate of interest like traditional Treasurys, but their principal, to which the interest rate is applied, is adjusted twice a year to reflect changes in inflation as measured by the Consumer Price Index (CPI). However, those increases are not paid until the end of the term.

Twice a year the interest rate is multiplied by the new principal, so the interest you receive will increase or decrease as well. Interest is federally taxable, as are any increases in the value of your principal.  The interest is exempt from state and local income taxes.

At maturity, you're repaid the inflation-adjusted principal or par value, whichever is more.

Treasury note

Like US Treasury bills, Treasury notes are debt securities issued by the US government and backed by its full faith and credit.

They are available at issue through Treasury Direct in denominations of $1,000 and are traded in the secondary market after issue.

Notes are intermediate-term securities, with a maturity dates of two, three, five or ten years. The interest you earn on Treasury notes is exempt from state and local, but not federal, taxes.

And while the rate at which the interest is paid is generally less than on long-term corporate bonds, the shorter term means less inflation risk.

Treasury stock

Treasury stock is stock that an issuing company repurchases from its shareholders.

The company may choose to repurchase if it has cash available, as an alternative to investing it in expanding the business. Or it may issue bonds to raise the money it needs to repurchase, which changes the company's debt-to-equity ratio.

In most cases, the company offers to pay a premium, or more than the market price, to build its cache of Treasury stock.

Reducing the number of outstanding shares boosts the per-share value of the remaining shares and tends to increase the market price of the stock. That results, in part, because no dividends are paid on Treasury stock and it's not included in earnings-per-share calculations, boosting that ratio.

A company may buy back its stock for a number of other reasons, ranging from preventing a hostile takeover to having shares available if employees exercise their stock options.

It may also choose to resell the shares or use them to meet the demand for shares from holders of convertible securities.

Trust

When you create a trust, you transfer money or other assets to the trust.

You give up ownership of those assets in order to accomplish a specific financial goal or goals, such as protecting assets from estate taxes, simplifying the transfer of property, or making provision for a minor or other dependents.

When you establish the trust, you are the grantor, and the people or institutions you name to receive the trust assets at some point in the future are known as beneficiaries. You also designate a trustee or trustees, whose job is to manage the assets in the trust and distribute them according to the instructions you provide in the trust document.

Trustee

A trustee is a person or institution appointed to manage assets for someone else's benefit.

For example, a trustee may be responsible for money you have trans-

ferred to a trust, or money in certain retirement accounts.

Trustees are entitled to collect a fee for their work, often a percentage of the value of the amount in trust. In turn, they are responsible for managing the assets in the best interests of the beneficiary of the trust. That's known as fiduciary responsibility.

Truth-in-Lending Act

The Truth-in-Lending Act requires every lender to provide a complete and clear disclosure of the key terms of any lending or leasing arrangement, plus a statement of all costs, before the agreement is finalized.

The statement must include the finance charges stated in dollars and as an annual percentage rate (APR).

For most loans, it must also include the total of the principal amount being financed, all the interest, fees, service charges, points, credit-related insurance premiums, payment due date and terms, and any other charges.

The consumer lending section of the Act, which was first passed in 1968 and then simplified and reformed in 1980, is also known as Regulation Z. The consumer leasing section is known as Regulation M.

Turnover ratio

A mutual fund's turnover ratio measures the percentage of holdings that the fund sells, or turns over, in a year.

For example, if a stock fund manager has a portfolio of 100 stocks at the beginning of the year, sells 75 of them and buys 75 different stocks, the turnover rate of the fund is 75%.

Some investors look for funds with lower turnover ratios, since limited trading may help to minimize capital gains taxes and trading costs. However, a high turnover ratio can also produce strong returns, which can offset the added costs and produce a net gain.

Uncovered option

An uncovered option, also known as a naked option, is an option that is not backed by another position.

For example, if you sell a call option without owning the stock that you would have to deliver if the option holder exercised, the call is uncovered.

Similarly, if you sell an uncovered put, you don't have adequate cash in reserve to fulfill your obligation to purchase the underlying instrument at exercise.

Writing uncovered contracts can put you at significant risk despite the premium you collect when you open the position.

For example, if a naked call option were exercised and assigned to you, you would have to buy the underlying instrument at its market price to be able to meet the terms of the contract. Because of the potential risk, your brokerage firm may restrict your right to write uncovered positions or may require you to trade these options in a margin account.

Underlying instrument

An underlying instrument is a security, such as a stock, a commodity, or other type of financial product, such as a stock index, whose value determines the value of a derivative investment or product.

For example, if you own a stock option, the stock you have the right to buy or sell according to the terms of that option is the option's underlying instrument.

Underlying instruments may also be called underlying products, underlying interest, or sometimes the underlying investment.

Underlying investment

The investments in a mutual fund, a variable annuity's separate account fund, or other fund makes are considered the fund's underlying investments.

The value of a single share or unit of the fund is based on the combined value of all its underlying investments, minus fees and expenses, divided by the number of outstanding shares or units.

In some cases, when the item underlying a derivative investment is a security, such as the individual stock underlying an equity options contract, it is also called an underlying investment.

However, when the underlying item is a consumable commodity, such as corn, or a financial product, such as an equity index, it is called the underlying product, the underlying instrument, or sometimes simply the underlying.

Undervaluation

Any stock that trades at a lower price than the issuing company's reputation, earnings outlook, or financial situation would seem to merit is considered undervalued.

Undervaluation may occur when investors lose interest in a company, perhaps because it hasn't kept pace with its competitors, or if there are management problems.

Some investors concentrate on identifying and investing in undervalued stocks, sometimes called simply value stocks, drawn by their bargain prices and the expectation of recovery.

Underwater

You're underwater when your employee stock options are out-of-the-money and so currently worthless.

For example, if you have options to buy your company stock at a strike price of $50, and the stock is currently trading at $30, you're $20 underwater on each option. You can see how the next step may be drowning—financially speaking, of course.

The term underwater is also used to describe situations where the principals are unable to meet their financial obligations.

For example, if an investor is unable to meet margin calls on a margin account that has lost a considerable amount of money, the account is said to be underwater. Similarly a firm that is having financial difficulty is described as underwater.

Underweighted

When you own less of a security, an asset class, or a subclass than your target asset allocation calls for, you are said to be underweighted in that security, asset class, or subclass.

For example, if you have decided to invest 30% of your portfolio in fixed-income investments, but the actual holdings account for only 10% of your portfolio, you are underweighted in fixed income.

In another use of the term, a securities analyst might recommend underweighting a particular security, which you might reasonably interpret as advice to sell.

Underwriter

An underwriter, typically an investment banker, may buy an entire new securities issue from the company or government offering it and resell the issue as individual stocks or bonds to the public.

Or, in a best-efforts arrangement on a stock IPO, the underwriter may commit to selling as many shares as possible without actually buying the securities.

Part of the underwriter's job is to weigh the risks involved in taking on the financial responsibility of finding buyers against the profit to be made on the difference between the price paid for the issue and the profit it will generate.

Typically, a number of bankers join forces as a purchase group, or syndicate, to spread the risk around and to reach the widest possible market.

Insurance policies also need an underwriter. In this case, the term refers to a company that is willing to take the risk of insuring your life, property, income, or health in return for a premium, or payment.

Underwriting

Underwriting means insuring.

An insurance company underwrites your policy when it agrees to take the risk of insuring your life or covering your medical expenses in exchange for the premium you pay.

An investment bank underwrites an initial public offering (IPO) or a bond issue when it buys the shares or bonds from the issuer and takes the risk of having to sell them to individual or institutional investors to recover its investment.

Uniform Gifts to Minors Act (UGMA)

Under the UGMA, you as an adult can set up a custodial account for a minor and put assets such as cash, securities, and mutual funds into it.

You pay no fees or charges to set up the account, and there is no limit on the amount you can put into it. To avoid owing potential gift tax, however, you may want to limit what you add each year to an amount that qualifies for the annual gift tax exclusion.

One advantage of an UGMA custodial account is that you can transfer to it assets that you expect to increase in value. That way, any capital gains occur in the account, and you avoid potential estate taxes that might have been due had you owned the asset at your death.

If you sell an asset in the account, taxable capital gains are calculated at the beneficiary's capital gains tax rate provided he or she is 18 or older. Taxable capital gains are calculated at the parents' rate if the child is younger than 18.

One potential disadvantage of a custodial account is that any gift to the account is irrevocable.

The assets become the property of the beneficiary from the moment they go into the account, even though as a minor he or she cannot legally control activity in the account or take money out. At majority, which typically occurs at 18 or 21 depending on the state, the beneficiary may use the assets as he or she wishes.

In addition, if you are both the donor and the custodian, and die while the beneficiary is still a minor, the assets are considered part of your estate. That could make your estate's value large enough to be vulnerable to estate taxes.

Uniform Transfers to Minors Act (UTMA)

The UTMA allows you as an adult to set up a custodial account for a minor, who owns any assets placed in the account. You may act as custodian of the account or name another adult to serve in that role.

The UTMA is similar to the Uniform Gifts to Minors Act (UGMA) in many respects, but you can use an UTMA to gift assets in addition to cash and securities, including real estate, fine art, antiques, patents, and royalties.

You may choose to transfer assets that you expect to increase in value into the UTMA account. That way, any capital gains occur in the account, and you avoid potential estate taxes that might have been due had you owned the asset at your death.

If you sell an asset in the account, taxable gain is figured at the beneficiary's capital gains tax rate provided he or she is 18 or older. Taxable capital gains above a certain limit that Congress sets each year are calculated at the parents' rate if the child is younger than 18.

One potential disadvantage of a custodial account is that any gift to the account is irrevocable. The assets become the property of the beneficiary from the moment they go into the account, even though as a minor he or she cannot legally control activity in the account or take money out.

At majority, which occurs typically at 18, 21, or 25 depending on the state, the beneficiary may use the assets as he or she wishes. To avoid owing potential gift tax, you may want to limit what you add each year to an amount that qualifies for the annual gift tax exclusion.

In addition, if you are both the donor and the custodian, and die while the beneficiary is still a minor, the assets are considered part of your estate. That could make your estate's value large enough to be vulnerable to estate taxes.

Unit investment trust (UIT)
A UIT may be a fixed portfolio of bonds with specific maturity dates, a portfolio of income-producing stocks, or a portfolio of all the securities included in a particular index.

Examples of the latter include the DIAMONDs Trust (DIA), which mirrors the composition of the Dow Jones Industrial Average (DJIA), and Standard & Poor's Depositary Receipts (SPDR), which mirrors the Standard & Poor's 500 Index (S&P 500). Index UITs are also described as exchange traded funds (ETFs).

UITs resemble mutual funds in the sense that they offer the opportunity to diversify your portfolio without having to purchase a number of separate securities. You buy units, rather than shares, of the trust, usually through a broker.

However, UITs trade more like stocks than mutual funds in the sense that you sell in the secondary market rather than redeeming your holding by selling your units back to the issuing fund.

Further, the price of a UIT fluctuates constantly throughout the trading day, just as the price of an individual stock does, rather than being repriced only once a day, after the close of trading. As a result, some UITs, though not index-based UITs such as DIAMONDS or SPDRs, trade at prices higher or lower than their net asset value (NAV).

One additional difference is that many UITs have maturity dates, when the trust expires, while mutual funds do not. A fund may be closed for other reasons, but not because of a predetermined expiration date.

Unit of trading
When you buy stocks, bonds, options and commodities futures, it's typical to buy in a particular volume or a particular dollar value, called a round lot or a unit of trading.

For example, stocks are usually traded in lots of 100 shares, or multiples of 100 shares, and bonds in multiples of $1,000. For some preferred stocks, known as ten-share traders, the unit of trading is ten shares.

Any variation from the standard unit of trading is known as an odd lot.

Unit trust
The category of investment known as a mutual fund in the United States is called a unit trust in other parts of the world.

Universal life insurance
Universal life insurance is a type of permanent insurance that offers flexible premiums and a flexible death benefit.

Your tax-deferred cash value account accumulates at least the guaranteed rate of interest, but may accumulate at a higher rate if market rates are higher than the guaranteed rate.

You can use the money in your cash value account to pay premiums if there's enough available. And you can also increase the amount of the death benefit without having to qualify for the additional protection. This alternative allows you to build inflation protection into your insurance.

As with other permanent policies, you may be able to borrow against your cash value account, though any outstanding loan reduces your death benefit. You also get a portion of the cash value back, minus fees and expenses, if you end the policy.

However, universal life is a more complex product than straight life and the premiums are higher for a comparable death benefit.

Universe

In the world of investments, the word universe refers to a specific group or category of investments that share certain characteristics.

A universe might be the stocks that are included in a particular index, the stocks evaluated by a particular analytical service, or all the stocks in a particular industry.

Unlisted security

A security, such as a stock, is unlisted when it does not meet the listing requirements or pay the listing fee of any of the organized exchanges or markets.

Unlisted stock may be traded over-the-counter (OTC), however, and its price and volume may be tracked in the Pink Sheets or on the OTC Bulletin Board (OTCBB).

In most cases, unlisted stocks are thinly traded because they do not get much attention from the media or financial analysts, and so may be too risky for many investors.

Unrealized gain

If you own an investment that has increased in value, your gain is unrealized until you sell and take your profit.

In most cases, the value continues to change as long as you own the investment, either increasing your unrealized gain or creating an unrealized loss.

You owe no income or capital gains tax on unrealized gains, sometimes known as paper profits, though you typically compute the value of your investment portfolio based on current—and unrealized—values.

Unrealized loss

If the market price of a security you own drops below the amount you paid for it, you have an unrealized loss.

The loss remains unrealized as long as you don't sell the security while the price is down. In a volatile market, of course, an unrealized loss can become an unrealized gain, and vice versa, at any time.

One reason you might choose to sell at a loss, other than needing cash at that moment, is to prevent further losses in a security that seems headed for a still lower price.

You might also sell to create a capital loss, which you could use to offset capital gains.

Unsecured bond

When a bond isn't backed by collateral or security of some kind, such as a mortgage, that can be used to repay the bondholders if the bond issuer defaults, the bond is described as unsecured.

However, most unsecured bonds pose limited risk of default, since the companies that issue them are usually financially sound. Unsecured bonds are also known as debentures.

Uptick

An uptick is the smallest possible incremental increase in a security's price, which, for stocks, is one cent. So when there's an uptick in a stock selling at $20.25 cents, the new price is $20.26 cents.

US savings bond

The US government issues two types of savings bonds: Series EE and Series I.

You buy electronic Series EE bonds through a Treasury Direct account for face value and paper Series EE for half their face value. You earn a fixed rate of interest for the 30-year term of these bonds, and they are guaranteed to double in value in 20 years. Series EE bonds issued before May 2005 earn interest at variable rates set twice a year.

Series I bonds are sold at face value and earn a real rate of return that's guaranteed to exceed the rate of inflation during the term of the bond. Existing Series HH bonds earn interest to maturity, but no new Series HH bonds are being issued.

The biggest difference between savings bonds and US Treasury issues is that there's no secondary market for savings bonds since they cannot be traded among investors. You buy them in your own name or as a gift for someone else and redeem them by turning them back to the government, usually through a bank or other financial intermediary.

The interest on US savings bonds is exempt from state and local taxes and is federally tax deferred until the bonds are cashed in. At that point, the interest may be tax exempt if you use the bond proceeds to pay qualified higher education expenses, provided that your adjusted gross income (AGI) falls in the range set by federal guidelines and you meet the other conditions to qualify.

US Treasury bond

US Treasury bonds are long-term government debt securities, typically issued with 30-year terms.

New bonds are sold at a par value of $1,000, and existing bonds trade in the secondary market at prices that fluctuate to reflect changing demand. These bonds, sometimes referred to as long bonds, are often used as a benchmark for market interest rates.

While interest on US Treasury bonds is federally taxable, it is exempt from state and local taxes. Treasury bonds are considered among the world's the most secure investments, since they are backed by the full faith and credit of the US federal government.

Valuation

Valuation is the process of estimating the value, or worth, of an asset or investment.

Sometimes it means determining a fixed amount, such as establishing the value of your estate after your death. Other times, valuation means estimating future worth.

For example, fundamental stock analysts estimate the outlook for a company's stock by looking at data such as the stock's price-to-earnings (P/E), price-to-sales, and price-to-book (net asset value) ratios.

In general, a company with a high P/E is considered overvalued, and a company with a low P/E is considered undervalued.

Value fund

When a mutual fund manager buys primarily undervalued stocks for the fund's portfolio with the expectation that these stocks will increase in price, that fund is described as a value fund.

A value fund may be limited to stocks of a certain size, such as those included in a small-cap value fund, or it may include undervalued stocks with different levels of capitalization.

Value Line Composite Index

Value Line, an independent investment research service, tracks the performance of approximately 1,700 common stocks in its composite index. The index, which is equally weighted, is considered a reliable indicator of overall market trends.

Value Line, Inc.

Value Line is an investment research company that provides detailed analysis on a range of stocks, mutual funds, and convertible investments.

Their publications include The Value Line Investment Survey and The Value Line Mutual Fund Survey, which contain regularly updated rankings of specific investments that the company covers.

The company uses a dual ranking system in its evaluations. For example, Value Line ranks stocks for their safety and timeliness, and mutual funds both for their overall performance and for their risk-adjusted performance.

Value stock

Value stocks, also known as undervalued stocks, trade at a lower price than the company's reputation, earnings outlook, or financial situation would seem to merit.

Investors who seek them out expect the company's fortunes to turn around, and the price of the stock to increase accordingly.

Variable annuity

A variable annuity is an insurance company product designed to allow you to accumulate retirement savings.

When you purchase a variable annuity, either with a lump sum or over time, you allocate the premiums you pay among the various separate account funds offered in your annuity contract.

The tax-deferred return on your variable annuity fluctuates with the performance of the underlying investments in your separate account funds, sometimes called investment portfolios or subaccounts.

You may purchase qualified variable annuities, which are offered as options within an employer sponsored retirement savings plan, or nonqualified variable annuities. Nonqualified annuities are those you purchase on your own, often to supplement other retirement savings.

You can also choose an individual retirement annuity, which resembles an individual retirement account except that the underlying investments are separate account funds.

Among the appeals of both qualified and nonqualified variable annuities are the promise of a stream of income for life if you annuitize the assets in your account and the right to make tax-exempt transfers among separate account funds.

If you purchase a nonqualified annuity, there are no federal limits on the annual amounts you can invest, no requirement that you purchase the annuity with earned income, and no minimum required withdrawals beginning at age 70½.

However, with both types of variable annuities, withdrawals before you reach age 59½ may be subject to a 10% early withdrawal tax penalty.

Variable life insurance

Variable life insurance policies are cash-value policies that allow you to choose how your premium is invested from among a package of alternatives offered by the insurer.

In many variable life policies, the face value of your policy depends on how well the investments you've chosen are performing.

Venture capital (VC)

Venture capital is financing provided by wealthy independent investors, banks, and partnerships to help new businesses get started, reach the next level of growth, or go public.

In return for the money they put up, also called risk capital, the investors may play a role in the company's management as well as receive some combination of equity, profits, or royalties.

Some venture capital also goes into bankrupt companies to help them turn around, or to companies that the management wants to take private by buying up all the outstanding shares.

Vesting

If you are part of an employer pension plan or participate in an employer sponsored retirement plan, such as a 401(k), you become fully vested—or entitled to the contributions your employer has made to the plan, including matching and discretionary contributions—after a certain period of service with the employer.

Qualified plans must use one of the standards set by the federal government to determine that period.

If you become entitled to full benefits gradually over several years, the process is called graded vesting. But if you have are entitled only when the full waiting period is up, the process is called cliff vesting. If you leave your job before becoming fully vested, you forfeit all or part of your employer-paid benefits.

However, you are always entitled to all the contributions you make to a retirement plan yourself through salary reduction or after-tax payments.

Viatical settlement

Technically speaking, a viatical settlement occurs when a life insurance policy is sold for cash to a third party before the original owner dies.

Most viatical settlements involve terminally ill people with life expectancies of less than two years who choose to sell their life insurance policies to raise money for their medical care.

In a viatical settlement, the third party pays the former policy owner an amount that is typically more than the surrender value of the policy, but less than the death benefit. When the insured person dies, the new policy owner collects the death benefit and makes a profit on the difference between the amount paid to the insured and the amount paid on the claim.

Some businesses specialize in viatical settlements, and may resell them as investments, arrangements that are regulated by the state in which the policies are sold.

Because viaticals are controversial, more complex than they seem, and have been aggressively and sometimes misleadingly marketed, both people considering selling their policies and people considering investing in them are advised to proceed with caution.

Virtual bank

A virtual bank offers of some or all the same types of accounts and services that traditional bricks-and-mortar banks do, but virtual banks exist only online. They typically charge lower fees and pay higher interest because of low overhead.

Virtual bank transactions can be checked in real time, as they happen, rather than at the end of the banking day or the end of the month—though those services may also be available through the online branches of traditional banks.

Virtual banks don't have branches or own ATM machines, so you make deposits electronically or by mail. Your virtual bank may reimburse your ATM fees for using other banks' machines. However, there may be a limit to the number of transactions a virtual bank will cover each month.

Volatility

The term volatility indicates how much and how quickly the value of an investment, market, or market sector changes.

For example, because the stock prices of small, newer companies tend to rise and fall more sharply over short periods of time than stock of established, blue-chip companies, small caps are described as more volatile.

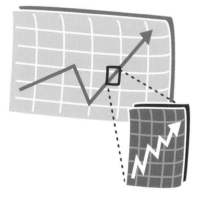

The volatility of a stock relative to the overall market is known as its beta, and the volatility triggered by internal factors, regardless of the market, is known as a stock's alpha.

Volume

Volume is the number of shares traded in a company's stock or in an entire market over a specified period, typically a day.

Unusual market activity, either higher or lower than average, is typically the result of some external event. But unusual activity in an individual stock reflects new information about that stock or the stock's sector.

Voting right

Investors who own shares of a common stock or shares in a mutual fund typically have voting rights, which allow them to participate in the election of boards of directors.

These shareholders can also vote for or against certain propositions put forward by management or by other stockholders. In contrast, investors who own preferred shares or corporate bonds have no voting rights.

Vulture fund

Like the scavenging bird of prey that lends its name to the fund, a vulture fund seeks out depressed or endangered investments.

Many vulture funds focus on real estate, but others invest in bonds that have been downgraded or are in default and other high-risk securities.

The strategy behind vulture investing is that such troubled securities have the potential to provide a large return eventually, in spite of their current vulnerable position. Most vulture funds are limited partnerships, but some are retail mutual funds that are open to individual investors.

Waiver of premium

If you have a waiver of premium provision in your long-term care or disability insurance policy, you may qualify to stop paying premiums once you've begun collecting benefits.

A waiver of premium provision increases the cost of your insurance, but means that you won't be left without coverage if you are no longer able to pay the premiums.

Warrant

Corporations may issue warrants that allow you to buy a company's stock at a fixed price during a specific period of time, often 10 or 15 years, though sometimes there is no expiration date.

Warrants are generally issued as an incentive to investors to accept bonds or preferred stocks that will be paying a lower rate of interest or dividends than would otherwise be paid.

How attractive the warrants are—and so how effective they are as an incentive to purchase—generally depends on the growth potential of the issuing company. The brighter the outlook, the more attractive the warrant becomes.

When a warrant is issued, the exercise price is above the current market price. For example, a warrant on a stock currently trading at $15 a share might guarantee you the right to buy the stock at $30 a share within the next 10 years. If the price goes above $30, you can exercise, or use, your warrant to purchase the stock, and either hold it in your portfolio or resell at a profit. If the price of the stock falls over the life of the warrant, however, the warrant becomes worthless.

Warrants are listed with a "wt" following the stock symbol and traded independently of the underlying stock. If you own warrants to purchase a stock at $30 a share that is currently trading for $40 a share, your warrants are theoretically be worth a minimum of $10 a share, or their intrinsic value.

Wash sale

When you purchase and then sell or sell and then repurchase the same security or a substantially similar security within 30 days, the double transaction is called a wash sale.

As an individual investor, you can't use any capital losses that the sale produces to offset capital gains from selling other securities in your portfolio.

For example, if you sold 200 shares of an underperforming stock on December 15 intending to use the loss on that sale to offset gains on other sales, your offset would be invalid if you repurchased the stock before the following January 15. But if you repurchased on January 16, the offset would be valid. In fact, avoiding wash sales is an important part of tax planning.

In a broader use of the term, purchasing and then quickly reselling a security may be described as a wash sale, whether the transaction is part of an innocent trading strategy or a pump-and-dump scheme.

Weather derivative

A weather derivative is a futures contract—or options on that futures contract—where the underlying commodity is a weather index.

These derivatives work much the same way that interest-rate or stock index futures and options do, by creating a tradable commodity out of something that is relatively intangible.

Analysts look at historical weather patterns—temperature, rainfall and other things—develop averages, and quantify the risk that weather will deviate from the average.

Corporations use weather derivatives to hedge their risk that bad weather will cause a financial loss. For a cereal company, bad weather might be a drought, which would cause wheat prices to go up. For a home heating company, it could be warm days in November, which could lower demand for home heating oil. And for an amusement park it could be rain.

The cereal company and the amusement park might buy futures contracts with an underlying weather index based on rainfall. The home heating company might want contracts based on a temperature index.

Weather derivatives are different from insurance, because they're linked to common weather events, like dry seasons, or a warm autumn, that affect particular businesses.

Insurance is still required to protect against major weather events, like tornadoes, hurricanes, and floods.

You can buy weather derivatives as an individual, but you'll want to consider the trading costs carefully to ensure that your risk of loss is worth the expense.

Weighted stock index
In weighted stock indexes, price changes in some stocks have a much greater impact than price changes in others in computing the direction of the overall index.

For example, in a market capitalization weighted index, such as the benchmark Standard & Poor's 500 Index (S&P 500), price changes in securities with the highest market valuations have a greater impact on the Index than price changes in stocks with a lower valuation.

Market capitalization of S&P indexes is calculated by multiplying the current price per share times the number of floating shares. Other market cap weighted indexes multiply the price by the number of outstanding shares. Market cap indexes may also be called market value indexes.

In contrast, in an unweighted index, such as the Dow Jones Industrial Average (DJIA), a similar price change in any

of the stocks in the index has an equal impact on the changing value of the index.

The theory behind weighting is that price changes in the most widely held securities have a greater impact on the overall economy than price changes in less widely held stocks.

However, some critics argue that strong market performance by the biggest stocks can drive an index up, masking stagnant or even declining prices in large segments of the market, and providing a skewed view of the economy.

Whisper number
A whisper number is an unofficial earnings estimate for a particular company that a stock analyst shares with clients to supplement the official published estimate.

If the company reports earnings in line with the official estimate when the whisper number has been higher, the stock price may fall anyway since investors were expecting something better.

The same is true in reverse. If earnings fall short of official expectations but meet a lower whisper number, the stock price may go up.

White knight
A corporation that is the target of a hostile takeover sometimes seeks out a white knight that comes to the rescue by making an offer to acquire the target company in a friendly takeover that suits the needs and goals of the target's management and board.

The hostile acquirer is called a black knight, and if the white knight is outbid by a third potential acquirer, who is both less friendly than the white knight and more friendly than the black knight, the third bidder is called a gray knight.

Whole life insurance

A whole life insurance policy is a type of permanent insurance that provides a guaranteed death benefit and has fixed premiums.

This traditional life insurance is sometimes also known as straight life insurance or cash value insurance.

With a whole life policy, a portion of your premium pays for the insurance and the rest accumulates tax deferred in a cash value account. You may be able to borrow against the cash value, but any amount that you haven't repaid when you die reduces the death benefit.

If you end the policy, you get the cash surrender value back, which is the cash value minus fees and expenses. However, ending the policy means you no longer have life insurance and no death benefit will be paid at your death.

Will

A will is a legal document you use to transfer assets you have accumulated during your lifetime to the people and institutions you want to have them after your death.

The will also names an executor—the person or people who will carry out your wishes.

You can leave your assets directly to your heirs, or you can use your will to establish one or more trusts to receive the assets and distribute them at some point in the future.

The danger of dying without a will is that a court in the state where you live will decide what happens to your assets. Its decision may not be what you would have chosen, and its deliberations can be costly and delay settling your estate.

Wire house

National brokerage firms with multiple branches were, in the past, linked by private telephone or other telecommunications networks that enabled them to transmit important news about the financial markets almost instantaneously.

Because of these lines, or wires, the firms became known as wire houses.

Although the Internet now makes it possible for all firms—and even individual investors—to have access to high-speed electronic data, the largest brokerage firms are still referred to as wire houses because of the technological edge they once enjoyed.

Wire room

When brokerage firm orders to buy and sell were handled manually, the firm's back office was called the wire room.

People who worked there received the buy or sell orders that came in from brokers and transmitted them to the firm's trading department or floor traders for execution. The wire room also received notifications when the transactions were completed and sent those notifications back to the brokers who took the orders.

However, as electronic systems increasingly handle these communications, wire rooms have essentially disappeared.

Withdrawal

A withdrawal is money you take out of your banking, brokerage firm, or other accounts.

If you withdraw from tax-deferred retirement accounts before you turn 59½, you may owe a 10% early withdrawal penalty plus any income tax that's due on the amount you've taken out.

In everyday usage, the term withdrawal is used interchangeably with distribution to describe money you take from your tax-deferred accounts, though distribution is actually the correct term.

Withholding

Withholding is the amount that employers subtract from their employees' gross pay for a variety of taxes and benefits, including Social Security and Medicare taxes, federal and state income taxes, health insurance premiums, retirement savings, education savings, or flexible spending plan contributions, union dues, or prepaid transportation.

Contributions to tax-deferred savings plans are withheld from your pretax income, as are amounts you put into tax-free flexible spending and prepaid transportation accounts. Those amounts reduce the taxable salary that your employer reports to the IRS.

Working capital

Working capital is the money that allows a corporation to function by providing cash to pay the bills and keep operations humming.

One way to evaluate working capital is the extent to which current assets, which can be readily turned into cash, exceed current liabilities, which must be paid within one year.

Some working capital is provided by earnings, but corporations can also get infusions of working capital by borrowing money, issuing bonds, and selling stock.

World Bank

Formally known as the International Bank for Reconstruction and Development (IBRD), the World Bank was established in 1944 to aid Europe and Asia after the devastation of World War II.

To fulfill its current roles of providing financing for developing countries and making interest-free and low-interest long-term loans to poor nations, the World Bank raises money by issuing bonds to individuals, institutions, and governments in more than 100 countries.

World fund

US-based mutual funds that invest in securities from a number of countries, including the United States, are known as world funds or global funds.

Unlike international funds that buy only in overseas markets, world funds may keep as much as 75% of their investment portfolio in US stocks or bonds.

Because world fund managers can choose from many markets, they are often able to invest in those companies providing the strongest performance in any given period.

World Trade Organization (WTO)

The WTO was formed in 1995 to enforce the regulations established by the General Agreement on Tariffs and Trade (GATT) and several other international trade agreements.

Composed of representatives from 150 nations and observers from additional nations, it regulates international trade with the goal of helping it to flow as smoothly and freely as possible.

Advocates praise the WTO for helping create an increasingly global economy and bringing prosperity to developing nations through increased trade.

Critics, however, assert that industrialized nations such as the United States, Canada, and the countries of the European Union have used the WTO to open trade with developing nations while disregarding these nations' environmental and labor-related practices.

Wrap account

A wrap account is a professionally managed investment plan in which all expenses, including brokerage commissions, management fees, and administrative costs, are wrapped into a single annual charge, usually amounting to 2% to 3% of the value of the assets in the account.

Wrap accounts combine the services of a professional money manager, who chooses a personalized portfolio of stocks, bonds, mutual funds, and other investments, and a brokerage firm, which takes care of the trading and recordkeeping on the account.

Writer

In the options market, a writer is someone who sells put or call options, an activity known as writing a call or writing a put.

Unlike the buyer, or holder, of an option, who can exercise an option or let it expire, as the writer you must meet the terms of the contract if the option is exercised and assigned to you.

You collect a premium for selling the option, which may provide a profit if the option expires worthless, and you always have the right, before exercise, to buy an offsetting contract and end your obligation to buy or sell.

Xenocurrency

Xenocurrency is currency that trades outside its own borders.

Yankee bond

Yankee bonds are bonds issued in dollars in the United States by overseas companies and governments.

The purpose is to raise more money than the issuers may be able to borrow in their home markets, either because there is more money available for investment in the United States, or because the interest rate the issuers must pay to attract investors is lower.

US investors buy these bonds as a way to diversify into overseas markets without the potential drawbacks of currency fluctuation, foreign tax, or different standards of disclosure that may be characteristic of other markets.

Yield

Yield is the rate of return on an investment expressed as a percent.

Yield is usually calculated by dividing the amount you receive annually in dividends or interest by the amount you spent to buy the investment.

In the case of stocks, yield is the dividend you receive per share divided by the stock's price per share. With bonds, it is the interest divided by the price you paid. Current yield, in contrast, is the interest or dividends divided by the current market price.

In the case of bonds, the yield on your investment and the interest rate your investment pays are sometimes, but by no means always, the same. If the price you pay for a bond is higher or lower than par, the yield will be different from the interest rate.

For example, if you pay $950 for a bond with a par value of $1,000 that pays 6% interest, or $60 a year, your yield is 6.3% ($60 ÷ $950 = 0.0631). But if you paid $1,100 for the same bond, your yield would be only 5.5% ($60 ÷ $1,100 = 0.0545).

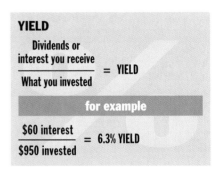

YIELD

$$\frac{\text{Dividends or interest you receive}}{\text{What you invested}} = \text{YIELD}$$

for example

$$\frac{\$60 \text{ interest}}{\$950 \text{ invested}} = 6.3\% \text{ YIELD}$$

Yield curve

A yield curve shows the relationship between the yields on short-term and long-term bonds of the same investment quality.

Since long-term yields are characteristically higher than short-term yields, a yield curve that confirms that expectation is described as positive. In contrast, a negative yield curve occurs when short-term yields are higher.

A flat or level yield curve occurs when the yields are substantially the same on bonds with varying terms.

A negative yield curve has generally been considered a warning sign that the economy is slowing and that a recession is likely.

Yield to maturity (YTM)

Yield to maturity is the most precise measure of a bond's anticipated return and determines its current market price.

YTM takes into account the coupon rate and the current interest rate in relation to the price, the purchase or discount price in relation to the par value, and the years remaining until the bond matures.